RILKE, MODE
POETIC TR

WITHDRAWN
UTSA LIBRARIES

If the rise of modernism is the story of a struggle between the burden of tradition and a desire to break free of it, then Rilke's poetic development is a key example of this tension at work. Taking a sceptical view of Rilke's own myth of himself as a solitary genius, Judith Ryan reveals how deeply his writing is embedded in the culture of its day. She traces his often desperate attempts to grapple with problems of fashion, influence and originality as he shaped his career during the crucial decades in which modernism was born. Her book is the first systematic study of Rilke's trajectory from aestheticism to modernism as seen through the lens of his engagement with poetic tradition and the visual arts. The book is full of surprising discoveries about individual poems. Above all, it shifts the terms of the debate about Rilke's place in modern literary history.

Judith Ryan is Harvard College Professor and Robert K. and Dale J. Weary Professor of German and Comparative Literature at Harvard University. Her books include *The Uncompleted Past: Postwar German Novels and the Third Reich* (1983) and *The Vanishing Subject: Early Psychology and Literary Modernism* (1991).

WITHDRAWN

CAMBRIDGE STUDIES IN GERMAN

General editors: H. B. Nisbet and Martin Swales
Advisory editor: Theodore J. Ziolkowski

Recent series titles

Seán Allan *The Plays of Heinrich von Kleist: Ideals and Illusions*
0 521 49511 3

W. E. Yates *Theatre in Vienna: A Critical History, 1776–1995*
0 521 42100 4

Michael Minden *The German "Bildungsroman": Incest and Inheritance*
0 521 49573 3

Todd Kontje *Women, the Novel, and the German Nation 1771–1871*
0 521 63110 6

Stephen Brockmann *Literature and German Reunification*
0 521 66054 8

RILKE, MODERNISM AND POETIC TRADITION

JUDITH RYAN

CAMBRIDGE
UNIVERSITY PRESS

CAMBRIDGE UNIVERSITY PRESS
Cambridge, New York, Melbourne, Madrid, Cape Town, Singapore, São Paulo

Cambridge University Press
The Edinburgh Building, Cambridge CB2 2RU, UK

Published in the United States of America by Cambridge University Press, New York

www.cambridge.org
Information on this title: www.cambridge.org/9780521661737

© Judith Ryan 1999

This publication is in copyright. Subject to statutory exception
and to the provisions of relevant collective licensing agreements,
no reproduction of any part may take place without
the written permission of Cambridge University Press.

First published 1999
This digitally printed first paperback version 2006

A catalogue record for this publication is available from the British Library

Library of Congress Cataloguing in Publication data

Ryan, Judith, 1943–
Rilke, Modernism and poetic tradition / Judith Ryan.
p.   cm. – (Cambridge studies in German)
Includes index.
ISBN 0 521 66173 0 (hardback)
1. Rilke, Rainer Maria, 1875–1926 – Criticism and interpretation.
2. Modernism (Aesthetics)   3. Aesthetics, Modern – 20th century.
I. Title.   II. Series.
PT2635.165Z8528   1999
831'.912 – dc21   99-11717   CIP

ISBN-13 978-0-521-66173-7 hardback
ISBN-10 0-521-66173-0 hardback

ISBN-13 978-0-521-02511-9 paperback
ISBN-10 0-521-02511-7 paperback

Library
University of Texas
at San Antonio

Contents

Acknowledgments

Rilke's poetry always calls forth a response, sometimes sympathetic, sometimes critical; but it is rare to study a text of his without becoming fully engaged, one way or the other. While I was working on *Rilke, Modernism and Poetic Tradition*, I had the chance to present my thoughts about Rilke in a variety of different forums. At an early stage in the project, Paola Mildonian invited me to speak at the International Comparative Literature conference in Venice. I am grateful to her for the opportunity to present my reading of Rilke's poem on Saint Mark's cathedral in the watery city itself. Two seminars at the Center for Literary and Cultural Studies at Harvard University invited me to speak; in both cases, the audience was lively, perceptive and not inclined to let me get away with anything. I learned a great deal from those discussions and have done my best to incorporate the suggestions that emerged from them into the book. I am very grateful to the seminar organisers, Beatrice Hanssen, Nicholas Jenkins, Jesse Matz and Joshua Esty for inviting me to test my ideas before their groups. At a crucial juncture, when the book was very close to completion, I was invited to speak at Oxford University on 'Rilke, Modernism and Mourning', where I received helpful suggestions from T. J. Reed, Ray Ockenden, and others who attended the talk. I owe thanks to Paul Kerry for having mediated the invitation and made my stay such a delightful one. Finally, a conference in Mainz on 'Rilke and World Literature' in September 1998, just before I put the finishing touches on my manuscript, affirmed my sense that this is the moment for a more international vision of Rilke's writing. I would like to express my appreciation to the organisers, Manfred Engel and Dieter Lamping, for inviting me to participate, and to thank the other speakers and members of the audience for broadening my understanding of Rilke's manifold links to other literary traditions.

I am grateful to several journals for permission to include here revised versions of material that first appeared in their pages: *Modern Language*

Quarterly, for an adaptation of 'Dead Poets' Voices: Rilke's "Lost from the Outset" and the Originality Effect' (volume 53, 1992, 227–245); *Comparative Literature Studies*, for a reworking of 'The Intertextual Maze: Rilke's "Der Turm" and His Relation to Aestheticism' (volume 30, 1993, 69–82); and *PMLA*, for a version of 'More Seductive Than Phryne: Baudelaire, Gérôme, Rilke, and the Problem of Autonomous Art' (1993, 1128–1141). I am also grateful to Bulzoni Editore for permitting me to reprint here in revised form my 'Pasticcio and the Incrusted Style: Ruskin, Rilke and Saint Mark's', in *Parodia, Pastiche, Mimetismo*, ed. Paola Mildonian (Rome, 1997), pp. 219–229.

Students in three graduate seminars at Harvard University suffered through various stages of my thinking on intertextuality in Rilke; my dialogue with these groups was invaluable in helping to form the central ideas of the book, as well as the readings of individual poems. Conversations with Joseph Metz, Christina Pugh, Daniel Reynolds, and William Waters have been illuminating and inspiring. Christina Pugh kindly read a section of the book and made perceptive suggestions for its improvement. Daniel Reynolds provided valuable research assistance during my work on the project; Xiaojue Wang and Claudia Bohner continued this help during the final months of the book's production.

Colleagues and friends have borne patiently with my enthusiasms over the years of the book's gestation. Peter Bloom advised me about Pászthory's musical setting of Rilke's *Cornet*. Marshall Brown read the first version of my argument about 'Lost from the Outset' with extraordinary care and subtlety. Sharon Copperwheat rescued material from a seemingly ruined computer disk. Karl S. Guthke provided the clue that helped me identify Rilke's Madame Lamort. Ingeborg Hoesterey reassured me about one of my forays into art history, and helped me refine my ideas about pastiche. Helmut Leppien took exceptional trouble with an unannounced visitor to the Hamburger Kunsthalle who was not even an art historian. Peter Nisbet talked with me about Paul Klee and Emilie Norris showed me the Klee holdings of the Busch-Reisinger Museum. Reinhold Grimm, Egon Schwarz, Hans Vaget and Theodore Ziolkowski were among the earliest supporters of the project. The two readers of my manuscript at Cambridge University Press responded encouragingly to my ideas and made a number of crucial suggestions and corrections. Linda Bree has been a superb guide through the editorial maze.

James O'Neil showed me photographs from his visit to the mausoleum at Halikarnassus and helped me understand more about the monument and its location. Vanessa Ryan shared an interest in many aspects of the book and was always willing to help me think through my ideas. Antony Ryan cast a critical eye on the penultimate version of the text and made sure I did not forget that not everyone is as deeply familiar with the material as I have become. Lawrence A. Joseph read reams of drafts and continued to remain optimistic even when the project eluded easy shaping. My mother, Kath O'Neil, who first introduced me to the world of poetry, has been linked in my mind with this book from the outset; to my great sorrow, she did not live to see its completion.

Introduction: Rilke's writing desk

When Rilke's older friend Ellen Key, a well-known Swedish social reformer, wrote to him that his poetry smacked of the writing desk,[1] she meant that it was too meagrely rooted in actual experience. She thought of poetry as the result of personal suffering, and she wished her friend Rilke had had more of it. Rilke himself thought he suffered quite enough: he had been a lonely little boy and he led a somewhat isolated adult life. Whenever real experiences loomed, he shied away from them: from building a life with his wife and baby daughter, from the troubling events of his trip down the Nile, and from service at the front during the First World War. Still, at the end of his life, when he had to endure the terrible pains of leukemia, he refused heavy doses of drugs that would prevent him from fully experiencing his suffering. His final poem, an expression of this suffering, is devastating to read; but in formal respects it is also a highly literary production.

Lack of personal experience is not the only reason for the 'writing desk' effect. Part of it comes from Rilke's use of unusual vocabulary, his fondness for exotic rhymes, his love of tight forms like the sonnet. More than anything else, the 'writing desk' effect derives from echoes of other writers' poems. He read extensively, mostly in recent literature, and he engaged in a lively exchange of literary enthusiasms and discoveries with his friends and patrons. Reminiscences from his reading repeatedly find their way into his work.

Rilke, Modernism and Poetic Tradition is the story of Rilke's complex path toward modernism. Like many other young writers, Rilke began as an imitator. But these early imitations have a curious quality that makes one wonder whether their tone is admiring or mocking. Rilke was indebted to tradition at the same time as he tried to free himself from it. As time went on, Rilke's dependence on other people's work became less evident. In part, his move to Paris and the cross-linguistic nature of his borrowings meant that they were far less evident. Later, when he

I

immersed himself once more in his native literary tradition, he grew more concerned about his imitative impulses.

Much of the special resonance of Rilke's poetry comes from the density with which he distilled effects from other poets' work and recombined them with his own unusual turns of phrase and mind. His relation to poetic tradition is complex, not to say ambivalent. One way of explaining this ambivalence would be to point to the body of literature that sustained his interest most consistently throughout his life: the aestheticist movements of the late nineteenth century. Aestheticist poetry trod a delicate line between originality and imitation, casting its private frames of reference in mannered and often traditional forms. Both Rilke and his public had a highly developed taste for stylised modes of expression. Still, the Romantic conception of originality continued to play a powerful role in literary value judgments of his day.

Debates about originality in our own time still defer in many ways to the Romantic ideal. The shift in scholarly usage during the nineteen-seventies and -eighties from 'influence' to 'intertextuality' was partly an attempt to reconceptualise literary debts in more positive terms. It was also intended to replace the notion of an author's individual psychology with the concept of texts as forms animated by a life of their own. Moving away from an assumption that literary echoes were the result of mechanisms at work in the depths of an author's subconscious mind,[2] newer theorists saw them more in terms of rhetorical strategies located in texts themselves.[3] More recently, we have rediscovered that texts are not the only elements involved in cultural exchange: paintings, photographs, films, historical events, fashion and much else are now recognised as part of a vast and complex dynamic.

Rilke's poetry becomes more vibrant when seen against this conceptual backdrop. In fact, Rilke was not quite as tied to his desk as Ellen Key's comment implies. He was a frequent visitor to art museums, a careful student of architecture and monuments, a knowledgeable writer about the decorative arts; he went through phases of interest in theatre and dance; he read avidly about religious, mystical and occult traditions; he travelled widely and devoured travel guides; he loved history; he was attracted at various times by alternative lifestyles; he was interested in psychology and psychoanalysis. In the ebb and flow of cultural fashions, he sometimes let himself be carried along; at other times, he mounted resistance. He was susceptible to market forces, yet never quite managed to free himself from the aestheticist vogue to which he owed his first major successes. Although we are accustomed to think of Rilke in the way he wished to be seen, as a figure aloof from mundane affairs, the only way to understand Rilke's writing fully is to see it in its cultural context.

This study traces the many ways in which contemporary culture is 'constituted and contested'[4] in Rilke's work. Literary texts and works of visual art dominate the discussion, since these were what was most often uppermost in his mind, if not actually present on or pinned above his writing desk. Other cultural phenomena, such as fashions in dress, theories of sexual pathology, ancient religions or the ballet mania of the early twentieth century, are drawn in along the way. Texts, discourses, visual iconography, performance arts and other cultural productions are often difficult to separate as they manifest themselves in Rilke's writing. Where Rilke contests contemporary fashions, rather than letting himself be swept away by them, he often seems to protest too much. The more he finds fault with aestheticism, the more he seems infected by it. When he explores ancient Egyptian religion, he assimilates it to his own quirky system of belief, or perhaps more accurately, to his idiosyncratic aesthetic practices.

In tracing Rilke's poetic development, I diverge in certain ways from received opinion. The *Neue Gedichte* [New Poems] are not presented as a clean break from his previous poetry; *Die Aufzeichnungen des Malte Laurids Brigge* [The Notebooks of Malte Laurids Brigge] is studied in terms of its earliest origins; and the *Duineser Elegien* [Duino Elegies] are not regarded as a fully coherent project. The borderlines between what have been conventionally considered separate 'periods' in Rilke's work are deliberately broken down. While biographies of Rilke have done something of this already – especially with respect to *Malte Laurids Brigge* and the *Elegies*, both composed over a period of years – studies of his poetry have tended to consider Rilke's published works in terms of the cyclical structures in which he liked to present them.

The book is divided into four chapters, each concerned with a different creative strategy. The first chapter, 'Fashioning the self', looks at Rilke's earliest attempts to shape his professional identity, which move from gentle parodies of German Romantic models to a pronounced alignment with turn-of-the-century art and culture. The chapter goes on to examine Rilke's involvement with Pre-Raphaelite aesthetics, Nordic novels about sensitive young artists and early modernist ideas about psychological development. The second chapter, 'Arts and crafts', explores Rilke's critique of, and simultaneous dependence on, the concept of the well-wrought and autonomous art object. His interest in French and Belgian Symbolism, Rodin's concept of fragmentary sculpture and Ruskin's heterodox art criticism are treated in this chapter. Rilke's poetic and personal crisis is the focus of the following chapter, 'Writing troubles'. Here we see him worrying about the connection between madness and creativity, dabbling in theories of sexual pathology, returning desperately to aestheticist fashions and practices while casting about among canonical writers for new ideas and formal models. The fourth chapter, 'The modernist turn', studies the fragile emergence of experimental tendencies in Rilke's work. At the same time, it highlights his renewed engagement with the traditional debate between painting and poetry, as well as about the ways in which poetry can be said to form a monument that lasts beyond death. The conclusion situates Rilke within the broader context of the second and third decades of the twentieth century and from the perspective of current debates about what constitutes the modernist movements.

Each chapter focusses on a small cluster of separate texts.[5] One of these is a prose poem, another an excerpt from Rilke's novel *Malte Laurids Brigge*. Most of them are verse poems of varying lengths. In most cases, the analysis explores outward from individual texts to their contributory artifacts and the contemporary fashions that go into their making. The analyses are not close readings or explications; I make no pretence of commenting on every interesting feature in the chosen texts. Rather, I visualise each text as a kind of comet, attracting a certain amount of cosmic dust and incorporating it within its own visible trajectory.

Arranged around texts, the book samples characteristic work from different phases of his career. The translations are my own. Current fashion prefers translations to be unrhymed, but this method ignores an essential feature of much of Rilke's work: he adored esoteric rhyme words. At the risk of losing some nuances, the translations given here reproduce as much as possible of the formal structure of Rilke's poems. They are intended as an aid to understanding my argument, not as a basis for further work with the poems, which can only be fully understood by reference to Rilke's originals.

Rilke was well aware that his manner laid his works open to misuse: he was disturbed by all the young people who wrote to him for advice about the conduct of their personal lives. German-speaking soldiers took his *Cornet* into the First World War, and his *Duino Elegies* into the Second. Even today, many readers of Rilke's writing feel it speaks directly to them. Still, it would be wrong to think of Rilke's works as a self-help manual in disguise.

Nor is Rilke's poetry a product of pure inspiration. It is also the result of hard work, sometimes against immense odds. Rilke lived from his royalties, his publisher's advances, and the support of wealthy patrons. Poetry was his profession, and he pursued it zealously; though his work often smacks of the writing desk, it is permeated by the cultural context in which he lived. At the same time, it also provides a lens through which the genesis of modernism comes into unusually clear focus.

CHAPTER I

Fashioning the self

RILKE'S DRESS

Rilke's earliest poetry is scarcely known to modern readers. Yet his beginnings not only reveal his conscious shaping of a poetic career, they show him absorbing and adapting multiple aspects of the culture around him. He had a good sense of the niches in which a beginning poet could lodge his work, from fashionable Viennese magazines to the souvenir shelf of Prague bookstores. From his emergence as a child prodigy, he situated himself within the framework of a progressively conceived 'feminine aesthetics' – today we would speak of an androgynous gender ideal – that was widely fashionable at the time and that continued to resonate throughout his works. His first volume of poems articulates a crisis of marginality common to artistic self-stylisation at the turn of the century. Far from being derivative, Rilke's early verses are in fact an attempt to disengage himself from the clutch of German poetic tradition. By giving his neo-Romanticism a slightly critical edge and thus underscoring his half-affectionate, half-alienated depictions of conventional scenes, Rilke implicitly declares his readiness to embark on a new kind of poetry.

Throughout his development, Rilke follows the cultural interests of his day. His almost seismographic response to fashion in every sense of the word lies at the heart of his early self-styling. He worked hard to attune his projects to current demand and 'package' his works to ensure their success. In the early years of the century, when his cousins discontinued the stipend he had been receiving from the inheritance of his uncle Jaroslav, he was entirely dependent upon what he earned through his writing. Only later, once he was under the wings of a distinguished publishing house, Insel, did he have more financial leeway in the form of advances for work in progress. By then he had also cultivated friendships with rich or well-to-do people who subsidised his work in various ways, mostly by inviting him to spend time in their houses and castles. Rilke's letters provide ample testimony to his attempts to secure patronage.

Altogether, Rilke's career presents an intriguing example of a writer poised between patronage and the market. His Paris years, in particular, show him moving towards a new professionalism, assiduously developing his talents as a literary and art reviewer. Accepting an assignment from the prominent art historian and editor of popular books about art, Richard Muther, was an important ingredient in this attempt to create, as it were, his own by-line. Under the influence of Rodin, he consciously shifted from what Louis Menand has called the 'innocence of design'[1] affected by the Romantics and neo-Romantics to the cultivation of a specialised profession characteristic of the modernist movements.

Like much aesthetic modernism, Rilke's poetry disguised its susceptibility to fashion by an ostensible rejection of it. In the first poem Rilke published (in 1891, when he was sixteen), he shows a spirited and playful approach to fashionable women's dresses:

> Die Schleppe ist nun Mode –
> verwünscht zwar tausendmal,
> schleicht keck sie sich nun wieder
> ins neueste Journal!
> Und so dann diese Mode
> nicht mehr zu tilgen geht,
> da wird sich auch empören
> die 'strenge' Sanität;
> ist die dann auch im Spiele
> und gegen diese Qual,
> daß man geduldig schlucken
> soll Staub nun sonder Zahl –
> schnell, eh man es noch ahndet,
> die Schlepp' vergessen sei,
> eh sich hinein noch menget
> gar ernst die Polizei.
> Die müßte an den Ecken
> mit großen Scheren stehn,
> um eilends abzutrennen,
> wo Schleppen noch zu sehn.   (3: 415)

The train is now in fashion –
a thousand times be cursed,
into the latest newspaper
it boldly slips, head-first!
And seeing that this fashion
is not to be erased,
we'll see stern public hygiene
indignant and red-faced:
once it's been alerted
to defy this torture-rack
that makes you calmly swallow
dust enough to make you hack –
quick, before they fine us,
let's just forget the train,
policemen might get serious
and interfere again.
They'd need to stand on corners
with monstrous pairs of shears,
prepared to sever hastily
whatever train appears.

An offence against practicality and hygiene, the train forces upon its viewer the idea of fashion pure and simple, form exaggeratedly in evidence for nothing but its own sake. Dragging behind its elegant wearer, the train draws attention to itself more than to her. Though flamboyant, it is also sneaky: it slips into fashion reports as if it were illicitly following the dress it is attached to. Unlike a poem, newspaper article or fashion illustration, the vogue for wearing dresses with trains cannot so easily be expunged or 'erased'. And although the train is the newest of fashion, the verses Rilke uses recall something more traditional: German Romantic imitations of mediaeval songs. The poem echoes the rhythms of a lyric in Eichendorff's novella *Aus dem Leben eines Taugenichts* [From the Life of a Good-for-Nothing] (1826), the protagonist's song of praise to a beautiful woman, a servant he has mistaken for an elegant lady. The ironic implications of parodying this well-known serenade in a piece of occasional verse about fashion would not have been lost on Rilke's readers.

The notion that trains stir up dust and present a danger to the health of others is ludicrous, of course. But these lines also contain a play on the word 'swallow', in the sense of resigning oneself to something unpleasant. The speaker is a curmudgeon for whom the trailing cloth is an extravagance, a sin against the better judgment of people like himself.

But he goes on to suggest that if we do not dwell too much on the idea of the train, it might slip out of existence as suddenly as it has slipped in. The concluding image envisages the police lying in ambush to snip off ladies' trains as they go by. Throughout the poem, the fashionable accoutrement seems to be strangely detached from any human wearer. The poem itself is also a train, dragging its length down the page and ending at the very moment when its speaker imagines the police snipping off the hateful extra fabric.

'The train is now in fashion' appeared in a Viennese paper in 1891 over the signature of 'René Rilke in Prag, Smichov' ('René Rilke, of Smichov, Prague'; 3: 801). Rilke must have written the poem in the interval between his departure from military academy in June of that year and his enrolment at a commercial school in September. He had lost all hope of receiving the officer's commission he had once desired; but he was not entirely crushed. His light-hearted poem even won a prize.

Glimpses of humour surface here and there in Rilke's early work. Three years after the publication of 'The train is now in fashion', the nineteen-year-old author of *Leben und Lieder* [Life and Songs] (1894) expressed the fear that his verses were primarily destined to be bought as Christmas presents for young girls (3: 443). Rilke's mother, herself not free from literary ambitions, appears to have been the instigator behind this approach to poetic success; and she was doubtless also behind his awareness of women's fashion.

Rilke's mother has received rather bad press.[2] This negative image derives more from Rilke's novel, *The Notebooks of Malte Laurids Brigge*, and possibly also the influence of his psychoanalytically trained friend Lou Andreas-Salomé, than from any objective perception of the case. Yes, Rilke's mother had lost a baby girl before the birth of her son, but was her way of dressing the young Rilke really the product of a pathologically disturbed psyche? There are certainly photos of Rilke as a small child wearing a dress – but this was progressive and fashionable at the time. Young boys not only wore tunics over pleated skirts, they also wore smocks and dresses trimmed with lace, tied with silk sashes, and decorated with bows. In daguerrotypes and photographs from the period, Oscar Wilde, at the age of three (1857), appears in a velvet dress trimmed with white broderie anglaise; Marcel and Robert Proust at five and three respectively (1896) sport double-breasted tunics over skirts, one of them quite lacy. In Mallarmé's fashion magazine, issued between September and December 1874 (just one year before Rilke's birth), paper patterns and line illustrations of young boys' clothing follow an androgynous model until the children reach the age of about seven or eight. Smocks, skirts, and dresses were not only worn by boys in families with an artistic bent: even royal princes, including Prince Wilhelm of Prussia and Napoleon's son, the Prince Imperial, wore lacy dresses in their early years. If royalty dressed their young sons this way, can it really have been child abuse when Phia Rilke did so?

If we explore nineteenth-century fashion more closely, we discover that the combined influence of fashion and hygiene created a new style for male children in the period around 1870. The appearance of 'die strenge Sanität' (stern public hygiene) in Rilke's poem is not as far-fetched as it may seem. In the late nineteenth century, dress was increasingly linked to health. Reformers argued for easily-fitting clothing for young children, just as they railed against corsets and other forms of tight-lacing on grown women. At the same time, an androgynous style of upbringing was being advocated in many quarters. In Victorian England around the mid-nineteenth century, for example, what was then called a 'feminine ethic' was proposed as a way of reducing the supposedly innate wildness of young boys and imbuing them with ideals of 'manly purity'.[3] Elizabeth Barrett Browning adopted this ideal for her son, Pen, whom she hoped to keep in delicate fabrics and long hair until the age of ten.

Rilke wore smocks and dresses until he was seven. A photograph taken in 1882 is inscribed on the back by Phia Rilke: 'My darling in his very first pants'. This shift to trousers may have taken place somewhat late by Prague standards (to judge from photographs, Kafka seems to have worn pants at the age of five), but it was certainly not late by those of fashionable Paris. Phia Rilke's book of aphorisms shows her to have been ahead of her time in many ways, and the androgynous model of child rearing fits well with her other progressive attitudes.

In his earliest published volume of poetry, Rilke writes without embarrassment about having played with dolls as a child: he describes the blue silk drawing room where he looked at picture books, where 'ein Puppenkleid, mit Strähnen dicken Silbers reich betreßt, Glück mir war' (a doll's dress, richly decked with thick silver strands, was a joy to me; 1: 41). There, too, he writes in the same poem, he liked to read verses and play tram or ship on the window ledge; sometimes he waved to a little girl in the house opposite. Activities we think of today as gender-specific (dressing dolls versus playing tram) are part of a single, undifferentiated complex in this nostalgic picture of a Prague childhood.

Attending military academy, a plan Rilke later said he accepted mainly because his father told him of the impressive uniform he would wear there, must have clashed dramatically with his androgynous childhood years. Rilke's prose sketch, 'Pierre Dumont' (1894), and his powerful short story, 'Die Turnstunde' [The Gym Lesson] (1902) render this conflict vividly. Still, even after he left military school and began to attend commercial school, Rilke liked to wear his uniform. We know much less about Rilke's sartorial interests than we do about Kafka's,[4] but both spent their adolescent years steeped in the aesthetic cult imported from France via Vienna. The Houghton Library has a drawing by Rilke from his cadet years depicting a dandy and a lady; the sketch, though artistically inept, pays careful attention to the finer details of its two figures' clothing, thus testifying eloquently to Rilke's interest in fashionable attire. Rilke's novella *Ewald Tragy* (written in 1898 but not published until after his death), a slightly transposed autobiographical narrative about the young poet's decision to leave Prague for Munich, opens with reflections on the women's dresses Ewald sees on his Sunday afternoon walk with his father. Some of the ladies are wearing last summer's colours and fabrics, while a lovely young woman in up-to-the-minute pink crepe de Chine spoils the effect by wearing refurbished old gloves (4: 512).

Despite Rilke's affectations during his Prague years, he did not really embark on a radical course of self-fashioning until he met Lou Andreas-Salomé in 1897. A former lover of Nietzsche and now the wife of a distinguished professor of Persian, Lou was an independent and impressive woman. It was Lou who suggested that he change his name to something more 'Germanic', Rainer (perhaps not coincidentally, also less androgynous than his given name René); it was Lou who sent him to Italy in 1898; and it was Lou who took him with her on two trips to Russia (in 1899 and 1900) that were to be crucial for his aesthetic self-development. Even more significantly, she insisted that he model his handwriting after her own, developing the elegant style he was later to use for copies of poems offered to friends as gifts.

Rilke's self-fashioning proceeded quite consciously. In moving first from Prague to Munich, then to Berlin and finally to Paris, Rilke had been approaching, stage by stage, the centre of fashion and culture. When planning his trip to Russia with Lou, he thought of himself as stripping off all his accustomed habits and guises, reducing himself to an essential nakedness. In actual fact, he startled his new Russian friends by appearing everywhere in a Slavic peasant blouse.

Rilke's fascination with the arts-and-crafts movement, as well as with alternative lifestyles such as those represented by the artists' colony in Worpswede, Ellen Key's experimental school in Sweden, and the artists' studios in Hellerau, a garden suburb of Dresden, are all part of his effort to keep up with the latest cultural trends. He was one of the first to write an informed and genuinely insightful essay on the neo-Impressionists (1898), and he was also among the first to review Thomas Mann's *Buddenbrooks* and appreciate its accomplishment (1901).

His ideas for developing his own writing projects were consciously guided by cultural fashions. Rilke admired the actress Eleanora Duse, whom he had hoped to see in the title role of his stylised verse drama *Die weiße Fürstin* [The White Princess] (1899, revised 1904). Since he did not see her on stage until he attended a performance of Ibsen's *Rosmersholm* in 1906, he was going solely on her reputation. Following the *Rosmersholm* performance, he apostrophised her in a famous passage in *Malte Laurids Brigge* (6: 924); he also presented a portrait of her acting in one of his *New Poems* (1: 608). In 1914, she seems to have suggested that she might give a recitation of his *Marien-Leben* [Life of the Virgin Mary] (1911), dressed as a shepherdess or – according to some versions of the story – a nun; but although Rilke managed to secure the support of the director Max Reinhardt for the project, it did not in fact materialise.

Lou encouraged him to 'work through' his memories of childhood along the model of the Freudian analytic techniques that were beginning to capture her attention. His novel *The Notebooks of Malte Laurids Brigge*, begun in 1902 and published in 1910, was in part the result of this effort. Here he attempts to recover the childhood that seems 'wie vergraben' (as if buried; 6: 721), reinterpreting his androgynous upbringing as the product of a psychologically disturbed mother:

Es fiel uns ein, daß es eine Zeit gab, wo Maman wünschte, daß ich ein kleines Mädchen wäre und nicht dieser Junge, der ich nun einmal war. Ich hatte das irgendwie erraten, und ich war auf den Gedanken gekommen, manchmal nachmittags an Mamans Türe zu klopfen. Wenn sie dann fragte, wer da wäre, so war ich glücklich, draußen 'Sophie' zu rufen, wobei ich meine kleine Stimme so zierlich machte, daß sie mich in der Kehle kitzelte. Und wenn ich dann eintrat (in dem kleinen, mädchenhaften Hauskleid, das ich ohnehin trug, mit ganz hinaufgerollten Armeln), so war ich einfach Sophie, Mamans kleine Sophie, die sich häuslich beschäftigte und der Maman einen Zopf flechten mußte, damit keine Verwechslung stattfinde mit dem bösen Malte, wenn er je wiederkäme. (6:800)

It occurred to us that there had been a time when Mama had wished I were a little girl and not the boy that I happened to be. I had somehow guessed this, and I hit upon the idea of knocking on Mama's door on occasional afternoons. When she then asked who was there, I happily called out 'Sophie', making my little voice so delicate that it tickled in my throat. And when I stepped inside (in the little girlish house dress that I wore anyway, with sleeves rolled up all the way), I was simply Sophie, Mama's little Sophie, busy with household tasks, who had to braid Mama's hair so that there could be no confusion with naughty Malte, if he were to come back again.

However close this scene from the novel may be to games René Rilke actually played with his mother, it is an interpretation of reality, not a simple transcription. Dress is a distinct motif in the novel, frequently connected with questions of identity (though not always with issues of gender), as in the scene where Malte dresses up in old clothes that have been stored away in guest rooms, and then rushes away in horror when he sees his unfamiliar image in the mirror (6: 806). Disguises, masks, and various forms of clothing give shape to Malte's probing of identity, his own and others', as the novel progresses. Even the idea of an 'eigener Tod' (personal death), which Malte believes has been lost in the impersonal atmosphere of modern hospitals, is seen through the metaphor of a custom-made suit: 'voilà votre mort, monsieur' (here is your death, sir; 6: 714).

At the same time, fabrics and laces are also metaphors for aesthetic pleasure and the free play of the imagination. When Malte comes upon the old clothes in the guest rooms, he feels almost drugged by their drape and textures:

Was mich aber in eine Art von Rausch versetzte, das waren die geräumigen Mäntel, die Tücher, die Schals, die Schleier, alle diese nachgiebigen, großen, unverwendeten Stoffe, die weich und schmeichelnd waren oder so gleitend, daß man sie kaum zu fassen bekam, oder so leicht, daß sie wie ein Wind an einem vorbeiflogen, oder einfach schwer mit ihrer ganzen Last. (6: 805)

What put me into a kind of trance, though, were the roomy coats, the scarves, the shawls, the veils, all these yielding, expansive, unused fabrics, soft and flattering or so fluid that one could hardly keep hold of them, or so light that they flew past one like a breeze, or else simply heavy with their entire weight.

Rilke himself was attracted by the dancer Isadora Duncan, who had used a gallery in the Hotel Biron for her rehearsals when Rilke was living there in 1908. Perhaps her scarf dances are reflected in Malte's delight in floating lengths of fabric. Later, Rilke was enraptured by Nijinsky and his Russian Ballet, and even began to conceive a pantomime in which Nijinsky would play a central role.

This preoccupation with moving fabric, costume and decorative motifs is the Rilkean equivalent of Kafka's 'pleats, pockets, buckles and buttons',[5] with their implications of aestheticist ornamentation and disorienting detail. In the Louvre, Malte observes young women who have left home to study painting. Their sense of dislocation in a big city that pays them no attention is captured by the two or three undone buttons that cannot be reached in the upper back of their dresses (6: 831). In another scene, Malte and his mother look at rolls of old lace, transforming each in turn into imaginary scenes of cloisters, prisons, gardens and hothouses (6: 835). Imagination, pattern and the survival of the past in the present are the leading ideas in this scene, not only drawing on a contemporary interest in lace and lacemaking, but also indebted to aestheticist ideals in a broader sense.

Rilke never lost his interest in beautiful fabrics and interior decor. As a guest at the castle of Princess Marie von Thurn and Taxis, he amused himself by taking a meticulous inventory of all the old lace, veils and scarves that had belonged to the princess's mother and grandmother. He gathered tiny objects – unusual perfume bottles, porcelain cosmetic pots, little needlework cases – and arranged them artfully in a small glass curio cabinet. He even furnished an outdoor pavilion with an ancient fringed reading chair.[6]

His fascination with fabric and design continued into the final years of his life. In 1923, after viewing a collection of Kashmiri shawls in the Bern Historical Museum, he wrote two poems titled 'Shawl' (2: 476–477); a third poem on the same topic followed a year later (2: 488–489). Now the primary emphasis is on pattern: the shawl's design, perceived as constant motion around a still centre, is read as an objective correlative for the course of the viewer's individual life. At the same time, the shawl continually unfolds an entire panoply of traditional motifs, both natural and more abstractly figural. Simultaneously an art object and a historical document, it takes us out of ourselves and demonstrates a kind of permanence our own lives can never attain.

The idea that tradition and history – the very opposites of fashion – are falling out of modern consciousness is a pervasive motif in Rilke's writing, but whenever he tries to conjure up this past it is transfigured into the static and stylised form familiar to us from pre-Raphaelite painting. What he 'rescues' from the past through poetry was precisely that which had become fashionable in turn-of-the-century art and literature; but in regretting the loss of vitality in modern life, Rilke's early poetry continues to reduce it to formal configurations that are the very opposite of breathing actuality. This paradox constitutes the underlying tension in *Das Stunden-Buch* [The Book of Hours], written between 1899 and 1903, precisely during the years when Rilke was performing his most deliberate act of self-construction. Images of building and pilgrimage are its poetic correlatives, and the dichotomy between creating *ex nihilo* and preserving sacred relics from the past says much about Rilke's struggle during that transitional period to decide between tradition and originality. A similar tension, with the balance tipped in the direction of tradition, is evident in *Malte Laurids Brigge*. Here, as Robert Jensen has shown for modern painting, 'the "alienation" of the artist was [. . .] largely a fiction that served rather than denied the commodification of art'.[7] Today's readers of Rilke tend to fall into one of two groups: those who identify with his alienation and those who are made uncomfortable by his aestheticism. Both of these effects must be seen, however, as related parts of a single attempt to gain a grip on the market by constructing a professional identity.

Rilke's translations from other languages, projects he mostly pursued during lean moments in his own career, make this effort especially evident. Well aware that his readership was largely to be found among proponents of 'feminine aesthetics', he created, in 1908, a poetic version of Elizabeth Barrett Browning's *Sonnets from the Portuguese*; in 1913, he published a translation of the *Letters of a Portuguese Nun*, at the time still thought to have been written by Marianna Alcoforado, and in 1917, he translated twenty-four sonnets by Louise Labbé. Rilke came to think of femininity as an aspect of all human beings that needed to be cultivated and saved from its unfortunate polarisation in the man–woman dichotomy.[8] His devotion to female admirers and patrons, his self-identification with a series of women writers, his development of an idiosyncratic theory revolving around abandoned women and unrequited female love, testify to an interest in the feminine that runs through his entire life and work.[9] In all these ways, Rilke continued to cultivate ideals that had characterised his early childhood.

Rilke's simultaneous pursuit of fashion and his self-presentation as marginal to it is central to the persona he creates. The two main art centres at the turn of the century were Berlin and Paris. As a student of art history, Rilke naturally moved to Berlin; but once he discovered that the most important art historians of his time, Richard Muther and Julius Meier-Graefe, saw French art as the model on which to base a historical understanding of nineteenth-century European art in general, he quickly shifted his focus to Paris. Writing about, working for and staying with

Rodin gave Rilke access to a large number of artists based in Paris at the time. Yet although he was in the thick of conversations about aesthetic principles and practices, Rilke never became an exclusive disciple of any particular school. His poetry belongs to none of the many movements that rapidly followed one another in the development of twentieth-century modernism. Even when Rilke was in a culturally central location, as was certainly the case in Paris, he took up a position on the margins, preferring to remain unaffiliated.

As Stephen Greenblatt has shown for sixteenth-century England, self-fashioning 'is achieved in relation to something perceived as alien, strange, or hostile'.[10] He argues that 'if both the authority and the alien are located outside the self, they are at the same time experienced as inward necessities, so that both submission and destruction are always internalized' (p. 9). Greenblatt's description of Renaissance self-fashioning applies remarkably well to Rilke, especially during his Paris years, when the 'authority' was located for him in French art and poetry, and the 'alien' manifested itself every day in the sights and sounds of the chaotic foreign city. Rilke's cultivation of an aesthetics of femininity was well suited to this situation, since it allowed him to re-evaluate his marginality and lack of genuine control by converting them into positive capacities of intuition and receptivity.

This analysis of Rilke's self-creation places him firmly in the context of aesthetic modernism. In the chapters that follow, we will see him struggling with central issues of the period: autonomy and engagement, originality and borrowing, tradition and technology. Above all, Rilke was an early participant in the internationalising movement that swept through the arts in the first decades of the twentieth century. In this venture, his work shows more clearly than that of many others the strain internationalism placed on modern writers. At the same time, this strain is precisely what ultimately produces Rilke's most accomplished poetry. The ways in which he interacted with current cultural trends throughout his career are remarkable for a writer who, as a young man on Europe's cultural margins, had proposed in light verse that one might wish to clip the train of contemporary fashion.

OLD PRAGUE

In sharp contrast to the remarkable early poems produced by his Viennese counterpart, Hugo von Hofmannsthal, Rilke's verse of the mid- to late eighteen-nineties was highly uneven: by turns trite, precious, sentimental, naive and curiously knowing, it was the work of a young person accustomed to being treated as a prodigy. Stefan George once commented that Rilke had started to publish too early, a judgment Rilke himself later cited with agreement.[11] Yet even these very earliest productions of Rilke can tell us much about the way he positioned himself within the German-language literary canon.

Characteristic of Rilke's early work is his second collection of poetry, *Larenopfer* [Sacrifices to the Lares] (1895), with its charming little portraits of old Prague. Most of the poems in *Sacrifices to the Lares* were written in late autumn 1895, presumably in the hiatus between Rilke's matriculation exam and his first semester at Prague University. He had already published another collection of poems, *Leben und Lieder* [Life and Songs], the year before.

Why did Rilke call the volume *Sacrifices to the Lares?* Critics have paid curiously little attention to this question. We know, however, that Rilke was to move to Munich in 1896, the first geographical displacement designed to help him escape his peripheral position. *Sacrifices to the Lares* is a collection of verbal postcard views, as if Rilke felt obliged to propitiate the household gods before he left his native city for good.[12] The volume takes us on a guided tour, stopping at historic monuments (the Hradshin, the chapel of St. Wenceslas, the monument to Emperor Rudolf, the Town Hall clock and so forth), noting the mixture of religions (from Ursuline nuns to Rabbi Löw), recalling principal figures from Prague's history and literature (Kajetan Týl, Dalibor, Julius Zeyer), and observing the city at different seasons of the year. The main focus is on Prague's historic charm and its linguistic and cultural multiplicity.

Characteristic of the volume is 'Auf der Kleinseite' [In the Little Quarter], about a section of Prague that lies across the Moldau from the main business centre of the city. The quarter's dominant architectural style is baroque, and it is full of magnificent palaces and villas with richly decorated façades, elegant balustrades, and a proliferation of statues, niches and interior courtyards:

> Alte Häuser, steilgegiebelt,
> hohe Türme voll Gebimmel, –
> in die engen Höfe liebelt
> nur ein winzig Stückchen Himmel.
>
> Und auf jedem Treppenpflocke
> müde lächelnd – Amoretten;
> hoch am Dache um barocke
> Vasen rieseln Rosenketten.

Spinnverwoben ist die Pforte
dort. Verstohlen liest die Sonne
die geheimnisvollen Worte
unter einer Steinmadonne.   (1: 9–10)

Ancient houses, steeply gabled,
lofty towers full of bells, –
Heaven, flirting with the fabled
narrow courtyards, weaves its spells.

And on every porch and stair,
languid, smiling, cupids breathe.
Baroque, on rooftops in the air,
vases rustle round with wreaths.

Spider webs obscure the portal
in that place. The furtive sun
reads the mystic words immortal
on a Virgin's pedestal of stone.

'In the Little Quarter' recalls Eichendorff's poem 'In Danzig', of 1842, a text that had become a staple in school anthologies. It would not be fair to describe Rilke's text as derivative; neither is it a parody, like 'The train is now in fashion': rather, it presents itself as a deliberate rewriting of an existing text using its external form and some of its stylistic peculiarities. In fact, a number of poems in the same volume are reworkings of familiar texts.[13] The poem's charm lies in the way it reconfigures Eichendorff's text while retaining its rhythms and some of its imagery. Here is Eichendorff's poem:

Dunkle Giebel, hohe Fenster,
Türme tief aus Nebeln sehn,
Bleiche Statuen wie Gespenster
Lautlos an den Türen stehn.

Träumerisch der Mond drauf scheinet,
Dem die Stadt gar wohl gefällt,
Als läg zauberhaft versteinet
Drunten eine Märchenwelt.

Ringsher durch das tiefe Lauschen,
Über alle Häuser weit,
Nur des Meeres fernes Rauschen –
Wunderbare Einsamkeit!

Und der Türmer wie vor Jahren
Singet ein uraltes Lied:
Wolle Gott den Schiffer wahren,
Der bei Nacht vorüberzieht![14]

Sombre gables, lofty windows,
Towers peering deep from mist,
Pallid statues, ghost-like figures,
Stand at doors in silent tryst.

Dreamily the moon shines down,
Taking pleasure in the town,
As if what lay there, petrified,
Were a fairy countryside.

All around the deepest listening
In the houses' interlude,
Just the ocean's constant rustling –
Wondrous solitude!

And the watchman as of yore
Sings his ancient song of prayer:
May God keep the sailor safe
Whose boat is passing over there!

In Eichendorff's Danzig poem, the architectural elements of the town are transformed by the mysterious powers of mist and moonlight into a fairy-tale world that no longer seems like the product of human hands. As the silence of the sleeping town is overlaid by the distant sound of the sea, the speaker is filled with awe at the 'wunderbare Einsamkeit' (wondrous solitude) it seems to embody. The final stanza of Eichendorff's poem deconstructs its own Romantic myth, however, by invoking a traditional watchman's prayer for the safety of ships passing by at night. 'In Danzig' expresses the late German Romantics' sense of profound ambiguity about the relations between reality and imagination, past and present, human and natural life. Poetry, symbolised by the night watchman's song, has the power both to heal these rifts and to reveal them in all their terror.

Rilke's adaptation of Eichendorff's model says a great deal about how Rilke saw his relation to this tradition during his early years. Prague and Danzig share the steep gables mentioned in the opening lines of both poems, but the mysterious Gothic effects of Eichendorff's Danzig are replaced by more playful baroque decorations in Rilke's Prague.

In Eichendorff's poem, the city's living spirit seems to have been turned to stone: statues stand beside doorways like paralysed ghosts, and the moonlit buildings look like a kind of petrified forest. In a paradoxical and even logic-defying way, however, everything is also somehow animated. What begins as simple anthropomorphism, with towers peering out from the mists and the moon taking a dreamy pleasure in the sight of the city below, shifts to a strangely disembodied version of the pathetic fallacy, as the atmosphere above the houses fills with listening. We do not know who breathes the rapt exclamation, 'wondrous solitude!' that closes the third stanza, nor whether it refers more to the silence of the city or the distant sound of the ocean. Only the fourth and final stanza of Eichendorff's poem returns to a more conventional perspective in which the watchman in the tower is heard singing his prayer for those at sea.

Like Eichendorff, Rilke also anthropomorphises some elements in his scene: the sky that flirts its way into the courtyards in the opening stanza and the sun that sneaks a glance at the words on the stone madonna in the poem's conclusion. The spider-webs on the door suggest a sleeping-beauty world scarcely touched by modern life. But unlike the stone statues of Eichendorff's Danzig, the stone cupids of Rilke's Prague are full of languid motion, and even the ropes of carved roses on the baroque vases seem to ripple or rustle as if touched by the breeze.[15] The emphasis is on make-believe, playfulness, delicacy; the Little Quarter is charmed into a moment of fleeting life by the fanciful gaze of the spectator. The scene is expressive, communicative, full of meaningful sounds, glances and gestures. Yet none of these signs can be fully decoded, at least not by their human observer. The cupids smile to no one in particular, and the words on the madonna's stone pedestal, though furtively read by the sun, remain mysterious to the speaker. Whereas Eichendorff's poem puts a name to the emotions aroused by the scene he describes ('wondrous solitude') and repeats a line from the watchman's prayer, Rilke's text stops short of articulating a response to its scene, and although it does not hesitate to anthropomorphise both natural and architectural elements, it neither explicates nor moralises. At times, the syntax itself is sketchy and the descriptive method impressionistic; the enjambements in the third stanza close, rather than open, the door to meaning. The eye moves rapidly about the scene without putting together a coherent whole. At first, the characteristic features of the quarter seem to be repeated everywhere alike: houses, towers, courtyards, cupids and vases appear quintessentially plural. When the observer does try to gain optical purchase on a single spot, as in the final stanza, the ancient architecture seems to offer resistance. He cannot look beyond the cobwebbed door or understand the words on the base of the statue.

The history of place is differently conceptualised in Eichendorff's and Rilke's poems. In Eichendorff's Danzig poem, history underlies the present just as the gables and towers hide behind the mists; by the same token, a primitive fear of the demonic, represented by the possibility of shipwreck, forms the obverse of poetic delight in solitude and silence. The schema behind Rilke's 'In the Little Quarter' is not dualistic in this way. Instead, the entire scene is composed of surfaces without depth. We cannot see through to the old town's historic origins, which appear only in the form of mysterious vestiges and unreadable signs.

The young Prague poet regards himself as part of a distinguished poetic lineage, yet he also sees himself as a latecomer who does not have complete access to this heritage. He speaks partially in Eichendorff's voice, but his world is no longer invested with the same – or perhaps indeed with any – significance. Eichendorff's vision of Danzig provides a schema that superficially applies to Rilke's Prague, but in the last analysis it does not help to make sense of the Czech city. In contrast to the speaker of Eichendorff's poem, whose listening is homologous with the greater 'listening' of the atmosphere, Rilke's observer stands at one side, unable to enter the scene even as much as the sky is able to insinuate its way into Prague's narrow courtyards. The sense of inauthenticity, superficiality, detachment, and frustration that speaks here is the expression of a young poet's feeling of exclusion from the cultural centre. The crisis expressed here is a crisis of marginality.

A mild irony threads its way through much of the volume's homage to Bohemian folk songs and Czech poets. In the Bohemian Ethnographic Exhibition of 1895, which was energetically boycotted by the German-speaking population of Prague, the room in which Kajetan Týl had composed his patriotic poem 'Kde domov můj' [Where is my homeland?] (later to become the Czech national anthem), was recreated in faithful detail. Rilke's poem about Týl describes the room as small and furnished only with a chair, a trunk that served as a writing desk, a bed, a wooden cross and a jug (1: 38–39). Still, the last stanza tells us, so strongly attached was he to his native land that he would not have left it 'für tausend Louis' (for a thousand Louis; 1: 39). Rilke himself was soon to move away.

Another poem in *Sacrifices to the Lares* draws out the irony explicitly, this time in connection with the Czech writer Jaroslav Vrchlický (1853–1912). The speaker of Rilke's poem describes himself as leaning back in a comfortable armchair and reading a book of poems by Vrchlický until dusk falls (1: 20).[16] Rilke's speaker falls under the spell of the verses, feeling that they allow him to overhear solutions to 'divine problems' – yet he also has enough presence of mind to ask whether he might not just have been drugged by the scent of chrysanthemums in a vase nearby. Unlike Kajetan Týl, the speaker of Rilke's poem enjoys not only a life of comfort but also of aesthetic pleasure. In a poem about another Czech poet, Julius Zeyer, Rilke contrasts political struggle with the equilibrium of art (1: 36).[17] Zeyer, he claims, leads his people in their attempt to achieve national identity, but has also mastered the art of aesthetic balance.

The poems of *Sacrifices to the Lares* forge an aesthetic of marginality by looking at home from the perspective of a tourist. A conscious discrepancy between German literary language and Czech folk tradition runs through the entire volume. If the opening poems rework Eichendorff, the concluding poem recalls Heine. 'Vom Feld klingt ernste Weise;/ weiß nicht, wie mir geschieht...' (From the field a solemn melody resounds / I don't know what's happening to me...; 1: 68). The 'Märchen aus alten Zeiten' (tale from olden times) that Heine recounts in his 'Lorelei' is transposed here into a Czech melody, sung not by a Rhine maiden on the cliff top but by a girl from the Czech people mowing hay in the fields. The song she sings is Týl's 'kde domov můj', and it not only brings tears to her own eyes but elicits a copper coin from her listener. The reader of this pastiche knows, however, that the Lorelei lures men to their deaths. The past, transposed in Heine's ballad into a beautiful and seductive fairy tale, is an attraction that can only cause shipwreck. No wonder Rilke fled from Prague to Munich less than a year after composing *Sacrifices to the Lares*.

THE CULT OF YOUTH

Rilke's construction of a poetic persona went forward rapidly after his move to Berlin in October, 1897. In November of the same year, he began work on a volume of poetry, titled *Mir zur Feier* [To Celebrate Myself], that was to establish a tone quite different from that of his previous two volumes.

Here, playfulness and self-irony disappear as Rilke steeps himself in turn-of-the-century art. The flowing lines and decorative surfaces of Jugendstil art give new shape to Rilke's language and imagery.[18] Jugendstil's abolition of clear distinctions between background and foreground, nature and the human figure, subject and object, presents a seductive but troubling vision for the young writer trying to fashion a new lyric identity. Moving in from the cultural margins means immersing oneself in this flux. No longer does Rilke look quizzically at women's dresses or wistfully at city architecture; he is much more involved in the culture around him. Two aspects of the Jugendstil movement attract his attention: its fascination with floral decor, and its cult of youth. To represent his new sense of interrelation with this culture, Rilke develops the image of the 'inner garden'.

A sequence of three garden poems, written in November and December, 1897, follow the epigraph that opens Rilke's volume, *To Celebrate Myself*.[19] They set forth a new poetic credo that proclaims a removal from vulgar reality and a heightened degree of sensitivity, an increasing involvement with Jugendstil, and, above all, the first development of Rilke's ideas about interior landscape. Here is the first in the sequence:

> Ich bin so jung. Ich möchte jedem Klange,
> der mir vorüberrauscht, mich schauernd schenken,
> und willig in des Windes zartem Zwange,
> wie eine Ranke überm Gartengange,
> will meine Sehnsucht ihre Schwingen schwenken.
>
> Und jeder Brünne bar will ich mich brüsten,
> solang ich fühle, wie die Brust sich breitet.
> Denn es ist Zeit, sich reisig auszurüsten,
> wenn aus der frühen Kühle dieser Küsten
> der Tag mich tiefer in die Lande leitet. (3: 205)

> I am so young. And trembling, I incline
> to every sound that rustles through the air,
> and in wind's tender clasp, like columbine,
> or vines across the garden path that twine,
> my longing sends forth swaying pinions there,
>
> And free of armour I will make my way,
> as long as I can feel my lungs expand.
> For it is time to leave, not time to stay,
> when, from this early coastal coolness, day
> guides me more deeply on the road inland.

The idea of the 'inner garden' – a projection of the poet's psyche into the external world – had already become a staple of French Symbolism.[20] German and Austrian poets influenced by that movement, notably Stefan George and Hugo von Hofmannsthal, picked up the motif and worked it out more intricately.

Rilke had read George's poetry with Lou in her Berlin apartment in the autumn of 1897, and met him personally at a reading in the salon of the painters Reinhold and Sabine Lepsius.[21] George's two volumes of poetry, *Algabal* (1892) and *Das Jahr der Seele* [The Soul's Year] (1897), make copious use of garden imagery. For Rilke's 'I am young' sequence, *Algabal* is a crucial point of departure. George's emperor Algabal is depicted as a young, handsome, but cruel potentate, given to a life of luxury and sensuality. His subterranean palace, with its artificial gardens, is a timeless realm totally removed from the sphere of real life and action. Its underground garden is composed of petrified trees and lifeless birds; only the glimmer of lava and the dusty scent of incense lend a semblance of life to his artificial paradise. Algabal's sole frustration in this crystallised kingdom of his own making is his inability to create the dramatic and sinister blossom he dreams of, the 'dark, large, black flower' that symbolises poetry itself. Baudelaire's *Les Fleurs du Mal* [The Flowers of Evil] were doubtless prototypes of the black flower Algabal longs to create.

In 1892, Rilke's Austrian contemporary, Hugo von Hofmannsthal had already pulled off a brilliant contrafacture of Algabal's petrified garden. Called 'Mein Garten' [My Garden], it was written after he first met George in 1891 when he was only sixteen.[22] Hofmannsthal begins by creating a pastiche of George's artificial and lifeless garden, but then goes on to compare it unfavourably with the original garden, paradise. In its ironic inflection of George's precious effects, Hofmannsthal's poem is a brilliant example of aestheticist self-critique.

Rilke's takes a different tack in his engagement with George. Instead of the unchanging garden George creates for his underground ruler Algabal, Rilke's garden is full of motion. George's trees of coal, fossilised birds, and fruits made of lava are replaced by rambling vines, blowing breezes, and rustling leaves. The shapes invoked are the curvilinear forms of Jugendstil art, and the speaker's insistence on his youthfulness refers to the cult of youth promulgated by the movement. Indeed, just a year before, Rilke had already described himself for an entry in a lexicon of poets as editor of a journal called *Jung-Deutschland und Jung-Österreich* [Young Germany and Young Austria] (6: 1204), a move clearly designed to align him with the late nineteenth-century youth cult.

Despite an element of self-indulgence, these poems mark an important way-stage in Rilke's development. In them, he stakes a new claim to a sensitive, supple, and mobile kind of writing that will include increased responsiveness, change and growth.

Rilke's garden poems retain George's tight, rhymed forms while countermanding his constraints on the expression of emotion. The receptive posture of the speaker in Rilke's poems replaces George's controlled subjectivity. To use the terms of the day, Rilke substitutes a 'feminine aesthetics' for a 'masculine' one. Rilke's garden poems are suffused with indeterminacy: longing, dreaminess and numbness are their most pervasive qualities. The speaker gives himself up to the sounds wafted in by the wind and lets himself be led by the emerging daylight. The poem's self-reflexivity creates some logical problems. Are the vines that creep across the garden path projections of the speaker's desire, or are they obstructions on his way through the land-scape? There is something threatening about this apparently easy commerce with nature. Why does the poet shudder when he yields himself up to the sounds borne by the wind? Why does he even imagine freeing himself from armour? Everything in Rilke's sequence remains vague and abstract, and the poem even flaunts its essential passivity.

At the same time, a new conception of the relation between experiencing subject and poetic object begins to emerge. Alliteration, assonance, rhyme, and other self-echoing effects enhance the reflexivity between speaker and garden to create an interior landscape in which subject and object are suspended in complex interaction. Apparently countermanding this self-reflexivity is the summons to travel; yet the trip, far from leading into the open, will take the speaker inland into a topography of enclosure.

In the second poem of the sequence, he metamorphoses into a garden himself, and does no more than attend to the sensations of his and its growth:

> Ich will ein Garten sein, an dessen Bronnen
> die blassen Träume neue Blumen brächen,
> die einen schwarmgesondert und versonnen,
> und die geeint in schweigsamen Gesprächen.
>
> Und wo sie schreiten, über ihren Häupten
> will ich mit Worten, wie mit Wipfeln rauschen,
> und wo sie rasten, will ich den Betäubten
> mit meinem Schweigen in den Schlummer lauschen.

> (3: 205)

I wish to be a garden at whose spring
the pallid dreams would find new blossoming,
some grouped apart and veiled in fancy's fog,
and others clasped in silent dialogue.

I'd like my words to rustle where they tread,
and sound like tree tops whispering overhead;
I'd like to listen, silent, where they rest,
drugged in the heavy slumbers of the blest.

As in the first poem, the train of thought remains loose. If the speaker is
– or wishes to be – a garden, whose are the dreams that enter upon the
scene? What does it mean when dreams become drugged? In the third
poem, similar problems emerge:

Ich will nicht langen nach dem lichten Leben
und keinen fragen nach dem fremden Tage:
Ich fühle, wie ich weiße Blüten trage,
die in der Kühle ihre Kelche heben.

Es drängen Viele aus den Frühlingserden,
in denen ihre Wurzeln Tiefen trinken,
um, krank und dürstend, in die Knie zu sinken
vor Sommern, die sie niemals segnen werden.   (3: 206)

I will not grasp toward life's light-filled crowd
nor ask about another's days or hours:
I sense that I am bearing pure white flowers,
lifting their throats in morning's cooling shroud.

Many, in spring, thrust upward from the earth
in which they drink the depths with thirsty roots,
only to sink exhausted from the dearth
of moisture in dread summers with no fruits.

If the speaker is a garden 'bearing' white flowers, how can he describe
them lifting their calixes as if he were seeing them from outside? Will the
poet's own productions sink in exhaustion at some later point? We sense
a troubling undercurrent to these poems about beginning anew. Rilke
works better with the paradoxes of self-reflexivity in his later poetry.
These early poems make us acutely aware of the machinery of self-
projection – what we now call the pathetic fallacy – that he had
inherited from Romanticism.

These poems in fact form part of a frame around the volume *To
Celebrate Myself*. Its middle section consists of poems about young

women, either spoken in their own voices or addressed to them by the poet. Suffering from the loss of a mother or a lover, beset by nameless anxieties, praying to the Madonna for aid, the girls are also compared with flowering gardens. The image combines two well-known motifs: one, the metaphor in which adolescent girls are seen as budding plants, and the other, the mediaeval tradition in which the Virgin Mary is depicted within an enclosed garden. The volume's frame is closed by a series of poems about dreams, reading, solitude, silence, nightfall and the almost imperceptible movement of time.[23] Who is the speaker of these poems? We are not told. Coming after the songs of the young women, they have the effect of mask lyrics. Are the opening poems mask lyrics as well? Rilke gives no indication. The speaker of the first poem casts aside his armour, emblem of traditional manliness, in favour of merging with the garden and its twining vines. The speaker of the third poem 'bears', or possibly even 'wears' flowers (the German word 'tragen' means both) but whether we are to imagine a woman's corsage or a man's floral buttonhole is not clear. It seems inappropriate even to enquire about the speaker's gender. Although the precise status of the poems' speaker (or speakers) remains ambiguous, it is fair to say that, in the last analysis, these poems confirm, rather than criticise, the cult of passive receptivity and 'feminine aesthetics'.

Situating themselves within the context of the Jugendstil art movement, the poems are part of a contemporary re-evaluation of sensitivity not as a weakness but a strength. They capture a newfound sense of unity between human and natural life and embody a belief that organic growth was essentially aesthetic. Appropriately, the first edition of *To Celebrate Myself* contained numerous vignettes and arabesques by Heinrich Vogeler, one of the artists whom Rilke was soon to study in the course of writing his monograph about the Worpswede art colony. Like Jugendstil itself, these poems trust in the power of youth to revivify all around it, turning everything into a single, flowing whole in which individual parts can no longer be clearly distinguished. Rilke's self-alignment with Jugendstil could scarcely have been more effectively realised. The price, however, was that once again he had written a volume suitable for a young woman's night table.

RUSSIAN ICONS

Through his relation to Lou Andreas-Salomé, Rilke began to find more effective ways of developing his own poetic persona. In the first chapter of her autobiography, *Lebensrückblick* [Looking Back], Lou describes her own difficult struggle for identity by setting it into a more general psychological context: 'Unser erstes Erlebnis ist, bemerkenswerter Weise, ein Entschwund' ('Our first experience, remarkably, is of loss').[24] The experience of birth is one of separation, marked by a sensation of emptiness and experienced as a rift in consciousness.

Before her training in psychoanalysis, however, Lou had seen her identity formation as the result of a spiritual crisis during young adulthood: her first book appeared under the title *Im Kampf um Gott* [In the Struggle for God]. She encouraged Rilke to see his own psychological development in similar terms.

In Rilke's poetic transposition of Lou's ideas, God is in essence a projection of human consciousness. An entire panoply of conventional relationships – centre and periphery, active and passive, container and contained, root and branch, light and dark, surface and depth – is reversed in the world of *Das Stundenbuch* [The Book of Hours]. God becomes another version of the devotional artifacts created by the monks into whose mouths Rilke places the poems of this volume.

Conceived under the influence of Rilke's two trips to Russia with Lou Andreas-Salomé in 1899 and 1900, *The Book of Hours* was published in three volumes composed in 1899, 1901, and 1903 respectively. Though inspired by the spirituality Rilke believed he found in Russia, *The Book of Hours* in fact presents a heretical anti-mysticism. God becomes a metaphor, not for the creative act, but for the art object. *The Book of Hours* conducts an exploration of the nature of poetic rhetoric in which the structure of prayer is identified with the figurative structures of poetry itself.[25]

Rilke's discussions of Russian icons and religious artifacts with Lou Andreas-Salomé, which led to the beginnings of his own collection of Russian objects, were an important factor in his unorthodox view of God as an objective correlative for art. Lou's view of Russian spirituality was the product of her orientalising perspective. While Rilke saw her as an authentic mediator between Russian culture and himself, much of her knowledge about Russia was second-hand.[26] Perhaps the most important element in the ideas she promulgated about Russian religion was her conviction that the Russians would do best if they reconceived God as an abstraction. Rilke does just this in *The Book of Hours*.

Superficially a volume of devotional poetry, *The Book of Hours* is in fact a meditation on the development of personal identity in an age where 'God is dead'. Its appeal lies precisely in the link it makes between

precarious self-knowledge and fundamental doubts about God's existence and powers. Creative art becomes an icon that substitutes for the
divine in a sceptical age. The following poem, written in 1899, presents
Rilke's theory of God as a creation of the human subject:

> Du, Nachbar Gott, wenn ich dich manchesmal
> in langer Nacht mit hartem Klopfen störe, –
> so ists, weil ich dich selten atmen höre
> und weiß: Du bist allein im Saal.
> Und wenn du etwas brauchst, ist keiner da,
> um deinem Tasten einen Trank zu reichen:
> Ich horche immer. Gieb ein kleines Zeichen.
> Ich bin ganz nah.
>
> Nur eine schmale Wand ist zwischen uns,
> durch Zufall; denn es könnte sein:
> ein Rufen deines oder meines Munds –
> und sie bricht ein
> ganz ohne Lärm und Laut.
>
> Aus deinen Bildern ist sie aufgebaut.
>
> Und deine Bilder stehn vor dir wie Namen.
> Und wenn einmal das Licht in mir entbrennt,
> mit welchem meine Tiefe dich erkennt,
> vergeudet sichs als Glanz auf ihren Rahmen.
>
> Und meine Sinne, welche schnell erlahmen,
> sind ohne Heimat und von dir getrennt.　　　　(1: 255–56)

> You, neighbour God, if I, from time to time,
> disturb you in the night with knocking loud, –
> it's just because your breathing's hard to hear:
> I know: you're in the room there all alone.
> And if you have a need, there is no one
> to pass your searching hand a cup to drink:
> I'm always listening. Give a little sign.
> I'm quite near.
>
> Between us there is but a narrow wall,
> coincidentally; for it might be:
> your mouth or maybe mine might give a call –
> and it falls down
> quite without noise or sound.
>
> The wall's constructed of your images.

> Images keep you hidden just like names.
> And if sometime the light in me burns out,
> with which my depths take cognizance of you,
> it will be spent like shine upon their frames.
>
> And all my senses, quickly going numb,
> have lost their homeland and parted from you.

Reversing the relationship of the human subject to the divinity, the poem describes God as if he were a frightened child trying to go to sleep in the next room. Human prayer, presented here through the image of knocking on the wall at night-time, overwhelms God and makes him still more aware of his inability to take care even of his own needs. The human speaker, the monk who is the mouthpiece of most of the poems in *The Book of Hours*, consoles God as if he were a loving parent.

The extended metaphor that constitutes the poem is a peculiar one. On the one hand, customary attributes of God are attributed to the human speaker: the notion of being ever-present and always listening. By the same token, human attributes, such as needing comfort in the night, are attributed to God. On the other hand, in accord with more conventional thinking about the relation between human beings and the divine, the speaker is the one who tries to make contact with God at night, and God is the one who is asked to give a sign. Yet communication between God and the human speaker is constantly frustrated, even though they are neighbours separated only by a fragile wall. The poem goes on to define this wall as the images that keep God hidden instead of revealing him more clearly. But it also consists in the consciousness of the speaker himself: as long as the speaker's mental activity persists, God can be perceived, but when it ceases, nothing is left but lifeless images of the divine.

'You, neighbour God' is quite remote from conventional theology. Prayer, in these poems, is directionality itself rather than directed toward a specific goal.[27] Speaking of God, the poems also speak of themselves and of poetry in general. In many ways, they are one of the earliest avatars of Rilke's later notion of 'intransitive Liebe' (intransitive love), the love that has no object and that, because it is projected infinitely outward, allows the subject to achieve a kind of self-transcendence. *The Book of Hours* oscillates between ideals of divine inspiration and human construction. Not until his work on the Rodin monograph did Rilke begin to separate the idea of 'work' from that of 'inspiration'.

The question whether art is inspired or constructed (or some mixture of the two) had become acute for Rilke during the final years of the century. In 1897, Tolstoy had published an essay entitled 'What is Art?', in which he argued that art must have a religious or ethical component. Finding that he strongly disagreed with the views Tolstoy had presented in that essay, Rilke wrote a response, 'Über Kunst' [On Art] (1888–89; 5:426–434).

In 'What is Art?', Tolstoy argued that we should 'cease looking at [art] as a means of pleasure' and recognise its function as 'a means of communion among people'.[28] The term 'communion' includes both spiritual union and a more general notion of communication. Precisely because art is capable of reproducing in others the original feelings and impressions of the artist, Tolstoy argues, it is also able to bring people together in an essentially religious way. Art is thus not disinterested or purposeless, but an organ of social and spiritual transformation.

Rilke's essay 'On Art' is his response to this idea of art as a vehicle of social reform. Here, he claims that Tolstoy is defining art by its effects rather than by its essence (5: 426). In opposition to Tolstoy, Rilke sees the work of art as 'ein tiefinneres Geständnis' (a deep inner confession) that is externalised and given a viable existence independent of its creator (5: 428). Rilke defines the aesthetic in terms of its autonomy: 'Diese Selbständigkeit des Kunstwerkes ist die Schönheit' (Beauty is this self-sufficiency of the art work; 5: 428). Rilke does not deny that art may have social and political effects, but he prefers to think of these effects as being less direct. They are the result of a resistance between the artist and his time, Rilke claims, 'und erst aus diesem Zwiespalt zwischen der gegenwärtigen Strömung und der zeitfremden Lebensmeinung des Künstlers' (and only out of this discrepancy between the present trend and the artist's timeless view of life) does a certain emancipatory effect of the artwork arise (5: 427–428). Arguing against Tolstoy's opinion that the 'art of the future' will no longer speak only to an elite, but also to the masses, Rilke describes the true artist as one who is always alone and always ahead of his time (5: 431–432). Rilke's essay concludes with a vision of the artist as a tragic figure, unable to attain consonance with his time and constantly constrained by it: 'ein Tänzer, dessen Bewegung sich bricht an dem Zwang seiner Zelle' (a dancer whose movement is broken by the force of his cell) and who must 'die noch ungelebten Linien seines Leibes mit wunden Fingern in die Wände ritzen' (scratch the still unrealised lines of his body with wounded fingers on the walls; 5: 434).

It is easy to see how Rilke has adapted this idea of the artist as a prisoner in *The Book of Hours*. Here, the prisoner has become a monk, tapping desperately on the walls in a vain attempt to summon God's presence. Despite their ostensible other-directedness, these poems really revolve around the self: God ceases to be when the poet no longer exists.

Much of the appeal of *The Book of Hours* derives from the way in which it connects its reflection on the divine with a precarious search for self-identity and an exploration into the nature of artistic creativity. The highly abstract terms and apostrophic forms in which this complicated construct is cast allow the reader considerable interpretive latitude. *The Book of Hours* contains some of Rilke's most brilliant early developments of the appellative structures that give his poetry its charisma.

Rilke saw his trips to Russia as an attempt, in part, to reconnect with the Slavic side of his Prague childhood and to identify more closely with Lou Andreas-Salomé and her heritage. In the course of these trips, Rilke acquired a number of religious artifacts – a seventeenth-century silver cross and various Russian icons – with which he subsequently decorated his study.[29] Rilke's two essays on Russian art continue a discussion that had begun several decades earlier about the relative merits of ancient icons and modern attempts to revitalise their spirit for a new age. Collecting Russian artifacts, creating a shrine-like Russian museum in his study, and recalling the objects of his collection and the spirit in which they had been created was a way for Rilke to work through his own relation to questions of belief, community, and creativity.

Despite his insistence on creativity as an act of the will, the monk Rilke uses as his mouthpiece in *The Book of Hours* still maintains some affinities with the essentially passive speakers of *To Celebrate Myself*. Like them, he is infinitely sensitive, receptive, registering the slightest nuance. But unlike them, he has greater strength of will and sees himself more distinctly as a shaper and definer. *The Book of Hours* is at once a meditation on creative powers in general and a waystage in Rilke's own exploration of his individual capabilities. Constructing the divine also constructs the voice and the mode that will become inimitably Rilke's: a personal tone modulated by a virtuoso command of rhetoric, expressions of intense anxiety combined with grandiose self-assurance, and a devotion to past tradition refracted through idiosyncratic forms of turn-of-the-century free-thinking.

HISTORIC PROJECTION

In his prose-poem, *Der Cornet* [The Cornet] (1899), Rilke shifts his focus to a more conventionally 'masculine' topic, battle. Still, he retains many of the emphases that had predominated in *To Celebrate Myself*: the cult of youth, the androgynous mode, a decorative manner and an emphasis on the life of the senses. At the same time, he continues to explore the questions of passivity and activity at the heart of *The Book of Hours*. *The Cornet* was Rilke's most resounding commercial success. First composed in 1899 and revised for publication five years later, the poem went through numerous reprintings during Rilke's lifetime.[30] In 1912, the text became the first volume in the Insel publishing house's still popular series, 'Insel Bücherei'; in the space of three weeks, the little book had sold eight thousand copies. Even Rilke himself was astounded: 'Wer hätte das gedacht' ('Who would have thought it'), he exclaimed in a letter to the publisher.[31] Recent biographies of Rilke devote only a few lines to *The Cornet*, or, to use its revised title, *Die Weise von Liebe und Tod des Cornets Christoph Rilke* [The Lay of Love and Death of the Cornet Christoph Rilke].[32] Scholarship on the text has been sparse. But although Rilke later disparaged *The Cornet* as an immature work not up to the standards of his subsequent poetry, he made no attempt to suppress the continued re-publication of this money-making book. *The Cornet* is a key text for understanding Rilke's professional development. It is no accident that it enjoyed such enduring popular success.

'Rilke, René Maria Cäsar, entstammt einem uralten Kärntner Adelsgeschlecht' (Rilke, René Maria Caesar, descends from an ancient Carinthian noble family). These had been the opening words of Rilke's self-written entry for the 1896 edition of Franz Brummer's lexicon of German poets (6: 1204). In presenting himself this way, Rilke had perpetuated a myth of family origins started by his father's oldest brother, Jaroslav, and much promulgated by his mother, who enjoyed the idea of a noble heritage. The chronicle Rilke cites, or rather adapts, at the beginning of *The Cornet* was among historical material Jaroslav Rilke had found in his attempt to confirm the family's connections to the nobility. In fact, however, their family was quite unrelated to that of the chronicle.

Rilke opens his prose poem in chronicle format:

'Appel Rilke, Herr auf Langenau, Gränitz, Greußen u.s.f. hat drei Söhne. Der Jüngste, Otto, tritt in oesterreichische Dienste. Er fällt, 18 Jahre alt, als Cornet in der Compagnie des Freiherrn von Pirovano gegen die Türken in Ungarn (1664)'. (3: 291)

'Appel Rilke, Baron of Langenau, Gränitz, Greussen etc. has three sons. The youngest, Otto, enters Austrian service. He falls at the age of eighteen as

standard-bearer in the regiment of Baron von Pirovano in battle against the
Turks in Hungary (1664)'.

The strategy of using old chronicles, real or invented, has a long
tradition: it was a particular favourite among the German Romantics.
The *Cornet* consists of twenty-nine sections of varying length, most of
them quite brief. This lyrical narrative about a young Austrian standard-bearer who dies in battle after a passionate night of love during a
billet in a castle seems to have struck an immediate chord in its readers.
After the carefully wrought first section, the poem develops its quasi-
historical narrative in an often banal manner: memories of blond girls
left behind, the cherished rose petal given him by a comrade, a young
woman tied to a tree and rescued by a stroke of the cornet's sword, an
unknown lady bending over him in the castle at night, an old woman
weeping after the cornet's death. Even in the more original parts of the
poem, the historical setting remains highly stylised.

I focus here on the first version of *The Cornet*, composed in 1899, which
Rilke later revised for re-publication in a Prague journal in 1904 and as a
free-standing book in 1906. It differs from later revisions in several ways.[33]
Of these, the most important is the narrator's comment about dual modes
of reading, wedged between the opening quotation from the chronicle
and the beginning of the narrative proper: 'Man kann sie so lesen, oder
auch auf folgende Art' (One can read it that way, or else in the following
manner; 3:291). The narrator is fully aware that his tale is an exercise of
imagination rather than a historical account. By insisting on this distinction, he urges us to abandon the chronicle-reader's objective stance and
enter the mind of his protagonist. Rilke's omission of this detail in the later
version tells us that by 1904 Rilke could be more confident of his readers'
familiarity with psychological modes of narration.

Turning away from the chronicle genre, the *Cornet* rapidly shifts into
the consciousness of the young standard-bearer:

Reiten, reiten, reiten durch den Tag, durch die Nacht, durch den Tag. Reiten,
reiten, reiten. Und der Mut ist so müde geworden und die Sehnsucht so groß.
Es giebt keine Berge mehr, kaum einen Baum. Nichts wagt aufzustehen.
Fremde Hütten hocken durstig an versumpften Brunnen. Nirgends ein Turm.
Und immer das gleiche Bild. Man hat zwei Augen zuviel. Nur in der Nacht
manchmal glaubt man, den Weg zu kennen. Vielleicht kehren wir nächtens
immer wieder das Stück zurück, das wir in der fremden Sonne mühsam
gewonnen haben? Es kann sein. Die Sonne ist schwer, wie bei uns tief im
Sommer. Aber wir haben im Sommer Abschied genommen, freilich. Die
Kleider der Frauen leuchteten lang aus dem Grün. Und nun reiten wir lang. Es

muß also Herbst sein. Wenigstens dort, wo traurige Frauen von uns wissen.
(3: 291)

Riding, riding, riding, through the day, through the night, through the day.
Riding, riding, riding. And courage has become so weary and longing so great.
There are no mountains any more, hardly a tree. Nothing dares to rise up.
Unfamiliar huts cower thirstily by swampy wells. Nowhere a tower. And always
the same image. One has two eyes too many. Only sometimes, in the night, one
thinks one knows the way. Perhaps we return at night, again and again, along
the same stretch of way that we have painfully gained in the foreign sun? It may
be. The sun is heavy, as in high summer at home. But, of course, we took our
leave in summer. The women's dresses shone out of the green for a long time.
And now we have been riding a long time. So it must be autumn. At least where
sad women know about us.

Something peculiar is at work here. On the one hand, we have a
modern attempt to tell the story very largely from within the protagonist's psyche. On the other, we have the poem's mannered style, which
partially countermands its modern point of view. How can we explain
this paradoxical effect?

Some of its artificial staging bears a resemblance to Adalbert Stifter's
novel *Witiko* (1865–67), a narrative set in twelfth-century Bohemia. Rilke
had long had a particular fondness for Stifter and owned a copy of his
novel *Der Nachsommer* [The Indian Summer] (1857); I do not know
whether he had read *Witiko*.[34] Given the novel's thematic connection
with Prague, Rilke may have read it (or excerpts from it) during his
studies for the matriculation exam. The stylised and highly visual mode
of description, the attention paid to hair, and the androgynous character
of the figure, are elements common to Stifter's novel and Rilke's version
of a later period in Austrian history.

If we look at the poem from a more visual perspective, seeing it as a
sequence of elegantly composed vignettes, it also closely resembles
Pre-Raphaelite mediaevalism. The figures and trappings of *The Cornet* –
the very young knight, the beautiful lady, the bright banner, the desperate ride into battle – recall numerous Pre-Raphaelite paintings and
drawings. One might think of Dante Gabriel Rossetti's *Before the Battle*
(1858), a highly stylised painting dominated by a lady in a red robe
attaching a pennant to the standard of a youthful, blond and pensive
knight; Elizabeth Siddal's more informal *Lady Affixing a Pennant to a
Knight's Spear* (1856); Edward Burne-Jones's *Going to the Battle* (1858), a
drawing of three ladies saying farewell to a troop of departing knights;
and Edward Burne-Jones's *The Knight's Farewell* (1856), a drawing show-

ing a lady embracing a kneeling knight in an enclosed garden.[35] Illuminated mediaeval psalters, mediaeval ballads and the chronicles of
Jean Froissart, among other things, were central influences on these
mediaevalising exercises by the Pre-Raphaelites. Rilke shared these
interests, especially during the period when he was first composing *The
Cornet*, and they stayed with him well into the first decade of the
twentieth century.[36] In his capacity as an art historian, he was of course
well acquainted with the Pre-Raphaelites' adaptations of mediaeval
materials in their visual art.

'It is a finer ideal, extracted from what in relation to any actual world
is already an ideal. Like some strange second flowering after date, it
renews on a more delicate type the poetry of a past age, but must not be
confounded with it', writes Walter Pater in his essay 'Aesthetic Poetry'
(1889).[37] He is talking about Pre-Raphaelite verse, but his words apply
equally well to Rilke's *Cornet*. The main part of Pater's essay is devoted to
a discussion of poetry by William Morris, which he sees as examples of
'aesthetic poetry' in his own day; a subsequent chapter of Pater's
Appreciations identifies Dante Gabriel Rossetti as another 'aesthetic poet'.
The leading sentiment of both writers Pater sees as 'the continual
suggestion, pensive or passionate, of the shortness of life. This is contrasted with the bloom of the world, and gives new seduction to it – the sense
of death and the desire of beauty: the desire of beauty quickened by the
sense of death' (p. 198). A closer approximation to the spirit of Rilke's
Cornet would be hard to find.

Rilke's prose-poem is in fact a superb example of what Carolyn
Williams terms 'aesthetic historicism' – a 'homology and interdependence of aestheticism and historicism'.[38] In Pater's scheme, the later
productions, those of his own day, are richer, more sophisticated, and
more profound than the earlier, mediaeval works. This effect he attributes to the process of secularisation that has intervened between the
Middle Ages and his own time, so that religion is now displaced into a
sense for the aesthetic object. 'Aesthetic poetry' is more aware than its
predecessors of the loss this shift has involved: a loss, primarily, of direct
sensory contact with the world.

Pater's account of this development is echoed in Rilke's concern over
what he saw as a loss of immediate relation to the earlier times. The
exploration of the relation between inner and outer realities, an attempt
to transfigure loss, and an understanding of the aesthetic as a phenomenon of displacement are all characteristic features of *The Cornet*, as of
Rilke's later writing.

The famous first section of the poem, 'reiten, reiten, reiten...' (riding, riding riding...), depends upon internalisation, displacement and transfiguration. The passage slides subtly between an inner and an outer perspective: in part, we seem to be inside the young knight's mind, riding through the strange countryside with him and seeing it with his eyes. At the same time, there is a distinct uneasiness about our identification with him, as it hinges in part on the use of the German word 'man' (one). One has, indeed, 'zwei Augen zuviel' (two eyes too many), as the speaker observes, alerting the reader, as it were, to the factitiousness of the empathy between the reader and the horseman. Even when the voice shifts to the first person plural, in the phrase 'vielleicht kehren wir nächtens...' (perhaps we return at night...), the pronoun seems to imply something more widely generalising than just the experience of the regiment riding through unfamiliar territory. How specific to the described situation or (on the contrary) how general is this statement? It is hard to tell. The pronoun 'wir' (we) seems more expansive here than in its subsequence uses: 'wir haben im Sommer Abschied genommen' (we took our leave in summer), 'nun reiten wir lang' (we have been riding a long time). But even these later phrases, though they strictly refer to the horsemen in the narrative, invite a certain degree of identification: 'Aber... freilich' (But... of course). Now the reader is in the mind of the horseman, thinking along with him, speculating about the lapse of time that may have taken place between the regiment's departure and their present predicament.

It would not be quite accurate, however, to describe what takes place in this section simply as internalisation. Projection of the interior into the exterior world is also at work: 'Und der Mut ist so müde geworden und die Sehnsucht so groß' (And courage has become so weary and longing so great). As the emotions of the rider turn into almost disembodied abstractions, the landscape becomes anthropomorphised: 'Nichts wagt aufzustehen' (Nothing dares to rise up), 'fremde Hütten hocken durstig...' (unfamiliar huts cower thirstily...). Dislocation works in two directions at once, moving the reader partially into the experiencing mind, while the emotions of the experiencing psyche are projected onto external nature. Like the mediaeval verse Pater describes in 'Aesthetic Poetry' (p. 193), 'the things of nature begin to play a strange delirious part' in these peculiar distortions of the landscape.

Dislocation occurs on several different planes beside the interior–exterior axis. One of these is geographic. But while everything is strange and unfamiliar, it is also 'immer das gleiche Bild' (always the same image). The rider knows that he is no longer at home, but he does not have the ability to identify landmarks, perceive differences, or in any way 'know where he is' in the foreign countryside. Simultaneously, he is troubled by a highly unsettling sense of temporal indeterminacy. He becomes aware of a discrepancy between his inner sense of time ('es muß also Herbst sein' (it must be autumn)) and the unreadable weather of these foreign parts ('die Sonne ist schwer, wie bei uns tief im Sommer' (the sun is heavy, as in high summer at home)). Knowledge itself, finally, is dislodged from the experiencing consciousness and cast backward into the minds of the women left behind ('wo traurige Frauen von uns wissen' (where sad women know about us)). The passage as a whole moves increasingly into an imaginary realm where nothing is fixed or certain and the only possible response is speculation.

Internalisation and externalisation form a complex knot here that is difficult to unravel. It is an extraordinary tour de force. We see here the origins of certain early texts by Kafka, who would have read the 1904 version of the *Cornet* in the Prague journal where it appeared and to which he also contributed.[39] Many years later, Robert Musil created similar tangles of interior and exterior reality, though without the sentimental overtones of Rilke's prose-poem.[40] To what extent these similarities have to do with an actual impact of the *Cornet* on later writing or to a common cultural climate is difficult to determine.

Rilke liked to claim that he had written *The Cornet* in the course of a single stormy night. That may well have been the case; but his insistence on it was also a way of distracting from the more consciously artificial techniques used in the poem. To claim that *The Cornet* had burst forth in a single torrent was to locate its origins in an individual rush of emotion and inspired creation. It was to claim it as the very opposite of professional design.

Even so, there was a literary precedent for Rilke's attempt to reproduce the emotions of a man riding through the countryside. This was an inset text in Achim von Arnim's novel *Die Gräfin Dolores* [Countess Dolores] (1810). Arnim's prose poem, extending over several pages and embellished by lavish use of internal rhyme and assonance, is an astonishingly early version of interior monologue, although of a very artificial kind. At times the text becomes rhymed verse written along the line, at other times the echoing elements of the language are less regularly arranged; my translation is somewhat free in order to render these effects:

Über Stock, über Stein, drein, drein, ohne Bewußtsein; knackts, brichts, wirfts um, ich sitze stumm; meiner Blicke einzige Sprache ist ewiges Wachen, ein nordischer Tag ohne Nacht in hallender rastloser Jagd.[41]

Over stick, over stone, on, on, consciousness gone; cracking, breaking, whacking, I sit tight; my eyes' only speech endless waking, a Nordic day without night in clattering restless riding without stay.

As the poem continues, it reproduces the Count's thoughts as he tries to banish his suspicions about his wife's relationship with a sinister friend. Gradually – if not immediately – the reader becomes aware that the Count has been driven mad by his jealous thoughts. The language rushes forward, stumbling over itself, ensnaring itself in excessive rhyme and jangling nervousness. There is no attempt at realistic representation, but rather at a form of language that frankly admits that it can be no more than a translation of thoughts that are essentially inchoate. It is a daring, if not sucessful, experiment.

Arnim had originally published two different sections of the poem as independent texts in 1808; in the novel of 1810, however, they function as stylised stream-of-consciousness narration. Like the first version of Rilke's *Cornet*, Arnim's prose poem is broken into numbered sections. Like Rilke's protagonist, Arnim's protagonist is spooked by the interreaction of his thoughts and the landscape, and divided from himself by geographic and psychological disorientation. Instead of an actual sexual experience, as in Rilke's poem, Arnim's text includes an erotic hallucination.

The most remarkable link between Arnim's prose-poem and Rilke's can be seen in a crucial scene that Rilke altered radically when preparing the text for publication. This is an episode in *The Cornet* where the castle catches fire and begins to burn uncontrollably as the young standard-bearer wrenches himself out of deep sleep after his night of love. In the 1899 version of this section (original number 23), a cluster of alliterative phrases in the style of old Germanic verse suddenly yields to a proliferation of internal rhymes:

Kommt der Morgen *so*? Plötzlich ist Alles hell: Wände und Waffen, Stimmen und Stirnen, Helme und Hörner, Lager und Land. Noch wälzt das Schloß den roten Gedanken in seinem Hirn, den ungeheuren, der heimlich reift und die Tore ergreift, bis sie alle schreien:
Brand!
Was hilft da verrammeln? Jetzt ist es verraten. Ganz nahe waren Jannitscharen. Taten! Taten! Taten! bedarfs. Schande den Schwachen, die zaghaft erwachen.

Schmach! Langsam erlangt der Drachen das Dach, es schwankt: Krachen.
Und im Hof erschrockene Hörner stammeln: Sammeln, sammeln, sammeln . . .
(3: 302)

Does morning come *this way*? Suddenly all is light: walls and weapons, voices
and visions, helmets and horns, camp and countryside. Still the castle turns the
red thought over in its mind, the monstrous idea that ripens late, grasps hold of
the gate, till everyone cries out:

Fire!

What use are barricades? Now it is all betrayed. Janissaries were near here.
Deeds! deeds! deeds! that's what one needs. A shame on those who quake,
hesitantly starting awake. Disgrace! Slowly the fire-trace reaches the roof of the
place, it staggers: crashing. And in the courtyard terrified horns tremble:
assemble, assemble, assemble . . .

The form of this section is remarkably close to that of Arnim's prose-
poem from *Countess Dolores*. As if to cover the traces of Arnim, Rilke
completely rewrites the section about the burning castle in the final
version of the *Cornet*, eliminating almost entirely the internal rhymes,
assonance and alliterations of the original. He shortens sentences, increases disjunctures and gives the passage a more impressionistic quality.

Why does Rilke not take his experiment one stage further and hazard
a more sustained attempt at interior monologue? This is a puzzle that,
oddly enough, has hardly been addressed in the discussion about Rilke's
relation to the modernist movements. Even his most distinctively modernist text, *Malte Laurids Brigge*, never shifts from its first-person perspective into interior monologue or stream-of-consciousness narration. In
those passages of *Malte*, as also of *The Cornet*, that move closer into the
mind of the protagonists, narrative perspective is maintained by use of
the simultaneous inside/outside pronoun 'one'.

We should not, however, overlook those aspects of the text that did
appear innovative to early twentieth-century readers. A scholarly essay
on *The Cornet* that appeared just three years after Rilke's death may help
us see the poem from a different vantage-point.[42] Here, the author
describes what strikes him as 'so bold, so new' about the text. If only we
had some way, he says, of writing a history of musical style in poetry.
Then 'one would recognise that the looser form of [Rilke's] work
approaches the freer style of modern music, that its meter changes
time-signature as often as the most disjointed work of Reger, indeed,
that it is able to utter word-chords that were in the mind of that brilliant
musical theorist, Arnold Schönberg, in the form of sound harmonies'

(p. 24). The constantly shifting and finely nuanced effects that Rilke creates in *The Cornet*, its allusive method, its shattering of conventional syntax, its significant omissions and pervasive indeterminacy, its subtle interweaving of inner and outer realities – all these features remind the scholar of 1929 of atonal music and cause him to rank the poem as a modernist piece strikingly in advance of its time. This view is reinforced by Kasimir von Pászthory's musical setting of the poem, the chromatic tonalities of which the author of the article regards as a brilliant representation of the linguistic effects of the original.[43] This reading of *The Cornet* as a 'modernist' atonal mood-piece contrasts strikingly with earlier readings of the poem in terms of its sexual thematics.

From today's perspective, it is easy to overlook what must have seemed, in 1899, a rather daring exploration of the relation between sexual desire and aggression. The fire scene forms a symbolic link between the erotic bedroom episode and the battleground, between what Freud was later to call the libido and the death wish. In bringing together these deep-seated impulses, Rilke situates his prose-poem in the context of a broader contemporary interest in human psychology. Hofmannsthal's 'Reitergeschichte' [Story of a Horseman], published just a year earlier (1898), develops similar linkages between violence and sexuality, aggressive action and passive sensuality. Somewhat differently, Frank Wedekind's drama *Der Erdgeist* [The Earth Spirit] (1895) had also drawn connections between sexual drives and violence (in Wedekind's play, not war but murder). *The Cornet* profits from an often sensationalist fascination with subconscious desires during a period where Freud himself was just beginning to work out his theories.

The Cornet hovers between historicism and aestheticism, the matter-of-factness of the old chronicle and the imaginative interiority of its modern recreation. It also hovers between neo-Romantic sensibilities and modernist understandings of the psyche. In this respect, *The Cornet* represents a crucial phase in Rilke's self-fashioning. His ability to combine psychological expression with decorative effects positions him between one cultural epoch and another. These paradoxical qualities make *The Cornet* a signal text for any discussion of Rilke's poetic development.

NORDIC CHILDHOODS

Rilke's most sustained reflection on the relation between psychology, creativity and literary and historical tradition is his 'prose book', *Malte Laurids Brigge*. Its lengthy gestation (over a period spanning almost six years, beginning in February 1904 and ending in January 1910) accompanied Rilke's work on the second edition of *Das Buch der Bilder* [The Book of Images], the first and second volumes of the *New Poems*, and the Requiems for Paula Modersohn-Becker and Wolf Graf von Kalckreuth. Several passages in *Malte Laurids Brigge* have near-equivalents in Rilke's correspondence, especially with Clara Rilke and Lou Andreas-Salomé, during his Paris period; some other sections are drawn from his childhood experiences, particularly his relationship with his mother. Themes such as loneliness, alienation and disgust reflect Rilke's concerns – and his psychological difficulties – during his work on *Malte Laurids Brigge*. The book's autobiographical character has led many readers to identify Rilke with Malte, despite Rilke's repeated warnings that his fictional protagonist was less a direct stand-in for himself than a negative alter ego.[44] By casting the novel as a record of a fictional writer's struggle with problems of reading, writing and professional development, Rilke takes the measure of what he sees as the simultaneous potential and limitations of narrative in the early years of the twentieth century.

Narrative issues, as well as larger issues about art in general, have long been the focus of critical attention to *Malte Laurids Brigge*.[45] But although there have been several studies of Rilke's adaptation of various works of literature and the visual arts in *Malte Laurids Brigge*,[46] the meta-poetic significance of this heavy dependence on other texts and art works has scarcely been explored. Yet the entire depiction of creative production in *Malte* revolves around a continued discussion of one's own creativity in its relation to that of one's predecessors. The book is not only about the process of 'learning to see', it is also about the process of learning to read. The connection between reading and writing, the extent to which writing is also re-writing is a central concern of Malte's notebook.

Rilke's prose book is precariously positioned on the boundary between naturalism and aestheticism. Malte knows, for example, that he is living in poverty and the only thing that distinguishes him from other poor people is that even his wrists are clean (6: 742). At the same time, he wishes he could still live in his noble country house among ancient family furniture, writing in a book bound in 'gelbliches, elfenbeinfarbiges Leder' (yellowish, ivory leather; 6: 746). The constant alternation between realistic descriptions of Malte's life in sordid Paris and his absorption in a world of fantasy, reading and recollections of earlier reading, gives the book its curiously disorienting quality.

Contextual evidence – primarily Rilke's letters and reviews – points to an early genesis of the passages in which Malte asks for his childhood to be restored to him. We can date them with reasonable certainty to around 1904. A remarkably realistic passage describes Malte's visit to a doctor at Salpêtrière following a general practitioner's suggestion that he be treated with electroshock therapy (6: 758). After waiting for a long time, observing the other patients and listening to doctors questioning another patient behind a partition, Malte flees in horror from the terrifying scene.

In several passages about Malte's illness, Rilke begins to work out a theory of psychological repression. One indication is his development of metaphors concerning surface and depth:[47]

Und mit dem, was kommt, hebt sich ein ganzes Gewirr irrer Erinnerungen, das daranhängt wie nasser Tang an einer versunkenen Sache. Leben, von denen man nie erfahren hätte, tauchen empor und mischen sich unter das, was wirklich gewesen ist, und verdrängen Vergangenes, das man zu kennen glaubte: denn in dem, was aufsteigt, ist eine ausgeruhte, neue Kraft, das aber, was immer da war, ist müde von zu oftem Erinnern. (6: 766)

And along with [an old habit or gesture] arises a whole tangle of confused memories, clinging to it like wet seaweed to a sunken object. Lives one had never heard of emerge and mingle among that which was real, and repress past events one thought one knew: for in that which arises is a new, restored energy, while that which was always there is weary from too frequent recollection.

Dangers are 'deep' and memories fished up as if from the bottom of the sea, while the thinking subject lies in his bed 'five floors up' from street level. Fictional lives 'emerge' from the depths ('emportauchen' means to rise up out of water) and push (or 'verdrängen': repress) past events back down into oblivion. The passage recalls one of Rilke's letters to Franz Xaver Kappus, a young poet who had written to him for advice. Writing (in 1904) of Kappus's puzzlement about fits of melancholy that come and go without any clear reason, Rilke compares them with illnesses that have not received the right medical treatment: they 'treten [...] nur zurück und brechen nach einer kleinen Pause um so furchtbarer aus; und sammeln sich an im Innern und sind Leben, ein ungelebtes, verschmähtes, verlorenes Leben, an dem man sterben kann' (merely recede and break out all the more terribly after a slight pause; and gather inside one and are life, unlived, despised, lost life that one may die of).[48] The metaphors he uses here, images of receding and breaking out again, of collecting internally and causing some kind of fatal festering, are ideas that have since become familiar from Freudian psychology. Rilke explores this type of thinking at an early point, well before Freud's theories were widely known. 'Hätte man doch wenigstens seine Erinnerungen. Aber wer hat die? Wäre die Kindheit da, sie ist wie vergraben' (If only one had one's memories. But who has them? If only childhood were there; it is as if it were buried; 6: 721).

Some of these ideas derive from Ellen Key. After reviewing her book, *Das Jahrhundert des Kindes* [The Century of the Child], in 1902, Rilke began a long correspondence with her, which deepened into a personal friendship.[49] While he did not take altogether kindly to Ellen Key's suggestions for the care of his daughter, he was impressed by her theories about the importance of childhood in general. It was Ellen Key who arranged for him to spend time in a country house in Borgeby Gård in 1904, when he needed a quiet refuge. During that time, he visited the Samskola in Furuborg, a progressive school that promulgated freedom of development. Rilke's essay on the school, written in November 1904, expresses his enthusiasm for the friendly relations between pupils and teachers, the children's enjoyment of their time at school, the comfortable, country house atmosphere of the schoolrooms, and the lack of conventional religious education (5: 672–681). How different it was from the military shool he had attended. In the Samskola, Rilke found a hopeful alternative to his own unhappy childhood experiences.

But more importantly for *Malte Laurids Brigge*, the idea of revisiting one's childhood as a crucial step in fashioning an adult identity takes its origin in a series of novels set in Scandinavia. Many of Malte's childhood recollections are not based on Rilke's own life at all. Often enough, they are 'borrowed' memories, drawn from 'Nordic' novels Rilke was devouring and sometimes also reviewing at the time when he first conceived his *Malte* project.

Rilke's interest in Jens Peter Jacobsen's novel *Niels Lyhne* is well known. Rilke's admiration for Jacobsen had much to do with the way in which the Danish author had depicted his childhood in this quasi-autobiographical novel. The early chapters of *Niels Lyhne* recount the protagonist's boyhood games and fantasies. At the age of twenty-three, when Niels sets out to become a poet, he falls back on memories of these early years: 'now, with the passion of an explorer, he began to seek himself out from childhood memories and impressions, from the living moments of his life, and with relief and astonishment he saw how it matched, piece by piece, and fit together to make a quite differently familiar person than the one he had chased after in dream'.[50] Jacobsen's

Frau Marie Grubbe, which Rilke also read, devotes its first seven chapters to Marie's childhood sufferings and shows how her later life is determined by these early experiences.

Other Danish novelists of the period also explored the relation of childhood experiences to adult identity formation. Herman Bang's novels, two of which Rilke reviewed and one other of which he read also trace the development of their young protagonists from their early years.[51] In his 1902 review of *The White House*, Rilke dwells on Bang's ability to conjure up childhood impressions of grown-ups' inexplicable moments of melancholy, as when the mother sits and sings to the piano, radiating sadness 'wie einen Duft, den gewisse Blumen ausatmen, ehe die Nacht kommt' (like a scent exhaled by certain flowers before night falls; 5: 584). As one who grew up 'ein Kind einsam unter Erwachsenen' (a lonely child among adults; 5: 581), Rilke identifies with Bang, the child who had listened to his mother's nameless sorrows at the piano and who grew up to write a book 'welches das Buch seiner Kindheit ist' (that is the book of his childhood; 5: 584).

What fascinates Rilke about Bang's *Tine*, which he reviewed in 1903, is its juxtaposition of the Danish-Holstein war of 1864 with the lives of the women and children who have been left behind. Frightening reports from the battlefield traumatise young Tine (5: 647). Rilke reads Bang's ability to present Tine from inside as a displacement of Bang's own childhood experiences: in Tine's home we recognise, Rilke says, Bang's 'schmerzlich verlorenes Vaterhaus' (painfully lost paternal house; 5: 648). Bang's artistic strengths in *Tine* derive, in Rilke's view, from his attempt to recover childhood memories and get closer to feelings that are bound up with these memories. 'So gewinnt er ein anderes Verhältnis zu seinen Stoffen: aus dem Dunkel der Kindheit kommt er zu ihnen wie aus ihrer eigenen Tiefe; er erlebt sie inniger, gerechter und ernster' (In this way, he gains a different relationship to his material: he comes to it from the obscurity of childhood as if from its own depths; he experiences it more passionately, justly, and earnestly; 5: 649). Rilke goes on to write that Bang 'will seiner Kindheit wieder mächtig werden und fähig, mit schlichter Klarheit von ihren Eindrücken und Bildern und Begebenheiten zu erzählen. Er ruft Erinnerungen' (wants to take possession of his childhood again and become capable of narrating its impressions and images and events. He summons up memories; 5: 649). Malte's name may derive from the hotel where Herman Bang, along with many another Scandinavian visitor, first stayed in Paris in 1893, the 'Hotel Malte',[52] across from the Bibliothèque Nationale, where, as we have already seen, Rilke's protagonist can be found reading poetry early in his own stay in the cosmopolitan city.

The strange air of melancholy that pervades the Danish novels finds its equivalent in Malte's psychological illness. Malte's preoccupation with deathbed scenes and untimely deaths reflects many similar scenes in Jacobsen and Bang. Rilke seems to have found the name of Malte's beloved youthful aunt, Abelone, in *Frau Marie Grubbe*, while her character and relationship to Malte is largely modeled on Niels Lyhne's aunt Edele, on whom Niels has a passionate crush. The death of aunt Edele is one of the most affecting scenes in *Niels Lyhne* and helps to explain the emotional ambience surrounding Malte's aunt Abelone. We cannot be sure what Abelone's status is in the haunting scene in Venice where Malte seems to see her double singing amidst a throng of eager listeners. Has Abelone died (like Niels Lyhne's aunt Edele) in the meantime? Malte does not tell us.

The most important – but hitherto unnoticed – 'Nordic' model for *Malte Laurids Brigge* is Franziska Reventlow's novel *Ellen Olestjerne* (1903). To be sure, this novel was not in fact Scandinavian; but it was certainly part of the 'Nordic vogue'. Essentially autobiographical, it displaces its author's life into Denmark and gives her a Scandinavian name. It is the story of a girl who has trouble fitting in, who fails to win the affection even of her own mother, and who has to fight to be permitted to go to Munich and study painting. Rilke knew Franziska Reventlow personally and corresponded with her before his own move to Munich to study art history. Not long after *Ellen Olestjerne* appeared, Rilke reviewed it in the form of a personal letter to its eponymous protagonist: 'Liebe Ellen Olestjerne, nun hat man Ihre Geschichte erzählt; und ich finde das gut' (Dear Ellen Olestjerne, now your story has been told; and I find that good; 5: 653). The fictive letter is full of affection for Ellen, viewing her obstinacy in a positive light, glossing over the wild bohemian life of free love she leads in Munich, and not even mentioning the stillbirth of her first, illegitimate baby during a temporary absence of the husband she has married in order to give the infant a name. Rilke does, however, gently criticise the novel's ending, in which Ellen is shown happily dreaming of the future after the birth of her second child, who is lying peacefully beside her.

Rilke combined elements from this novel with elements from *Niels Lyhne* and other Nordic texts from the years 1902–4 in *Malte Laurids Brigge*. In *Ellen Olestjerne* the protagonist, recently arrived in Munich and still finding her way in the unfamiliar city, decides to begin writing a diary. 'Ich möchte mir doch endlich angewöhnen, für mich selbst über mein Leben Chronik zu führen' (I would like to get into the habit, at last, of keeping a log of my life for myself).[53] At this point, her good intentions last only a couple of months, and cover less than ten pages; then the third-person narrator takes over as before. Towards the end of the novel, Ellen begins to keep a diary again: this time, her entries run for almost ten months and take up just over twenty pages. These two sets of journal entries bear many resemblances, in form and theme, to *Malte Laurids Brigge*, which is set forth as an intimate journal, even though only the first entry actually bears a date. More strikingly, even the third-person narrative in *Ellen Olestjerne* is broken up into small sections, as is the text of Rilke's prose book. There is a significant structural difference between the two novels, however: while Ellen's life is narrated in chronological order, Malte's memories of his childhood are interleaved with his experiences in Paris.

Thematically, *Ellen Olestjerne* and *Malte Laurids Brigge* have much in common. Both works explore the inner lives of a creative artist: Ellen is a painter, Malte a writer. Both young people are in their twenties: Ellen is twenty-three, Malte is twenty-eight. Neither enjoys family support and both must endure poverty and hardship in order to pursue their careers.

In some other respects, the two works are mirror-images of each other. Whereas the young Malte pleases his mother by pretending to be a little girl and chatting in a falsetto voice with her about the general nastiness of little boys, young Ellen causes an uproar in her family by saying she wants to be a boy. A maid consoles her by telling her that she will become a boy when she turns six, and Ellen innocently believes her. When her sixth birthday dawns she wants to put on boys' clothes, but everyone laughs at her and she realises 'daß sie immer ein Mädchen bleiben mußte' (that she must remain a girl forever; p. 18). Nonetheless, Ellen continues to play boys' games with her younger brother and another boy. Among these games is a ritual in which they swear blood brothership in the attic, dressed up in 'phantastische Gewänder aus weißen Bettüchern' (fantastic garments made out of white bedsheets; p. 28). The famous scene in Rilke's novel where young Malte dresses up in clothing found in unused guest rooms is clearly related to this scene in Reventlow's text, though Rilke introduces some new elements, notably the moment when Malte catches sight of his costumed figure in the mirror and flees in horror at the sight.

Like Malte, Ellen Olestjerne expresses great admiration for Ibsen. The sections of *Ellen Olestjerne* that deal with Ellen's membership in an

'Ibsenklub' (Ibsen club; p. 75), her promulgation of 'Ibsen und moderne Ideen' (Ibsen and modern ideas; p. 85) and her father's scornful linking of her desire to become a painter with thoughts of women's emancipation derived from the Ibsen club (p. 106), provide cultural details essential to understanding the full significance of the 'Nordic vogue' among young people around the turn of the century. Malte's adulatory address to Ibsen, which seems to surge up out of nowhere, is more readily intelligible when seen against this backdrop.

Indeed, Malte describes Ibsen in much the same terms that Rilke had used to describe Ellen Olestjerne in his review of Reventlow's novel: as a solitary figure whose influence can only be effective from a position of isolation. For Malte, Ibsen also functions as an illustrious model for his own attempts at writing, a tragic poet who 'unter dem Sichtbaren nach den äquivalenten suchte für das innen Gesehene' (sought to find equivalents in the visible world for that which he saw with his inner eye; 6: 785).

Ellen Olestjerne and Malte Laurids Brigge share an obsession with hard work and a desire to learn to see things anew. When one of Ellen's classmates helps her to improve her drawing skills by allowing her to use him as a model, she feels that he is teaching her to see (p. 167); and at the end of the novel, as she awaits the birth of her child, she begins to see with new eyes, feel with new senses, and finally, 'lesen zu lernen' (to learn to read; p. 231). Similarly, 'learning to see' becomes for Rilke's Malte a leitmotif that accompanies him throughout the book and is also connected with intensive reading projects. For Malte, 'learning to see' is a way of freeing himself from conventional aesthetics by accepting the fact that ugliness is just as much part of our world as that which is traditionally considered beautiful. It is a way, too, of quelling the anxieties that keep on rising to the surface of Malte's consciousness, of putting them to rest by casting visual experience into verbal form.

For Malte, however, the recovery of childhood memories does not mean a recovery of psychological health: 'Ich habe um meine Kindheit gebeten, und sie ist wiedergekommen, und ich fühle, daß sie immer noch so schwer ist wie damals und daß es nichts genützt hat, älter zu werden' (I have asked for my childhood, and it has returned, and I feel that it is still as burdensome as it was then and that it has been useless to grow older; 6: 767). The burden of the past is not lightened in the final sections of the novel. To the last, Rilke insisted that the book be read 'against the grain', taking into account the fact that Malte had still not managed to triumph over his illness. For all his increasing ability to write, Malte remains alienated. His final entry is a reworking of the Biblical story of the prodigal son. Here, Malte uses his empathetic powers to enter the psyche of the prodigal. In reinterpreting the story as that of a person 'who did not wish to be loved' (6: 938), he reads the prodigal as the opposite of Ellen Olestjerne, the girl who left home because she was not loved by her parents.[54] Unlike Ellen's ultimately happy escape to independence, the prodigal's story breaks off without resolution. The link between the prodigal son and Malte himself, though clearly enough implied, is never explicitly stated. In this sense, the novel concludes with a meta-narratological reflection on the problematic relation of texts to life and the questionable value of intertextuality. The therapeutic effect of reading, remembering, writing and rewriting is never shown.

In 1904 Rilke conceived *Malte Laurids Brigge* as a framework narrative, in which a friend reports on the life of the young poet. Two versions of a third-person opening are extant. Rilke may have hoped that this strategy would avoid some of the problems that troubled him in *Ellen Olestjerne*, in particular its use of first-person form (6: 1436). Had Rilke retained the framing structure, the fictional friend could have passed judgment on the outcome of Malte's development at the end of the book. It is significant that Rilke chose not to pursue this plan. For only by eliminating the framing device can the full ambiguity of Malte's life become evident. Only in this way can his disturbing vacillation between childhood and adulthood, mastery and impotence, reading and experience, the aesthetic and the real, achieve its most powerful effect.

CHAPTER 2

Arts and crafts

Rilke accompanied his *Neue Gedichte* [New Poems], published in two volumes in 1907 and 1908, with numerous pronouncements about their novelty. What was actually new about them? Rilke made several claims: they were the result of persistent labour and careful craftsmanship; they were created directly from nature; and they focussed on objects in all their three-dimensional reality, removing them from time and situating them in space. Rilke's first claim is certainly true: the *New Poems* are examples of poetic craftsmanship that rises at times to virtuoso heights. His second claim, bolstered by frequent subtitles referring to specific places, is not always accurate: in a number of instances, there was a considerable time lapse between Rilke's first visit to a place and his writing a poem about it. Rilke's third claim has been the topic of much critical debate, but the poems themselves, based on multiple and often quite fanciful analogies, demonstrate that representation of objects as such is not the ultimate effect of the *New Poems*.[1]

One thing is immediately apparent about Rilke's claims for his poems: he sees them in terms of the visual arts. Rodin's sculptures and, for the second part of the *New Poems*, Cézanne's painting are his two main models. His association with Rodin and his many visitors and house guests during the period of the *New Poems* was a crucial factor here; an important series of letters he wrote to his wife, herself a sculptor, about the 1907 Cézanne retrospective was another decisive element. In both artists, he was struck by the way in which objects seemed to acquire a self-sufficiency uncontaminated by sentimentality, a goal he wished to achieve for himself as he moved away from turn-of-the-century poetic models. In his studies of Rodin, which took shape as a book in 1902 and as a lecture in 1907, Rilke was especially interested in the interplay of surfaces in the sculptures. He saw Rodin as substituting for traditional compositional principles 'unzählbar viele lebendige Flächen' (innumerably many lively surfaces; 5: 150), reflecting light to create movement in what would otherwise be static (5: 218), and thus apprehending space in a radically new way (5: 220). At the Cézanne retrospective, Rilke was interested in the interplay of colours. 'Es ist, als wüßte jede Stelle von allen' (it is as if every spot [in the painting] knew about every other).[2] Writing to his wife about Cézanne, he comments that it was not so much the art itself that interested him (though he took great care to describe individual works to her in detail), but the new departure this art had taken. It was a 'Wendung' (turning), Rilke wrote, that he had just begun to approach in his own work.[3] But constructing texts in imitation of what he had learned from the visual arts was not a simple process.

Throughout the *New Poems*, Rilke conducts a debate about problems of representation and the relative virtues of the visual and the verbal arts. An art historian by training, he was thoroughly familiar with the ancient rivalry among the sibling arts and with the tasks to which they had traditionally been declared best suited. The poems we will look at in this chapter are all concerned with this debate: music, painting, architecture and sculpture are measured by turn against the powers of the verbal arts.

Approaches that minimise context do not reveal the full extent of Rilke's argument with symbolism and aestheticism, movements from which he repeatedly tries to fight free – not always with complete success. His implicit argument with the esoteric and hermetic strains of aestheticism emerges more clearly through comparison of his own poetry with that of his contemporaries.

Alongside discourses about the practice of art and the possibility of representation, Rilke also picks up a number of contemporary fashions: Biblical themes made popular by the Pre-Raphaelites; the colour blue, all the rage from the eighteen-nineties into the first decade of the new century (as in Picasso's Blue Period); travel to places like Venice, Capri or Bruges. Gothic architecture, mediaeval artifacts, ancient monuments, exotic flowers and zoo animals were all late nineteenth-century fetishes that still held their appeal in Rilke's day. The *New Poems* are full of these motifs.

IMAGINARY PICTURES

Among the most difficult to integrate into a coherent theory of the *New Poems* are the poems on Biblical themes, which diverge radically from Rilke's own proclamations about the nature of his 'new' poetry. They differ, for example, from the *New Poems* that are usually held up as models of the type: poems on a single object, such as 'Der Panther' [The Panther] (1903). The poems on themes from classical antiquity present a similar case, though some of these can be linked to an actual work of art such as a sculpture or a frieze. It is tempting to think of the two volumes of the *New Poems* as taking the form of two visits to museums, in which the viewer begins with objects or pictures from antiquity, proceeds to the Middle Ages, and thence to modern times. Not all of the Biblical poems, however, can be traced to identifiable pictures or art objects.

Rilke's *New Poems* include not only poems about actual pictures, but also poems about 'imaginary pictures', another popular poetic genre of the time.[4] In addition to those poems that can be traced to known works of art,[5] several of the *New Poems* treat themes that would have been familiar to his early twentieth-century audience from the visual arts: 'Die Genesende' [The Convalescent], 'Dame auf einem Balkon' [Lady on a Balcony], 'Übung am Klavier' [Piano Practice], 'Dame vor dem Spiegel' [Lady at her Mirror], and so forth. Thus the Biblical poems, though not necessarily referring to identifiable paintings, can be understood as exercises in the genre of 'imaginary pictures'. Many of them treat themes familiar from the pictorial tradition, with which Rilke was acquainted through his university studies of art history and his visits to museums and galleries.

What advantages did a poet gain from composing texts about pictures that had no real existence? Apart from the sheer demonstration of virtuosity, the genre allowed a poet to highlight the greatest strength of the verbal arts: their ability to mobilise the reader's imagination. Poems about 'imaginary pictures' privileged the mind's eye over that of the body. They also removed verbal works from an apparent dependency upon the visual that the fashion for 'poems about pictures' had encouraged.

At the time when Rilke was producing his *New Poems* he was not only a poet but an art critic, engaged in writing an important monograph on Auguste Rodin. After a brief period studying art history in Prague, Munich, and Berlin, Rilke had begun to earn his living by writing essays on art and literature, most notably his book on the artist colony of Worpswede. During the second half of the nineteenth century, the debate about the sibling arts had been catapulted into a central position, first by John Ruskin and then by Walter Pater. The problem of how to 'read' visual art and how to write about it was hotly debated. During Rilke's involvement with Rodin, the two discussed their personal aesthetics, their different ways of working, and the solutions they had found to problems of representation. Rilke felt that he had embarked on a new apprenticeship as he tried to adapt Rodin's principles to the very different medium of poetry. This gives many of the texts in *New Poems*, especially those written in the Jardin des Plantes while Rilke was there on an artist's pass, the character of exercises on set topics. Though not 'drawn from life', like the zoo poems, the Biblical poems share much of this character. Still, they have attracted much less attention than the poems about animals, antique sculptures, or people on Paris streets.

The Biblical poems in the first volume of the *New Poems* were written partly in winter 1905/06, partly in the period May-July 1906. Thus, apart from 'The Panther' (1903) and 'Orpheus. Eurydice. Hermes' (1904), these texts are among the earliest poems in the collection. In many respects, Rilke's Biblical poems reach back even earlier, to the prolific production of paintings on Biblical themes by the Pre-Raphaelites and Symbolists in the second half of the nineteenth century.

Rilke frequently creates an extended and quite complex narrative from a relatively simple and often quite brief Biblical original.[6] Perhaps the most remarkable of these imaginative extensions of the Biblical original is the 22-line poem 'Klage um Jonathan' [Lament for Jonathan] (1, 562-3) developed from a single verse of the second book of Samuel.[7] 'David singt vor Saul' [David sings before Saul] (1905/6) is a reworking of nine verses from the Old Testament (1 Samuel 16, 14–23). Yet Rilke uses only the most general features of the Biblical situation, refraining from reproducing any of the actual wording of the original. The poem follows immediately upon a two-part poem, 'Abisag' [Abishag], which treats King David's old age and his attempt to recover his sexual potency on his deathbed through the ministrations of the virginal young woman Abishag. The tripartite poem about David and Saul, which approaches the problem of ageing from the perspective of the youthful David, thus forms a kind of pendant to the treatment of fading power in 'Abishag'. It reveals a great deal about Rilke's use of the Bible as a way of exploring problems of creative potency during his Paris period.[8] The first of the poem's three sections is a kind of sonnet with supernumary lines:

> König, hörst du, wie mein Saitenspiel
> Fernen wirft, durch die wir uns bewegen:
> Sterne treiben uns verwirrt entgegen,
> und wir fallen endlich wie ein Regen,
> und es blüht, wo dieser Regen fiel.

Mädchen blühen, die du noch erkannt,
die jetzt Frauen sind und mich verführen;
den Geruch der Jungfraun kannst du spüren,
und die Knaben stehen, angespannt
schlank und atmend, an verschwiegnen Türen.

Daß mein Klang dir alles wiederbrächte.
Aber trunken taumelt mein Getön:
Deine Nächte, König, deine Nächte – ,
und wie waren, die dein Schaffen schwächte,
o wie waren alle Leiber schön.

Dein Erinnern glaub ich zu begleiten,
weil ich ahne. Doch auf welchen Saiten
greif ich dir ihr dunkles Lustgestöhn? –   (1: 488)

Do you hear, king, how my sounding strings
cast distances through which we make our way:
Haphazardly, stars whirl us into play,
and then at last we fall like rain or spray,
and where that water fell, a blossom springs.

Maidens blossom, girls who once were yours,
and now are women who'll seduce me hence;
the maidens' perfume wafts before your sense,
and youths are standing, silent and intense,
slender, breathing, at our secret doors.

Oh that my lyre might bring you back those sights.
And yet my notes still drunkenly careen:
Let them recall your nights, king, all your nights – ,
when, draining wordly doings of their might,
how very beautiful all bodies seemed.

In fancy I accompany your remembering,
for I have intimations. On what string,
though, can I pluck your dark desiring cry? –

Diverging from the Biblical text, Rilke depicts David identifying with Saul and embarking with him on an imaginary journey into the realm of memory. Problems of sexuality, fertility and poetic creativity are interwoven. Not only the aged Saul, but even the youthful David is tormented by fear of creative failure, a sense of personal inadequacy, and the awareness that it is impossible to enter completely into another person's psyche. The bewilderment and desperation in David's song is not in any way suggested by the book of Samuel, which simply describes, in the most laconic of terms, the calming effects of David's song upon Saul's troubled spirits and the keen affection that Saul conceives for the young musician.

By the same token, numerous motifs in the poem do not figure in the Biblical text. Most noticeably absent from the original are the maidens and youths that David attributes to Saul's recollections of his younger days. It is, of course, an easy leap of the imagination from the desolate figure Saul cuts in old age to his earlier years of sexual prowess. Indeed, a similar idea is expressed in Stefan George's poem 'Der Saitenspieler' [The String Player],[9] in which a handsome musician, warming the hearts of his elders with his youthful bashfulness, creates a stir among young people of both sexes.[10] Rilke's poem, however, reverses the configurations. George's young musician is brilliantly successful; Rilke's David is beset by doubts and overshadowed by the lifetime of experience that still radiates from the elderly King Saul. While George's poem limits itself almost entirely to what can be inferred from the scene it describes, Rilke's poem moves from the very outset into a more imaginary arena. A complex metaphorical network, combined with the dramatic monologue form of David's address to Saul, allows Rilke to transform George's static pictorialism into a more flexible, dynamic and expansive structure.

Altogether, Rilke opens up existing conventions in this early contribution to the *New Poems*. But, contrary to Rilke's later theorising, the poem does not aim for 'objectivity'; instead, it explores David's psyche as he attempts to imagine the thoughts and memories of the aged king for whom he is performing. If one were to seek an analogy for this effect, one might look at the way Gustave Moreau reworks the David theme in painting.

Moreau's 'David' (1878) represents the ageing musician remembering his past accomplishment.[11] Sunk in thought, David sits upon an elaborate throne surrounded by leafy potted bushes and trees; flowers are strewn on the steps of the throne, and on either side incense rises from exotic bronze containers. At David's feet sits a winged angel whose reddish halo picks up the colour of the semi-circular top of the throne's back. His hand supporting, but not playing, a harp that rests upon one of the steps, the angel seems to represent David's memory of his own youthful self. From the harp emerge leafy growths that mirror the potted plants behind the king; beyond the terrace on which he sits, the viewer can see the countryside spread out, marked by a river and gentle hills,

into the distance. The view is framed by decorated columns in the
oriental style topped in a more Gothic manner by various gargoyles
including an eagle, a lion's head, and a female caryatid that emerges like
a figure on a ship's prow; but here, too, leafy ornamentation predomi-
nates. From the roof of the terrace hangs a magnificent lamp, its flame
situated just above the middle of the picture. The angelic musician looks
straight out at the viewer, but David's eyes are clearly not fixed upon
anything real. Cast slightly downward, they seem to concentrate upon
some vision accessible to him alone. This posture turns the view into the
landscape beyond the terrace into a kind of window on his soul: the
viewer is drawn back into the distance in the same way as David's
thoughts draw him into his past.

More than the exoticism of the iconography, what makes this picture
a symbolist work is the implicit substitution of the background landscape
for the aged king's psyche and the identification thus established between the viewer's imagination and that of the painting's central figure.
Meditative isolation, interiority and the transfiguring power of the
imagination are familiar symbolist tropes.

Rilke's technique in 'David sings before Saul' is similar, though his
focus is on the younger David more familiar from the Bible. In the first
part of his poem, David's harp projects imaginary distances – like those
in the background of Moreau's painting – that enable him to embark
with Saul on a journey into the past. Blossoms emerge in this landscape;
and the girls Saul made love to in his youth still blossom for the singing
David. In the second part, David lays his harp to rest, overcome by a
sense of the old king's power and grandeur:

> König, der du alles dieses hattest
> und der du mit lauter Leben mich
> überwältigest und überschattest:
> komm aus deinem Throne und zerbrich
> meine Harfe, die du so ermattest.
>
> Sie ist wie ein abgenommner Baum:
> durch die Zweige, die dir Frucht getragen,
> schaut jetzt eine Tiefe wie von Tagen
> welche kommen – , und ich kenn sie kaum.
>
> Laß mich nicht mehr bei der Harfe schlafen;
> sieh dir diese Knabenhand da an:
> glaubst du, König, daß sie die Oktaven
> eines Leibes noch nicht greifen kann?   (1: 489)

My king, who have experienced these things
and who by force of sheer vitality
do overwhelm and overshadow me:
come from your throne and break apart my strings,
shatter my harp, which you have wearied so.

My harp is like a tree that's been cut down:
and through those branches on which fruit did grow,
a depth peers now as if from days and times
to come – , I hardly know their name.

Let me no longer drowse here by my harp;
look, king, at this, my boyish hand:
do you think it does not understand
how to grasp the octaves of a body?

The harp – like the leafy instrument of Moreau's angel – seems to Rilke's David like a tree that has been cut down and whose branches create a kind of grid through which one can see into another time. This time is identified, however, as the future: 'eine Tiefe wie von Tagen welche kommen' (a depth as if from days to come). The youthful David presents himself not as a singer, but as a lover, with all the experiences Saul has known still before him. The first two sections of Rilke's poem are thus related as thesis to antithesis, one looking into the past, the other into the future.

The third section, following what was to become Rilke's habitual way of structuring texts in the *New Poems*, enacts a synthesis of these two parts by means of transfiguration. Saul's wrath and David's youthful confusion are metamorphosed or reshaped into something like a constellation circling above the two figures clasping each other desperately for consolation:

König, birgst du dich in Finsternissen,
und ich hab dich doch in der Gewalt.
Sieh, mein festes Lied ist nicht gerissen,
und der Raum wird um uns beide kalt.
Mein verwaistes Herz und dein verworrnes
hängen in den Wolken deines Zornes,
wütend ineinander eingebissen
und zu einem einzigen verkrallt.

Fühlst du jetzt, wie wir uns umgestalten?
König, König, das Gewicht wird Geist.
Wenn wir uns nur aneinander halten,
du am Jungen, König, ich am Alten,
sind wir fast wie ein Gestirn das kreist.   (1: 489)

My king, you hide yourself in darkness' shroud,
and yet I have you firmly in my thrall.
Behold, my tight-wove song is not yet rent,
and round us both grows cold the firmament.
My heart, orphaned, and your heart, bemused,
remain suspended in a baleful cloud,
biting and clawing, rolled into a ball,
angrily enclasped and interfused.

Do you sense now how we become transformed?
King, o my king, weight turns into spirit.
If we hold fast just so, just as we are,
you to the younger, king, and I to the older,
we almost seem to form a circling star.

Written in Meudon during the time when Rilke had temporarily taken a position as Rodin's secretary, the poem doubtless reflects something of the tense relationship between the sixty-five-year-old sculptor and the thirty-year-old poet, a relationship that was to crumble just a few months later. David's sense of being overshadowed by Saul and rendered unable to play his music by the king's overwhelming influence captures Rilke's profound devotion to his artistic master Rodin and his inability to emulate his extraordinarily fecund productivity. The motif of the 'weary' harp, deprived of ability by the overwhelming power of a predecessor, indicates that Rilke was already concerned, even at this early point, with the problem of tradition.

More significant than this autobiographical connection, however, is the way in which the poem situates itself with respect to the debate about the sibling arts. Dominated by musical and visual imagery, the poem moves from repeated invitations to listen toward an increasing emphasis on sight. The sound of the harp conjures up spatial images, creating a fantasy landscape and calling forth recollected scenes of erotic desire. Still, sight does not completely dominate. The poem is built upon a typically symbolist conflation of the various sensory impressions, so that sound, in effect, is transformed into space. David's song itself becomes a kind of fabric, a screen onto which the final image of the circling constellation is enticingly projected. His poetic appeal to Saul argues for the power of the imagination to take us out of actual space and time. In doing so, it does not turn itself into a kind of sculptural object, as Rilke claimed his *New Poems* did. Rather, it allows the imagination to expand and create a space very different from that of three-dimensional reality. In this respect 'David sings before Saul' is a precursor of poems like 'Die Gazelle' [The Gazelle] (1907) which privilege the eye of the mind over concrete reality.

Throughout the poem there is a constant oscillation between the metaphorical and the actual. Sometimes the metaphors are openly indicated in the form of similes, at other times the language moves more boldly and directly into the imaginary sphere, as in the image 'die Oktaven eines Leibes' (the octaves of a body). Most remarkable is the final image in which the transfiguration of the singer and his sovereign is suggested – but only in the form of an approximation: 'fast wie ein Gestirn das kreist' (almost like a circling star). The reader is continually invited to plunge into the imaginary realm and continually pulled back again from the brink. The poem encourages its readers to think more closely about the precarious nature of metaphor and metaphor-making.

By choosing the youthful David as the speaker of his poem, Rilke also positions himself with respect to tradition. While David's song would not exist if he were not able to enter into the old king's memories, Saul would be overcome by wrath if his emotions were not softened by the sound of the young man's harp. Present and past subsist in a reciprocal relationship that permits the final transfiguration to occur: the emergence of the virtual constellation that will later come to represent, in Rilke's private language, poetry itself.

In this way, the poem becomes much more than merely a reworking of some verses from the Bible. It acquires the character of a programmatic utterance about the function of poetry and the nature of its genesis. 'David sings before Saul' takes a look at a frightening face of creativity: the arduous and even burdensome task of giving utterance when the presence of powerful elders makes the singer dwindle to insignificance. At the very moment, in other words, when Rilke – from the viewpoint of present-day criticism – is on the verge of achieving full poetic command, he is still fraught with doubts about his ability, his relation to other masters, and the complex nature of inspiration and accomplishment.

SYMBOLIST BLUES

In an important essay on Rilke, Ulrich Fülleborn argues that Rilke's development of a poetry about objects is a continuation of nineteenth-century realism.[12] From the standpoint of Rilke and his contemporaries, however, his claim to 'objectivity' was made against the poetic tradition of late nineteenth-century France, especially that of what we would now call its 'minor' practitioners. Typical of French poetry in the eighteen-eighties and -nineties was a mannered and sentimental style that tended to attribute human sensitivities to the things of the natural and domestic world. Rilke's new technique is directed against this subjectivising vision which assimilates the object entirely to the mental and emotional life of the poet. To a large extent, Rilke's *New Poems* share the minor French poets' fascination with ornamental furnishings, exotic plants and animals, artistic monuments from earlier times, and the pathos of those who live on the margins of modern urban society. But while he borrows from his French predecessors the rarefied language with which he describes these things, his poems also attempt to dismantle the very aura with which such language invests them.

One characteristic of this subversive technique is his use of rhyme: unusual words, frequently German equivalents of words culled from his French reading, are matched with deflating rhyme-words more suitable to everyday speech.[13] In this way Rilke simultaneously appropriates and implicitly criticises the precious tone of his French models. Similarly, when he reworks their characteristic themes and motifs, he shows both the attraction of the cult of beauty and the spiritual entrapment to which it frequently leads.[14]

We can take the measure of Rilke's engagement with French aestheticism of the eighteen-eighties and -nineties more fully by scanning some of the anthologies that appeared in the early years of the new century. When Rilke arrived in Paris in 1902, the influential two-volume selection of contemporary verse, *Poètes d'aujourd'hui* [Poets of Today],[15] had been in circulation for two years. The equally important three-volume *Anthologie des poètes français contemporains* [Anthology of Contemporary French Poets][16] appeared in 1906, as Rilke was beginning to think of gathering together his own recent poetry in the *New Poems*. While these collections included texts by Mallarmé, Rimbaud, Laforgue, Maeterlinck, Valéry and others of similar calibre, they also contained a generous selection from the works of poets now considered second- or third-rate. Much of this verse is mawkish, affected, and excessively sensitive.

Many of Rilke's titles in the *New Poems* – 'Die Genesende' [The Convalescent], 'Die Bettler' [The Beggars], 'Das Kapitäl' [The Capital], or 'Die Kathedrale' [The Cathedral] – pick up motifs from these anthologies.[17] In reworking these late nineteenth-century models, Rilke retains their emphasis on the complexity, fragility and evanescence of the object, but develops metaphors that are less clichéd and sentimental, more original, and even abstract. Reading Rilke's *New Poems* after *Poets of Today* and *Anthology of Contemporary French Poets*, one is struck by the efforts Rilke has made to concentrate imaginative energies that had remained dispersed and unfocussed in the poetry of many of his French predecessors. A case in point is Rilke's 'Blaue Hortensie' [Blue Hydrangea] (1906):

> So wie das letzte Grün in Farbentiegeln
> sind diese Blätter, trocken, stumpf und rauh,
> hinter den Blütendolden, die ein Blau
> nicht auf sich tragen, nur von ferne spiegeln.
>
> Sie spiegeln es verweint und ungenau,
> als wollten sie es wiederum verlieren,
> und wie in alten blauen Briefpapieren
> ist Gelb in ihnen, Violett und Grau;
>
> Verwaschnes wie an einer Kinderschürze,
> Nichtmehrgetragnes, dem nichts mehr geschieht:
> wie fühlt man eines kleinen Lebens Kürze.
>
> Doch plötzlich scheint das Blau sich zu verneuen
> in einer von den Dolden, und man sieht
> ein rührend Blaues sich vor Grünem freuen.   (1: 519)

> Like the last dregs of green in children's paint,
> so are these leaves, all dry and dull and rough,
> behind the flower heads with blue as faint
> as if it were reflected from far off.
>
> They mirror it like eyes that fill with tears,
> as if they wished to lose it once again,
> and like some old and faded writing gear,
> there's yellow in them, grey and violet stain;
>
> washed out colours like a children's smock,
> no longer worn, forever staying clean:
> how narrow seems the span of one short life.
>
> But suddenly the blue seems to revive
> in one hydrangea umbel, and a flock
> of touching blue takes pleasure in the green.

The main French point of departure for 'Blue Hydrangea' is a book of poetry that has all but passed into oblivion: *Les Hortensias bleus* [The

Blue Hydrangeas] by Robert de Montesquiou-Fezensac.[18] Montesquiou was a dandy, an interior decorator, and a poet. His 400-page
volume of poems capitalises on the contemporary mania for the colour
blue: as John Richardson comments in his discussion of Picasso's Blue
period, 'symbolist Paris had been in the throes of a blueish obsession
since the early 1890s'.[19]

The hydrangea was also becoming popular in the late nineteenth
century. Frédéric Bazille includes pots of pink hydrangeas in his painting of a greenhouse scene, 'Flower Pots' (1866); Jacques-Emile Blanche
painted a still-life titled 'Blue Hydrangeas' and a painting of a child
against a backdrop of blue hydrangeas titled 'La Petite Fille aux hortensias' [The Little Girl with Hydrangeas] (1887).[20] In an essay on Montesquiou, Proust writes about some hydrangea pictures by Paul Helleu that
were in his possession: 'Peintures et pastels, je possède sept panneaux
d'hortensias jardinés par Helleu, et dont les corymbes glauques ou
blondissants, mirent en des plateaux d'argent comme des bouquets de
turquoises mortes' (In the form of paintings and pastels, I own seven
baskets of hydrangeas cultivated [i.e. painted] by Helleu, whose glau-
cous or bleached out colours are reflected in silver platters like bouquets
of dead turquoises).[21] Along with a bowl titled *Blue Melancholia*, Emile
Gallé sent to the 1892 Salon a hydrangea dresser that he had created in
collaboration with Robert de Montesquiou.[22] Under the influence of the
artist Jean Grandville, whose volume *Les Fleurs animées* [The Flowers
Personified] invested flowers with human expressions and emotions,
Gallé rejected distinctions between animate and inanimate nature,
indulging freely in anthropomorphic fantasies.[23] Gallé believed that the
vegetable world partook of the same inner nervous vibrations as the
human psyche, and saw the veins in plant leaves as the literal equivalent
of human nerves. The hydrangea, with its multiple delicate blossoms
held above coarse, strongly-veined leaves, ambiguously suggested the
fragility of the neurasthenic coupled with taut and powerful nerves
visible, as it were, beneath the skin.

Victor Prouvé's *Portrait d'Emile Gallé* [Portrait of Emile Gallé] (1892)
vividly depicts the craftsman in a state of hallucinatory interaction
with a pink and blue vase, surrounded by other vases and fading
flowers. The period's 'blueish obsession' permeates the painting: a
group of vases on the right-hand side of the picture are in various
tones of blue, and there is a general blue undertone to the painting as
a whole. In the tallest blue vase rests a wilting blue flower head. A pale
blue book rests on the artist's table, which is strewn with faded sheets

of watercolour paper. Rilke's imagery of fading flower heads and old blue notepaper draws upon the same sort of ambience as Prouvé's picture.

Montesquiou's volume *The Blue Hydrangeas* is situated within a post-Romantic tradition that saw poetry as an exotic, rare, or artificial flower. Baudelaire's *Flowers of Evil* are the most obvious example of this tradition; Huysmans' elaborate descriptions of artificial flowers in *A rebours* [Against Nature] and Maeterlinck's *Serres chaudes* [Hothouses] are its direct descendents; Pierre Louÿs defines poetry as 'an oriental flower that cannot live in our hothouses'.[24] While the hydrangea does flourish in Europe – both in greenhouses and outdoors –, it comes originally from Asia, where it grows wild along the riverbanks in China and Japan. It was first introduced into Europe in the nineteenth century.

Only four poems in Montesquiou's volume make direct reference to blue hydrangeas, but, arranged as a sequence, they form a cluster that develops the exotic flower as an emblem of the entire volume. At the start of the sequence, Montesquiou invokes a muse-like figure who seems to be a compound of every conceivable form of Romantic and Symbolist imagery: she sings a mysterious song to the accompaniment of a lyre in the form of two swans' necks, and her head, set against an aureole of moonlight and graced by the flapping wings of an orbiting bat, is crowned with a somewhat improbable wreath of blue hydrangeas which, the poet says, she has picked in the field of dreams. The bizarre imagery of this poem clearly owes much to the proto-Surrealist out-reaches of Symbolism represented by late nineteenth-century artists like Max Klinger, Odilon Redon, Gustave Moreau, and Fernand Khnopff. The second poem describes the hydrangea's appearance as mysterious and enigmatic, and the third poem continues to highlight its exotic nature, dwelling on the plant's troubling 'metempsychoses' – its capacity to change the colour of its flowers. In the final poem of the sequence, Montesquiou tells the story of a blue hydrangea which his cousin Claude had carried with him on a crossing from Jersey: when a storm arose and threatened the passengers with shipwreck, the flower is credited with having saved Claude from a watery grave.

If the association of blue hydrangeas with the uncanny surprises today's reader, this is a measure of how familiar the flower has become in the meantime. The hydrangea's form – large, artificial-looking clusters of delicate little flowers – was responsible for the bizarre impression it made on nineteenth-century writers. Montesquiou is particularly interested in the clustering effect, a correlative for the structural principle of his volume, which brings together disparate fragile impressions in bolder groupings like the flower heads of hydrangeas.

Even in a more conventional deployment of the motif, like Jacques-Emile Blanche's 'The Little Girl with Hydrangeas', the subtle nuances of colour in the hydrangea umbels are echoed by the child's luminous blond hair, fair skin and delicate dress in the palest of blue checked fabrics.[25] Posed against the backdrop of a large hydrangea bush, the little girl holds one of its flower heads in her hand, but her eyes do not appear to be focussed on it at all: rather, they gaze dreamily elsewhere, into a space accessible to her alone. The painting is at once an aesthetic representation of idealised childhood and an implicit commentary on the complex relationship between nature and artifice.

In 'Blue Hydrangea', Rilke builds on these visions of hydrangeas by Montesquiou and Blanche. Although he surrounds the hydrangea with a number of similes from other realms of experience, his description of the flower is less grotesque than Montesquiou's, less aestheticised than Blanche's.[26] The rough leaves, the complex shadings of the florets, the variations in the colour intensity of the individual flower heads: all these aspects of the blue hydrangea are carefully represented.

But in addition to this horticultural accuracy, the flower is also portrayed as if it were something artificial that has been ineptly coloured. Its dull green leaves resemble dried-out slabs of colour in an old paintbox; its blue flowers look now like old blue writing paper (Rilke, incidentally, wrote final copies of the *New Poems* on blue manuscript sheets),[27] now like a child's faded blue apron. Rilke takes the sentimental elements of eighteen-nineties aestheticism but stops short of provoking an emotional response. The faded notepaper, the washed-out apron, the shortness of life are relatively abstract.

Rilke's poem speaks as if in shorthand of the passing of time, yet for the better part of the poem time is seen as something not passing but already gone: the water colours have dried out, the letters have faded, the apron is no longer worn. Only in the final tercet does anything actually happen, but even this turns out to be merely an effect in the eye of the beholder, who suddenly realises that the blue is more intense in one of the hydrangea's umbels. In Rilke's terms, this apparent renewal of colour is the 'transformation' that justifies the entire poetic operation. By the end of the poem, however, it is not the colours that have disappeared from the object, but the flower that disappears behind its colour effects. In the last tercet, the word 'umbel' is the only indication left that we are looking at a flower; blue and green, in the curious form of neuter nouns derived from adjectives, remain in the last line, virtually divorced from the object, like strokes of colour in an abstract painting.

Representation is seen as necessarily inadequate, and the theory of poetic mimesis is constantly called into question. Rilke repeatedly calls attention to the fact that his images are approximations, likenesses grasped in an almost desperate attempt to render what cannot be exactly reproduced. Just as the hydrangeas mirror the sky in a distant and diluted way, so the poem presents its object only imperfectly, painfully conscious of its inevitable inexactitude. Much of the poem's poignancy, though overtly attributed to the problem of transience, derives from this recognition of the inadequacy of representation. The more the poem tries for accuracy, the farther it removes itself from the actual hydrangea.

Not until details are abandoned, and blue and green are left to respond to each other in the abstract does the hydrangea's transformation occur. Rilke's final tercet revokes the notion of poetry as a vehicle for decadence. In contrast to the imagery of dried-out paints, discoloured notepaper, and the faded apron, the sudden renewal of colour in one of the flower heads represents a return to a more positive – but also a more abstract – mode.

Rilke's 'Blue Hydrangea' is thus directed against several notions dear to the late nineteenth century. First, it attacks the aestheticist conception of poetry as an exotic hothouse flower available only to the privileged few; second, it argues against the idea that poetry should be the expression of a fantastic and decadent imagination; and finally, the motif of renewal with which it concludes suggests that the material of eighteen-nineties poetry should not so much be discarded as placed in the service of a new aesthetic.

THE BELGIAN REVIVAL

In 1906, two of Rilke's friends, the sculptor Rodin and the poet Verhaeren, suggested that he take a trip to Belgium.[28] Rilke planned to find some small town there where he could spend time with his wife, Clara, and their small daughter; but he also hoped to find material for his poems: 'von gewissen Eindrücken in Furnes, Ypern und Gent erwarte ich Wichtiges und Gutes für eine kommende Arbeitszeit' (from certain impressions gathered in Furnes, Ypres and Ghent, I am expecting good and important things for the next phase of my work).[29] Oddly enough, he did not mention Bruges in this announcement of his travel plans, although the 'Venice of the north' was a popular destination in the early years of the century. Travel guides, histories, and cultural essays about Bruges proliferated. Rilke's trip was extraordinarily fruitful, giving rise not only to a substantial essay, 'Furnes' (5: 1005–1016), but also to a series of related poems (1: 532–538). Although the poems' subtitles indicate that the first two are set in Furnes, the second two in Bruges, and the last in Ghent, Rilke did not in fact write them until late July 1907, exactly a year after his trip (6: 1462). They are thus hardly written 'in the open air' and 'on the spot', as he liked to say of the *New Poems*.

In 'Der Turm' [The Tower] (1907) Rilke develops the critique of symbolism and aestheticism he had begun in 'Blue Hydrangea'. In the convoluted structure of this peculiarly extended sonnet,[30] one thing stands out clearly: the speaker experiences his climb inside the tower as a kind of rebirth:

> Erd-Inneres. Als wäre dort, wohin
> du blindlings steigst, erst Erdenoberfläche,
> zu der du steigst im schrägen Bett der Bäche,
> die langsam aus dem suchenden Gerinn
>
> der Dunkelheit entsprungen sind, durch die
> sich dein Gesicht, wie auferstehend, drängt
> und die du plötzlich *siehst*, als fiele sie
> aus diesem Abgrund, der dich überhängt
>
> und den du, wie er riesig über dir
> sich umstürzt in dem dämmernden Gestühle,
> erkennst, erschreckt und fürchtend, im Gefühle:
> o wenn er steigt, behangen wie ein Stier –:
>
> Da aber nimmt dich aus der engen Endung
> windiges Licht. Fast fliegend siehst du hier
> die Himmel wieder, Blendung über Blendung,
> und dort die Tiefen, wach und voll Verwendung,
>
> und kleine Tage wie bei Patenier,
> gleichzeitige, mit Stunde neben Stunden,
> durch die die Brücken springen wie die Hunde,
> dem hellen Wege immer auf der Spur,
>
> den unbeholfne Häuser manchmal nur
> verbergen, bis er ganz im Hintergrunde
> beruhigt geht durch Buschwerk und Natur.   (1: 532–533)

Earth-innermost. As if the place to which
you blindly climb were surface of the earth
to which you mount by crooked beds of streams
that slowly from the softly trickling search

of darkness issue forth, dark space in which
your face, as if arisen, pushes through,
and which you *see*, quite sudden, as if pitched
from this abyss that's overhanging you

and which you, as it monstrously careens
above you in the darkening roof beams,
you recognise, alarmed and scared, and feel:
oh when it rises, covered like a bull –:

Then you are taken from the narrow ending
by windy gusts of light. Seeming almost to fly,
brightness on brightness, now you see the sky
and there the depths, alert and all-intending,

and little days like those in Patenier,
all taking place at once, with hour by hour,
through which the bridges leap and bound like dogs
sniffing in search of that light-coloured track,

hidden at times, it seems, by clumsy shacks,
till in the very background of the scene,
it makes its way, relieved, through nature's screen.

Emerging from darkness into light, pushing face forward through a
narrow space, the speaker is shocked by a rush of light and air, overwhelming and relieving at once. Everything that has seemed frightening, monstrous, and unintelligible during the climb upward suddenly
falls into meaningful images once he emerges into the clear light at the
top of the tower stair. The birth metaphor that underlies this poem is the
expression of a desire for creative renewal.

The subtitle of 'The Tower' indicates that its subject is the church of St.
Nicolas in Furnes, or more precisely its thirteenth-century brick tower,
which houses a carillon including one of the oldest bells in Belgium. This
setting, however, fails to explain a number of puzzling elements in the
poem, notably the seemingly unmotivated image of a bull.[31]

Formally, the poem is a virtuoso performance. The better part of the
first three stanzas consists of a single sentence, as does all but a line and a
half of the last three stanzas. An isolated word stands at the beginning,

and an incomplete sentence, containing the surprising bull image, forms the pivot upon which the entire structure turns.

Most striking is the heteroclitic assemblage of images that seem to bear little relation to one another: the comparison of the tower's inner stairway to the bed of an underground river; the passing reference to resurrection; the idea of an abyss located above the climber; the mysterious bull image; and the concluding comparison of the landscape outside the tower with paintings by Patenier. Ill-assorted though this combination of imagery may seem, it has its own rationale. The images derive from a complex set of intertextual relations and form an implicit critique of an earlier aesthetic. Elements from Rossetti, Rodenbach, and Baudelaire can be detected in the presentation of the speaker's climb up the dark tower staircase.

Rossetti's *Sonnets for Pictures*, a group of poems about paintings by Leonardo da Vinci, Giorgione, Mantegna, Ingres and Burne-Jones, explore the relations between the sibling arts, a topic of great interest to Rilke during the period of his *New Poems*. Indeed, Rilke already shows his familiarity with Rossetti, both as a poet and as a painter, in his essay on Walter Pater (5: 599). Rossetti's poem 'The Carillon', subtitled 'Antwerp and Bruges', is preceded by two 'sonnets for pictures' designed to accompany paintings by Hans Memmeling at Bruges.[32] 'The Carillon' describes two climbs up a bell tower: one in Antwerp at sunset, the other in Bruges by daylight. It portrays the feeling of night against one's face, the presence of water, the experience of wind, the speaker's emergence into a bright white sky, the expansiveness of a landscape seen from the top of a tower.

Rilke's poem links these elements more closely than does Rossetti's, displacing the setting to Furnes, combining the two tower climbs into one, and making the transition from darkness into light part of a single experience. A reference to Flemish art in Rossetti's poem becomes, in Rilke, an allusion to Joachim Patenier. Rossetti's nostalgia for great Flemish painters and famous Flemish carillons becomes a more positive affirmation of rebirth and renewal in Rilke's poem.

The opening image of 'The Tower' envisages a dark, winding staircase as the bed of an underground river. Groping his way in the darkness, the climber seems to struggle upward through a sloping tunnel formed by the slow process of trickling water. This richly associative image may be traced back to Georges Rodenbach's novel *Le Carilloneur* [The Carillon Player] (1897), set in Bruges but with an important penultimate shift of the action to Furnes.[33]

At the beginning of Rodenbach's novel, the newly selected carillon player of Bruges takes up his task for the first time and is surprised to find that mounting the bell tower is more frightening than he had expected. Part of its terror consists in a sudden change in his sense of direction: although he is actually climbing upward, it seems as if he were going down, 'au long d'un escalier souterrain, dans une mine profonde, très loin du jour' (along a subterranean staircase, in a deep mine, very far from daylight).[34] From this image of a mine shaft, the text rapidly modulates to that of an underground river, a simile that becomes dominant in Rilke's depiction of the tower's interior as a subterranean landscape.

Apart from the river-bed image, several other motifs in Rilke's poem are inspired by Rodenbach's novel. Rilke's 'Abgrund, der dich über-hängt' (abyss that overhangs you) is an adaptation of a central motif in *The Carillon Player*, 'le gouffre d'en haut' (the abyss above; pp. 28, 93), which the carillon player experiences while climbing up the bell-tower. Other images in Rilke's 'The Tower' also owe much to Rodenbach's novel: the hulking roof beams in the darkness; the blinding light that meets the climber once he has arrived at the top of the tower; the wind that seems to bring a sudden illumination; and the transfigured country-side seen from the top of the tower.

Rilke does much more in 'The Tower', however, than merely re-assemble some motifs from Rodenbach. In effect, he turns Rodenbach's novel inside out. Rilke's decision to arrange his poem in the form of an ascent (or ascension) from the underworld into the light, from terror to relief is clearly an attempt to invert Rodenbach's schema, in which the carillon player begins in the ecstasy of a new marriage and ends in such despair that he commits suicide by hanging himself inside a bell.

The Carillon Player is above all a novel about art. It depicts a clash between two fundamentally different aesthetics. The carillon player becomes involved in a movement designed to restore the city of Bruges to its former glory. His two loves, his wife and her sister, are daughters of an antiquarian who represents the more conservative face of the restora-tive movement. Another faction takes a more modern view of restora-tion, aiming to revive the spirit rather than the letter of the city's former glory. Caught in this conflict, the carillon player ultimately opts for the antiquarian side of the argument. For Rilke, the debate between two factions of the aestheticist movement was still vividly alive. In reversing Rodenbach's structure, he opts for the progressive, as opposed to the more conservative position.

Rilke's poem ends by distinguishing between consciousness and its object, the viewer at the top of the tower and the landscape below. The self-reflexivity of the tower climb, experienced as a terrifying kind of self-enclosure, is replaced in the second half of the poem by a focus on external objects. In this way, Rilke's poem revokes the sense of irrevocable entanglement experienced by Rodenbach's carillon player.

Rodenbach does not account, however, for the incongruous image of a bull on which Rilke's poem pivots. How are we to understand this cryptic line? The allusion, I believe, is to a bullfight. Before the fight begins, the bull is covered with a cloth and placed in a narrow tunnel made of boards called the 'toril'. After the animal has waited there for a time, his head is uncovered and he is driven out of the toril into the bright light of the arena. In another poem, 'Corrida', Rilke gives a vivid description of the moment when the bull bursts out of the boarded tunnel (1: 615–16). Emerging from a dark tower into the blinding light is clearly an experience similar to that of the bull when his eyes are suddenly uncovered and he is released from the confines of the toril.

We would expect the image of the bull released from the toril to be linked with the climber's emergence from the tower. Instead, the abyss itself seems to be hurtling down the narrow passageway of the tower staircase toward the climber like a bull about to be let out into the ring. This displacement of the toril image from the climber to the darkness that looms above him is part of the confusion of subject and object developed in this part of the poem. Projection of one's own feelings into nature is what we call the pathetic fallacy; here, the pathetic phenomenon turns upon the speaker as if to attack. Self-reflection is here portrayed as potentially destructive.

A poetic image that may have summoned up the idea of the bull is the flight of Dedalus and Icarus from the labyrinth in Ovid's *Metamorphoses*. Climbing up the dark and winding tower stairway makes the speaker of Rilke's poem think, perhaps, of the labyrinth made by Dedalus to house the King Minos's bull-headed monster, the minotaur. Gripped by fear, he mentally transforms the looming roofbeams into the head of a bull. Ovid's narrative describes how Dedalus, himself held captive by King Minos, decides that the only way he and his son can escape is by way of the skies: 'terras licet inquit et undas obstruat: et caelum certe patet; ibimus illac: omnia possideat, non possidet aera Minos' (Though he may obstruct land and water, yet the sky is certainly open; we will go that way. Though Minos rules over all, he does not have supremacy in the air; *Metamorphoses*, 8: 185–187). In Rilke's poem, the climber's emergence into the light is presented as an experience akin to flying. In thus alluding to Dedalus' escape from a prison of his own making, Rilke suggests that a way must be found out of the solipsism of the aestheticist ideal.

A final element in Rilke's elaborate network of allusions in 'The Tower' is the reference to the Flemish artist Joachim Patenier (1480–1524) in the poem's penultimate stanza. Known for the importance he accords to landscape at a relatively early point in the history of art, Patenier was especially skilled at depicting vast and luminous spaces. Patenier's 'Rest on the Flight to Egypt' may have been the painting Rilke had in mind, since it contains several elements that reappear in 'The Tower'.[35] The Virgin Mary and infant Jesus are depicted in 'Rest on the Flight to Egypt' against a landscape that makes up the larger part of the painting. The terrain depicted is rocky, and in the background a peculiar mountain arises, cut away in the front to reveal an extraordinary complex of castles and other buildings inside; a winding road, clearly visible because of its light colour, leads towards it from the foreground. The strangely supra- and subterranean mountain with its complex and convoluted interior has become Rilke's tower that is simultaneously an underground river and a labyrinth; the pale roadway visible in the painting is also present in the Rilke's poem, wending its way through the landscape around the tower and finally disappearing 'in the background' (not accidentally, Rilke uses here a term proper to painting; when we observe real countryside we say 'in the distance', not 'in the background'). But despite the somewhat fantastic nature of Patenier's painting, Rilke's poem stresses, rather, its clarity, orderliness and connectedness. By implication, Patenier's paintings are contrasted with the murkier and more ambiguous aesthetic ideals represented in the rest of the poem.

When Rilke identifies the bell tower in the subtitle as that of the 'Tower of St. Nicolas, Furnes', this designation highlights the reality-oriented aspect of the poem. At the same time, however, Belgium had symbolic value for anyone of Rilke's generation: though Baudelaire heartily detested Brussels on the occasion of his lecture tour in that city, it was at least the one place that had dared to publish the six controversial poems that had been excluded by the censor from the original edition of *The Flowers of Evil*. Furnes, the location of a well-known annual procession of penitents that still takes place today, formed in the nineteenth-century mind a contrast to the more forward-looking Brussels of Baudelaire's day. At the conclusion of Rodenbach's *The Carillon Player*,

Furnes is presented as a place of spiritual renewal for the young wife wronged by the carillon player's adultery with her sister. The motif of resurrection in 'The Tower' is thus rightly associated with the town of Furnes, but more importantly, it is associated in Rilke's poem with a purified and clarified version of the Baudelairean aesthetic, one that would prevent the poet from falling into a murky and satanic gulf. As such, it would allow him to soar to safety like his creative predecessor Dedalus. In this sense, the resurrection adumbrated in 'The Tower' is the restoration of an aesthetic ideal that leads out of the ambiguous realm of solipsism and self-reflexivity into a new kind of object-relatedness. Emerging from the convoluted filiations of poetic influence, this poetry, 'The Tower' implies, will gain a new integrity that derives from the way in which it mediates between these traditions and a world that is somehow also actually 'out there'.

Still, the final stanzas of 'The Tower' do not actually present an objective picture. The pathetic fallacy is still at work here. The depths are 'wach' (alert), the shacks 'unbeholfen' (clumsy), and the path at the end 'beruhigt' (relieved). The bridges seem to leap and bound like hunting dogs, enacting the speaker's delight in his escape from the tower staircase. In this respect, Rilke is still very much a child of neo-Romanticism.

Like all of Rilke's *New Poems*, 'The Tower' is a document of his transition from one stylistic manner to another. Its multiple allusions are the trace left by his daring, but not yet fully successful attempt to enter the modern age. In 'The Tower', he envisages a revival of a clearer, less obscure form of art. The old Belgian masters, represented by Patenier, ultimately win out against the shadow existence of symbolism and aestheticism in the poem's allusive structure. Yet although the speaker announces his new ideals in the final stanzas, the poem itself is far from transparent. Throughout the *New Poems* Rilke puts the aestheticist mode into question, but never quite manages to fight free of it. The rebirth of his poetic powers is bought at the price of constant effort. Precisely the poems he most wished to see as fresh, direct, and tied to real locations, also smack very much of the writing desk. Excessively and intricately worked, they create new obscurities in their attempt to avoid old ones. 'Good and important things' did indeed emerge from Rilke's trip to Belgium in 1906, but the 'new phase' of his work was still fraught with nostalgia for an artistic movement that had reached its peak in the eighteen-nineties.

AUTONOMY AND AURA

'Die Flamingos' [The Flamingos] (1907/8), one of the best known and most impressive of Rilke's *New Poems*, continues to develop his critical concerns about aestheticism. Here Rilke puts the notion of aesthetic autonomy to the test. The self-absorbed and highly stylised beauty invoked in 'The Flamingos' suggests the ideal of autonomous art. The poem is far from self-contained, however. Its allusion to Phryne, striking because of the curious way in which it associates the birds with a human figure, is only one of several links to contemporary discourse about the nature of art and poetry that are embedded in 'The Flamingos'.

> In Spiegelbildern wie von Fragonard
> ist doch von ihrem Weiß und ihrer Röte
> nicht mehr gegeben, als dir einer böte,
> wenn er von seiner Freundin sagt: sie war
>
> noch sanft von Schlaf. Denn steigen sie ins Grüne
> und stehn, auf rosa Stielen leicht gedreht,
> beisammen, blühend, wie in einem Beet,
> verführen sie verführender als Phryne
>
> sich selber; bis sie ihres Auges Bleiche
> hinhalsend bergen in der eignen Weiche,
> in welcher Schwarz und Fruchtrot sich versteckt.
>
> Auf einmal kreischt ein Neid durch die Volière;
> sie aber haben sich erstaunt gestreckt
> und schreiten einzeln ins Imaginäre.   (1: 629–630)

> Mirror images like those of Fragonard
> no more evoke their gentle red and white
> than if a person speaking of his lover
> told you, simply, that she was still quite
>
> soft with sleep. And if, among the greenery,
> they stand on pink stems turned in graceful order,
> together, blossoming, as in a garden border,
> they lure, yet more alluringly than Phryne,
>
> themselves; until the pallor of their eyes
> nestles and hides among their own soft down,
> concealed in which are black and fruit-red streaks.
>
> Suddenly through the aviary envy shrieks;
> but they have straightened, taken by surprise,
> and enter, one by one, the imagined realm.

In part, 'The Flamingos' is a response to Baudelaire's 'Lesbos', one of six poems from *The Flowers of Evil* that provoked Baudelaire's 1857 trial for obscenity.[36] 'Phryne' is the key motif that links Rilke's poem with Baudelaire's, where it occurs in the third stanza, which begins and ends with the line: 'Lesbos, où les Phrynés l'une l'autre s'attirent' (Lesbos, where Phrynes draw one another near).[37] Clearly, Rilke's 'The Flamingos' alludes directly to Baudelaire's 'Lesbos'. Rilke's long-standing interest in Baudelaire, whom he read intensively during the period when he was writing the *New Poems*, is well-known. Most studies of this relationship have seen the German poet as an admiring follower of his French predecessor.[38] In 'The Flamingos', however, Rilke continues the implicit critique of aestheticism we have seen in 'The Tower'.

Rilke and Baudelaire use the figure of Phryne in somewhat different ways. A famous Greek courtesan renowned for her beauty, Phryne was also the model for Praxiteles' statues of Aphrodite. Baudelaire's 'Lesbos' hinges on a fundamental opposition between Venus (Aphrodite) and Sappho. Baudelaire's description of Sappho as 'more beautiful' than Venus provides the subtext for Rilke's description of his flamingos as 'verführender' (more alluring) than Phryne. In Baudelaire's 'Lesbos', Phryne is metonymic for courtesans in general. According to classical tradition, the island of Lesbos was a training school for young prostitutes, who were also educated in various other arts, notably poetry. Sappho was one of these pupils. The nineteenth-century *Larousse* encyclopaedia tells us that, owing to the large number of women concentrated on the island, it fell into disrepute for what were believed to be their shameful sexual practices.[39] Baudelaire uses the inhabitants of Lesbos as a metaphor to explore the problematic relation of beauty to its viewer. As long as Lesbos remains shut off from the outside world, mirroring itself alone, it gives off a hint of something more radiant that seems to derive from another realm. Yet at the same time, the speaker is aware that, because of the island's autonomy, the voluptuous beauty of its inhabitants is also necessarily sterile.

In 'The Flamingos', Rilke gives the Phryne motif a new twist. Placing the motif of seduction at the turning-point of his sonnet, Rilke is clearly aware of the shock value of his adaptation. Whereas Baudelaire's Phrynes are prostitutes living in a self-enclosed and sterile world, Rilke's Phrynes are birds in a zoological garden. We expect them to seduce the spectator – but instead, they seduce themselves. Their posture wards off, and finally excludes, the spectator, as the birds first hide their eyes in their feathers and then move out into an imaginary realm. In other words, Baudelaire and Rilke take different positions on the problem of artistic autonomy. Rilke's adaptation of the motif suggests that aura – the power of a beautiful object to hold the viewer under a spell – disappears when autonomy is taken to its extreme.

By taking up the motif of Phryne in his poem 'The Flamingos', Rilke pays homage to Baudelaire while developing his techniques in a way that is tantamount to a critique. 'The Flamingos' moves through a series of complex shifts as it attempts to describe the flamingos and to explore a variety of different possibilities for formulating this description.

The opening sentence of the poem calls into question two different methods of representing the object, both of them somewhat forced attempts to find equivalents for it. Fragonard's mimetic paintings, the speaker claims, would render the flamingos' red and white colouring no better than if we were to hear someone describing a loved one on the border of sleep and waking. Neither painting nor verbal expression, neither mimesis nor analogy, proves quite adequate, and the language of these lines, with its mediating comparisons, maintains a cautious distance from the modalities it invokes. Yet as if oblivious to the impossibility of description that has now been doubly postulated, the poem proceeds to seek yet another equivalent for the flamingos. The figure now suggested is that of pink flowers blooming on a green lawn; but there is something curious about the way in which this image is presented. Pink stems are mentioned before the notion of blossoming has been introduced, and the grassy bank is elided behind a strangely abstract reference to its colour. The entire image hesitates between the natural and the artificial, as well as between metaphor and simile. The disjunction between the flamingos and their observer reaches its most acute point during the moment of what the text regards as their self-seduction, ingeniously placed in an enjambement that both separates and links the octave of the sonnet and its sestet.[40] Beautiful though it is, their sleeping posture frustrates the spectator, who can no longer see the brighter colours – the black and red underfeathers – hidden beneath the flamingos' folded wings.[41]

Whereas Baudelaire's 'Lesbos' presents the self-echoing and self-contained culture of ancient Lesbos as a lost past to be lamented, Rilke's poem views the ideal of aesthetic autonomy as factitious from the outset. By visualising the flamingos as pink flowers the text suggests a measure of artificiality. In this way, it implicitly criticises those proponents of artistic autonomy who, in attempting to restore the wholeness of the work of art, cut it off from outside reality. By choosing an exotic bird in a

state of captivity as the subject of his poem Rilke takes issue, as well, with
a long tradition of poetry on natural topics. His silent and artificially
posed flamingos are far removed from the songbirds of Romanticism
that identify poetic inspiration with the voice of nature itself. In other
words, the way in which Rilke develops his image of the flower-
flamingos questions both the Romantic notion of 'organic' art and the
Parnassian notion of artistic autonomy.

The speaker of Baudelaire's 'Lesbos' presents himself as the elegiac
modern representative of an enclosed island world. His claim that
Lesbos has chosen him to sing 'le secret de ses vierges en fleurs' (the
secret of its budding virgins) is subverted in Rilke's 'The Flamingos'.
The 'budding virgins' become birds 'blühend' (blossoming) as if in a bed
of flowers, resembling nothing so much as the extravagant artifical
blooms of Huysmans' aestheticist recluse Des Esseintes, the protagonist
of his novel *Against Nature* (1884).[42] In fact, however, the flamingos'
autonomy is really an illusion. Whereas the 'secret' of Baudelaire's
inhabitants of Lesbos is their self-involved and sexually salacious culture, the 'secret' of Rilke's flamingos is the brightly coloured underside
of their wings. By associating the red feathers with fruit, Rilke removes
some of the sterility that had characterised Baudelaire's self-echoing
Lesbos.

The final tercet of Rilke's sonnet adapts the theme of rivalry between
beauties developed in Baudelaire's 'Lesbos' through the motif of
Venus's jealousy of Sappho. In Rilke's poem, it is the birds in the aviary
that envy the uncaged flamingos.[43] Yet even though the flamingos are
free to roam, they do not fly: they merely step in a dignified and
measured fashion into the realm of the imaginary. In effect, this movement betokens their increasing assimilation to a world of representation,
visual or verbal. Rilke's project of writing about the object as it appears
in nature is called into question.[44]

In the nineteenth-century tradition to which Rilke alludes, the story
of Phryne was understood as the story of a rivalry between the sibling
arts, rhetoric and sculpture, represented by Hyperides and Praxiteles
respectively.[45] According to a tradition that goes back to Athenaios of
Naukratis,[46] Phryne was accused and brought to trial for impiety.
Running out of arguments before an unfavourably disposed court, the
defending orator, Hyperides, hit upon the ingenious stratagem of lifting
her veil and revealing her splendid form. The astonished judges were so
struck by her beauty that they acquitted her. When words are no longer
adequate, the anecdote implies, beautiful form can 'speak' without

them. Of course, at Phryne's trial, it was her living body that won the day. But in the nineteenth-century debate about the virtues of the competing arts, the story was reinterpreted as the victory of sculpture over rhetoric.

Rilke's poem opens with a reference to the inadequacies of both visual and verbal representation. Far from arguing in favour of poetry over painting, 'The Flamingos' turns upon the irony that the rhetorician Hyperides won his case precisely by ceasing to use the art in which he was so skilled. Yet whereas the Greek orator allowed the woman's body to speak, as it were, for itself, Rilke's flamingos are no longer able to do so, however much they seem to adopt her alluring pose. For in contrast to Baudelaire's 'Lesbos', which assumes an original harmonious world that subtends fractured modern consciousness, Rilke's 'The Flamingos' creates a world in which it is frustratingly difficult to lift the veil of representation. Even though the poem's subtitle invokes the birds' real existence in the Paris zoological garden, the speaker of the poem persistently sees the flamingos in terms of other things.

Rilke's associative technique is his version of his French predecessor's use of allegory. If Baudelaire's poetry ruptures the 'illusory continuities in which it is embedded',[47] Rilke's poetry presents this crisis of continuity in a more acute form. Rilke's poetry is disturbing because its extreme textualisation makes us uncomfortably aware of its status as poetry. 'The Flamingos' sets up a paradoxical and highly self-conscious relationship with the reader, who, like the observer of the flamingos, is neither completely drawn into the text nor completely excluded from it. In this way, the autonomous artifact is presented as a contradiction in terms from the very beginning.

The story of Phryne was still well known in the nineteenth century. It was frequently treated by contemporary artists, notably in a statue by Jean-Jacques Pradier which Baudelaire admired in his critique of the 1845 Salon.[48] The most famous nineteenth-century treatment of the Phryne motif, Jean-Léon Gérôme's 'Phryne devant l'aréopage' [Phryne before her Judges] (1861),[49] is a dramatic depiction of the moment when the orator removes Phryne's garment, exposing her nakedness to the lascivious gaze of her judges. Submitted to the salon not long after the appearance of *The Flowers of Evil* and the trial it provoked, Gérôme's painting incited a furor of its own. The controversy over Gérôme's 'Phryne' hinged upon its depiction of the unveiled model in an attitude of shame: turning her brilliant white body slightly away from the ranks of red-robed judges looking on, the celebrated courtesan hides her eyes behind her right arm. This attitude, which Gérôme used several times in his paintings of oriental slave markets, was thought inappropriate for a Greek beauty who should have been proud to display her physical charms. Ignoring an ancient tradition according to which Phryne was particularly known for her modesty, nineteenth-century critics took Gérôme to task for this presentation, claiming that he had unduly modernised a classical subject.[50]

As a result of this controversy, the picture became widely known. Indeed, it was the most frequently reproduced, imitated and caricatured interpretation of the Phryne motif in the nineteenth century. Photographs of the painting circulated in the latter part of the century. Goupil's engravings of the painting and Falguière's small-scale bronze statue of Phryne taken from Gérôme's picture were very popular.[51] An operatic version of the story composed by Saint-Saens was presented in Paris in 1903, and a ballet version was performed in 1905.[52]

The pose of Gérôme's Phryne came to be synonymous with an ambiguous kind of modesty. This tradition continued into the first decade of the twentieth century. A 1909 French magazine article on the history of modesty is illustrated by a line drawing of a naked woman in the Phryne pose.[53] Later in the year, the same magazine published a cartoon subtitled 'Phryne before the aeroplane' (an allusion to the French title of Gérôme's painting, 'Phryné devant l'aréopage'): it shows a bathing beauty, suddenly revealed from beneath a huge towel which another woman is whisking from her body, distracting the attention of other bathers and even a press photographer from a demonstration of flying machines at a seaside resort.[54]

Many famous contemporaries commented on Gérôme's 'Phryné'. In his report on the Salon of 1861, Gautier described the painting in some detail, placing special emphasis on the presentation of the courtesan's body, 'shaped and polished like an ivory statue'.[55] Zola, by contrast, regarded the work as a cheap appeal to public prurience and predicted, not entirely inaccurately, that reproductions of the painting would flood the provinces and earn a fortune for engraver and publisher.[56] Degas condemned the painting, claiming that by depicting Phryne in the act of hiding her eyes, Gérôme had turned the work into a pornographic picture.[57]

Cézanne copied the figure of Gérôme's Phryne, using it to replace the central figure in a drawing he made after an engraving of another painting by Gérôme, 'Intérieur grec' (Greek Interior). Cézanne had greatly admired Gérôme's 'Phryne' upon its submission to the salon in

1861, and his own, much more fleshly adaptation of its central figure at about a decade's remove was an even more aggressive challenge to those who thought it wrong to present classical figures through the lens of modern attitudes to sexuality.[58] In short, Gérôme's 'Phryne' had become a *locus classicus* for the contemporary debate on the representation of beauty and the relation of aesthetics to ethics. The name 'Phryne' was more than merely a classical allusion: it conjured up an entire debate about the power and function of art.

Shortly before he wrote 'The Flamingos', Rilke noted in a letter to Clara that he had begun to go to the Bibliothèque Nationale almost every day 'mehr um nachzuschlagen als um zu lesen' (more to look things up than to read).[59] We know, from remarks in earlier letters,[60] how much he enjoyed poring over dictionaries and other reference works. Under the rubric 'Phryne', the most up-to-date French encyclopaedia then in the Bibliothèque Nationale, the *Nouveau Larousse Illustré* of 1899, reproduces an engraving of Gérôme's 'Phryne before her Judges',[61] and the previous edition of the same reference work gives a lengthy account of the debates the painting had provoked.[62]

Rilke's poem refrains from treating contemporary aesthetic problems by displacing them into classical antiquity. Although it contemplates for a moment a possible equivalence between the flamingos and the Greek courtesan, it ultimately discards this notion. Instead, it substitutes for it a complicated formulation that makes the birds something both more and less than the traditional motif allows: 'verführender' (more alluring) than the extraordinary beauty whose body made words superfluous, but also less effective, since their seductions are directed toward themselves rather than toward an audience. In other words, Rilke uses the Phryne motif in 'The Flamingos' to question the value of traditional models, which he sees as inadequate to modern aesthetic concerns. In this way, Rilke's poem goes beyond Gérôme's painting.

How does the poem's allusion to Gérôme relate to its opening reference to the visual arts, the mention of Fragonard? One of the special effects of Gérôme's 'Phryne' lies in the contrast between the judges' carmine robes and Phryne's marmoreal body;[63] the first quatrain of Rilke's poem speaks of Fragonard's much subtler use of the same colours, red and white. Whereas Fragonard's erotic paintings, which Rilke saw and admired at the Louvre in 1907,[64] allow us a delicate glimpse into a softly pink and white private realm,[65] Gérôme's painting of Phryne shows her in a theatrically illuminated public space characterised by dramatic effects of colour and composition. The contrast between Fragonard's soft intimacy and Gérôme's stark public display, chiastically linked with that between the delicate outer feathers and striking underfeathers of the flamingos, would be, in this reading, part of Rilke's attempt to demonstrate a fundamental ambiguity in the nature of art and its effect on the viewer: the tension between its self-enclosure or autonomy, on the one hand, and its openness to external reality, on the other.

In this sense, the ambiguous relation between art and reality becomes acute in Rilke's 'The Flamingos'. The live flamingos in the Paris Jardin des Plantes are linked with a conglomeration of associations, suppositions and fantasies that the viewer brings to them and that threaten to drain them of their corporeality. These associations are not only arbitrary and heterogeneous, the poem also comments on the problem of allegorising by repeatedly insisting on the disjuncture between these images and the object.

The poem also develops a complex set of ambiguities by showing something natural – birds – from an aspect that makes it seem more like an art work. Rilke's poem moves uneasily between the world of nature and the world of art. By linking the birds so flamboyantly with art and the imagination, he partially dislocates them from the natural world to which they belong. This discrepancy between the object and its metaphoric correlative is one reason why 'The Flamingos' appears so highly wrought. Yet only by creating this effect can the poem comment on the artificial nature of poetic figuration in general. In this way, 'The Flamingos' radically breaks down the aestheticist belief in the interdependence of autonomy and aura.

THE MEANINGFUL FRAGMENT

'Archaischer Torso Apollos' [Archaic Torso of Apollo] (1908), the opening sonnet in the second volume of *New Poems*, may seem to countermand this position. Yet the radiance that emanates from the sculpture is not an effect of wholeness, but rather of its fragmentary nature. Of all Rilke's poetry from his Paris period, 'Archaic Torso of Apollo' is his most radical extension and revocation of Baudelairean tenets. Whereas for Baudelaire the fragmentariness of the modern art work is a sign of mourning for a lost perfection, the observer in Rilke's poem responds with enthusiasm to the fragmentariness of the Apollo. Whereas for Baudelaire the past is accessible only in fleeting glimpses, the ancient work of art in Rilke's poem speaks directly to us.[66] Broken by its survival into the modern world, the statue nonetheless bursts 'aus allen seinen Rändern/ aus wie ein Stern' (out of all its borders/ like a star), reaching across the divide between art and life and testifying to Rilke's desire to break out of the self-containment urged by proponents of poetic autonomy:

> Wir kannten nicht sein unerhörtes Haupt,
> darin die Augenäpfel reiften. Aber
> sein Torso glüht noch wie ein Kandelaber,
> in dem sein Schauen, nur zurückgeschraubt,
>
> sich hält und glänzt. Sonst könnte nicht der Bug
> der Brust dich blenden, und im leisen Drehen
> der Lenden könnte nicht ein Lächeln gehen
> zu jener Mitte, die die Zeugung trug.
>
> Sonst stünde dieser Stein entstellt und kurz
> unter der Schultern durchsichtigem Sturz
> und flimmerte nicht so wie Raubtierfelle;
>
> und bräche nicht aus allen seinen Rändern
> aus wie ein Stern: denn da ist keine Stelle,
> die dich nicht sieht. Du mußt dein Leben ändern   (1: 557)

> We did not know the never-heard-of head
> in which his eye-ball-apples ripened. Yet
> his torso, chandelier-like, holds a glow
> in which his vision, turned a little low,
>
> persists and gleams. Or else his curving breast
> could not so blind you, nor the gentle turn
> of his shaped loins send forth a smile, suppressed,
> to that mid-point where once the passion burned.
>
> Or else this stone would be distorted, short
> beneath the shoulders' clear protective screen,
> and would not shimmer so like wild beasts' fur;
>
> and would not burst out, like a radiant star,
> beyond its borders: for there is no spot
> that does not see you. You must change your life.

By comparing the missing head of the archaic torso with something modern (a turned-down gas candelabra) and its still existing shoulders with something primitive (the shining pelts of wild beasts of prey), Rilke poses an agonising and unresolved question about the possibility of historic contextualisation. Poised between two worlds, the broken statue suggests a confrontation between ancient and modern culture that is never fully articulated: history is invoked, but also curiously elided.

Rilke's 'Archaic Torso of Apollo' is an important exploration of the relation between the work of art and its viewer. Yet as soon as we look at it more closely, it is hard to determine just what the poem proclaims. Its final sentence, 'Du mußt dein Leben ändern' (You must change your life), is its most puzzling pronouncement. To begin with, we cannot tell whether these words are a direct address by the statue or an interior monologue on the part of its observer. Beyond the ambiguous origin of the hortatory phrase, the change envisaged remains unspecified. All we know is that a change must be made; we are not told why or how.

The dedication to Rodin at the front of the volume (1: 556) complicates this effect. Not only had Rilke written a monograph on Rodin (published in 1903), he had worked for a time as his secretary (1905–1906). Rodin's views on art and, above all, his persistent manner of working, had impressed Rilke from the start. Rodin had advised Rilke to devote himself exclusively to work, and to develop patience.[67] Rilke liked to think of his *New Poems* as an attempt to put Rodin's aesthetic practices into effect. Writing about an ancient torso was in part inspired by Rilke's visits to the Louvre, but also by his constant exposure to the sculptures of Rodin, with their attempt to recreate deliberately the fragmentary effects of ancient statues. Seen against the backdrop of Rilke's dedication to the sculptor, the final words of the Apollo sonnet suggest not so much a turning away from poetry to the real world as a turning away from the poetics of inspiration to a poetics of craftsmanship.

In the concluding sections of Rilke's 1907 lecture on Rodin, incorporated into the second edition of his monograph on the sculptor, Rilke imagines a conversation with a visitor who observes those parts of Rodin's *La Porte de l'enfer* [The Gate of Hell] that had already been completed (5: 226). The visitor is Oscar Wilde, appearing under his Parisian pseudonym, Sebastian Melmoth; ravaged by a life of debauchery, the visitor still hopes to be able 'neuanzufangen' (to start over again; 5: 226). Rilke's monograph ends by suggesting that Rodin's sculptures are a response to the increasing secularisation of modern life, which, unlike the medieval cathedral, is unable to bring disparate elements together.

Rodin's *Gate of Hell* and the archaic torso of Apollo have one feature in common: their fragmentary nature. Rodin's sculpture is put together from a multitude of heterogeneous elements and Rilke's ancient torso has lost those parts that we commonly think of as most expressive. Above all, the statue of Apollo lacks organs of creativity, mental and physical: the head and the genitals.

Apollo is, of course, not only the sun god, but also the god of poetry; like Orpheus, Apollo is frequently depicted with a lyre. Rilke draws a central image of his sonnet, the idea of the smile on the torso, from an essay by Mallarmé on Théodore de Banville, whom Mallarmé regards as the supreme lyric poet of his time.[68] Mallarmé first extols the virtues of Banville in his 'Symphonie littéraire' [Literary Symphony] (1864), an essay on three poets, Gautier, Baudelaire and Banville. Describing Banville, Mallarmé compares him directly with the god of poetry: 'Ainsi dut être celui qui le premier reçut des dieux la lyre et dit l'ode éblouie avant notre aïeul Orphée. Ainsi lui-même, Apollon' (Just so must have been he who first received the lyre from the gods and spoke the dazzled ode before our ancestor Orpheus. Just so Apollo himself; Mallarmé, p. 265). In his later piece, 'Théodore de Banville' (1892), Mallarmé cites a long passage from the section on Banville in 'Literary Symphony' into which he silently interpolates a new sentence about the poetic genius of his contemporary: 'la Muse, vêtue du sourire qui sort d'un jeune torse, lui verse l'inspiration' (the Muse, clothed in the smile that emanates from a young torso, pours inspiration into him; Mallarmé, p. 521).

Rilke's appropriation of this image, the idea of the smile on the torso, is striking. By deploying it in a context that also suggests Rodin, he gives it an ironic twist. Banville, according to Mallarmé's vision of him, is directly inspired by the muse; Rodin, by contrast, rejects the notion of inspiration in favour of hard work.

Complicating this implicit debate about inspiration is a reflection on history, provoked by the statue's origin in classical antiquity. The charm of the torso, as Rilke presents it, derives from its damaged condition, which forces the viewer to reconstruct in imagination its missing parts: head, limbs, and genitals. Emphasising the creative power of imagination, the speaker of the poem argues against a view of the statue that would see it as impoverished by the loss of these elements. In effect, he rejects both a classicising aesthetics that would define the statue's beauty in terms of its formerly balanced physical proportions (he denies that its reduction to a torso has unduly shortened and distorted it) and a romanticist aesthetics that would seek to appreciate it in terms of organic wholeness (indicated by the missing eyeballs, that might otherwise have 'ripened' like apples beneath the viewer's gaze). Despite the fact that the statue is a relic from an early phase in the history of art, the speaker heretically compares the light it seems to shed with that given off by a modern gas light, dimmed but somehow blinding nonetheless.

The word 'zurückgeschraubt' (dimmed or turned down) provides the clue to this unexpected intrusion of modernity into a meditation on an ancient statue. Whereas electric light, before the invention of the rheostat, could only be switched on or off, gas light could be literally 'turned' higher or lower with a key that partially interrupted the flow of gas to the lamp.[69] Rilke clearly has in mind a gas candelabra of this sort when he describes the torso's glow, a displaced vestige of its missing eyes, as dimmed but still burning. The word 'Sturz' (rendered in my translation as 'protective screen') refers to a glass lampshade.[70] By Rilke's day, gas light had already begun to be replaced by electricity, in the form of arc lights illuminating city streets and incandescent bulbs used in domestic lamps. What is it about the classical torso that makes him think of a gas light?

I suggest that the association is a recollection of Mallarmé's sonnet, 'Le Tombeau de Charles Baudelaire' [The Tomb of Charles Baudelaire] (1895), with its presentation of the eternally illumined modern city wracked by debauchery and prostitution.[71] The twisting gas flame illuminates what the speaker of the poem ironically terms 'un immortel pubis' (an immortal pubis) of a prostitute standing beneath it (Mallarmé, p. 70). This image has been the subject of intense critical speculation and cannot be fully analysed here.[72] Rilke picks up several elements from Mallarmé's poem – the gas lamp, the pubis, the notion of seduction, and the combination of things ancient and modern – and redeploys them with a significant shift of emphasis.

Mallarmé's poem is a reflection on the problem of poetic succession. At the beginning of the poem, the tomb of Baudelaire is buried, like a sacred monument of the past that is unintelligible to the modern viewer; the gas lamps illumine only the less than immortal bodies of streetwalkers. At the end of the poem, the street lights become votive lamps consecrating the marble of Baudelaire's tomb, the figure of the prostitute is transformed into the consoling shade of the poet, and the deadly poison of his poetry becomes a 'tutelary' draught (un poison tutélaire; Mallarmé, p. 70) for the poet who succeeds him.

Both Rilke's and Mallarmé's sonnets meditate on the connections between antiquity and the present day, between sexuality and the aesthetic, destruction and inspiration. Both regard artworks of the past as simultaneously accessible and inaccessible: in Mallarmé, the 'buried' tomb nonetheless divulges the ghost of the poet whose body it contains; in Rilke, the missing head of the statue is replaced by a gaze that seems to emanate from its torso and a smile that can only be imagined as directed toward the absent genitals. Both poems reflect on the position of art with respect to cultural history and the manner in which art exerts its influence upon its receiver.

Rilke chooses the bright god Apollo rather than the dark Anubis as his vehicle for confronting ancient religion and modern aesthetics. Mallarmé's canine idol, the Egyptian god Anubis, cannot articulate any message other than a terrifying bark; Rilke's statue exhorts the viewer directly and in clearly intelligible words. Light, in Mallarmé's poem the source of unsettling ambiguity, becomes in Rilke's poem the brilliant shining of a star.

In 1908, when Rilke wrote 'Archaic Torso of Apollo', a critical debate was still raging about the value of Mallarmé's poetry. On the one hand, there were those who viewed Mallarmé's poetry as the effusions of a madman; on the other, there were those who defended Mallarmé against the charge of obscurity. In the early phase of the debate, André Gide had argued that Mallarmé's work required a slow and gradual initiation, but he was attacked by others who refused to concede that one could make any sense out of Mallarmé's difficult and seemingly disjunctive verses. The battle came to a peak in 1908 and continued into 1909.[73] 'Archaic Torso of Apollo' takes up the terms of the debate through its contention that the fragmentary art object, which can only be fully known by an act of imaginative reconstruction, is nonetheless capable of 'speaking' directly and clearly to its viewer.

To be sure, Rilke's Apollo sonnet is more obviously unified and aesthetically harmonious in the conventional sense than Mallarmé's sonnet on Baudelaire's tomb. Mallarmé's poem is densely packed with heterogeneous and often repugnant images whose curiously disconnected linkages are forged by means of creative syntactic displacements which make the text appear simultaneously torn apart and pieced together. Rilke retains some aspects of this heterogeneity: the disparate images, the daring imaginative leaps, the unusual enjambements. But his poem moves more smoothly, blending the various elements rather than juxtaposing them, and presenting the radiance of his object as an aesthetic compensation for its disconcerting fragmentariness.

In Mallarmé's poem, his precursor Baudelaire is curiously present and absent at once, a veiled and elusive shade reposing against the marble of the tombstone. In Rilke's poem, Baudelaire leads an even more ghostly existence. In the modern cityscape of *The Flowers of Evil*, objects disconcertingly return the gaze of their beholder, subverting the traditional supremacy of the viewer over the thing seen. For Baudelaire, this is part of an oppositional gesture that fundamentally puts into question the power relationships of modern society.[74] Rilke is less concerned with power relationships in the socio-political sense than with the subject-object relationship, conventional notions of which he had already turned upside down in *The Book of Hours*. Rilke's archaic object admonishes its viewer to recognise that the control exercised by the observing subject is only apparent: by making the eyeless torso 'see' its observer, Rilke reverses the terms of the relationship and places the source of control in the object rather than subject. From this perspective, one way of 'changing one's life' would be to reconceive subject and object so as to abolish their usual hierarchy. The 'regards familiers' (familiar glances) of Baudelaire's objects thus retain their disturbing edge, but have been broadened to an essentially philosophical, rather than a social application.

If we look back from this poem to its predecessor in the *New Poems*, 'Früher Apollo' [Early Apollo] (1906; 1: 481), we can see that Rilke has now formulated his aesthetic position more precisely. Indeed, 'Archaic Torso of Apollo' is not so much a companion piece as in many ways a revocation of 'Early Apollo'. The first Apollo poem has suffered somewhat by comparison with the more striking later piece. Still, Rilke had used it as the opening piece in the first volume of his *New Poems*.

'Early Apollo' presents a notion of poetry as the result of a development akin to natural growth: the rays of sunshine that peer through the bare branches of early spring in the first lines of the poem point forward to the luxuriant garden projected in the later sections. Like the early spring light, this statue of Apollo is rudimentary: his temples are 'zu kühl für Lorbeer' (too cool for laurel), Apollo's traditional attribute. More importantly for our context, the early Apollo almost intimidates the poet who views him: there is nothing about his head, the speaker says, 'was verhindern könnte, daß der Glanz aller Gedichte uns fast tödlich träfe' (which could prevent us from being almost fatally wounded by the radiance of all poems). This image is remarkable in its frank expression of an anxiety about poetic influence.

The final image of the poem is also interesting with respect to its implied aesthetics. Unlike the archaic Apollo of the later poem, the early Apollo has a head, and the smile we see is that of his almost living, trembling mouth. The Apollo's attitude is that of an infant being fed from a bottle or a cup: 'mit seinem Lächeln etwas trinkend/ als würde ihm sein Singen eingeflößt' (drinking something in with his smile/ as if his singing were being poured into him). The formulation is telling: singing is not a bursting forth, but a flowing in, quite literally an in-fluence. This brings us back to the passage from Mallarmé's essay on Théodore de Banville, the latter-day Apollo whose poetic powers are bestowed on him, or 'poured into him' by the muse. It is as if Rilke had taken Mallarmé's verb, 'verser', which means to bestow with prodigal generosity, in its literal sense, not entirely absent in Mallarmé's formulation, of 'to pour'.

Viewed in this light, 'Early Apollo' speaks directly to the problem of poetic influence and inspiration. It suggests a new and hesitant beginning, one that tremblingly awaits the arrival of inspiration but fears the deadly splendor of an accumulated poetic tradition; that is too young for the laurel wreath of fame but antedates the most renowned examples of an ancient cultural heritage. This fundamental ambiguity is heightened by the poem's hesitation between conceiving the Apollo as a marble object and a living being that trembles and blinks, a remote stone monument 'too cool for laurel' and a statue so overgrown by nature that it seems to be sprouting rose bushes from its brows. Nor is it clear whether poetry is itself a point of origin, emerging like leaves in the spring at a ray of light from the sun god, or whether it occurs at a cumulative moment, like the fall of rose petals when blooming is almost over. As god of poetry, Apollo is a predecessor of Orpheus and of all later poets and is thus the one who makes their singing possible; and yet this Apollo is himself only tremblingly on the brink of song, waiting for inspiration to be poured into him from some external source. Although he is the focus of the entire sonnet, Apollo is never the grammatical subject of any of its sentences, and even his singing, far from bursting forth at the end of the poem as one might have expected, is embedded in an artfully passive construction ('als würde ihm sein Singen eingeflößt', as if his singing were being poured into him). 'Early Apollo' never quite decides between two different conceptions of art: as artifact or natural organism.

The later Apollo poem, 'Archaic Torso of Apollo', takes a more decisive position on these questions. Its opening lines pick up imagery from its precursor, in which the head of the Apollo was the sole focus. By visualising the statue's eyes (or somewhat spookily,[75] the statue's eyeballs) as if they were apples ripening on a tree, the poem retains something of the vegetative imagery of 'Early Apollo'. Yet this natural image is immediately followed by the image of the gas lamp, just as the later description of the statue as a 'stone' is subsequently cancelled out by its description as a star bursting out of all its borders.

Reframing the imagery of the torso poem in terms of the earlier Apollo poem, one might ask, then: is the statue a tree or a lamp, a stone or a star? Here the two possibilities seem to be maintained at once, just as the statue's eyes are simultaneously absent in actual fact and present in the imagination of the beholder. By the same token, almost the entire sonnet, though redeeming the statue from the charge of aesthetic incompleteness by pointing to its extraordinary radiance and mobility, does so in phrases curiously couched as negative conditions. The poem's compelling effect stems from the way it asks us to hold two visions of the statue in our minds at the same time.

Rilke does something quite striking with the sonnet form as well. Its traditional contrastive structure, in which the tercets present a reversal of the situation described in the quatrains, is drastically destabilised, the crucial 'but' being shifted almost to the beginning of the poem, at the end of the second line. The word 'mid-point', positioned at the traditional turning-point of the sonnet form, deceives the reader into thinking that this is in fact the pivot of the poem; but the tercets merely continue the 'or else' construction that had begun in the second quatrain. As these continuities override the expectation of reversal at the mid-point of the sonnet, another important double vision emerges in the reference to the statue's missing genitals. To think in terms of procreative organs is to think of the statue as a body, to think in terms of a 'mid-point' is to think of it as an art work. The poem makes both claims at once.

'Early Apollo' had captured a moment in its statue's existence before it had been overgrown by vegetation, just as the statue itself had captured a moment in the god's mythogenesis before he had begun to sing. The speaker knows what is to come, but presents it as if it had not yet happened. 'Archaic Torso of Apollo' looks back at an ancient statue from a decidedly modern viewpoint. The poem poses questions about the statue's historical status, comparing it, on the one hand, with the translucent shade of a modern gas lamp, and on the other, with the shining fur of primitive beasts of prey. To put it in aesthetic terms, the broken Apollo is remote from its present-day viewers because it comes from a cultural epoch virtually inaccessible to us, yet its fragmentariness can also be read as a forerunner of modernist artistic concepts, most obviously those of Rodin.

The aesthetics it implies go beyond the alternatives posited by the earlier Apollo poem. Although the archaic Apollo withholds many of its secrets, still it speaks directly to the modern viewer. The message it sends, at least as interpreted by the speaker of the poem, is one that moves decisively away from the notion of creative inspiration. It gives a command, but oddly, the command is one that shifts control from the statue itself to its observer.

In this way, Rilke distinctly modifies the classical ideal of a 'monument more lasting than bronze' (Horace). Certainly he was fascinated by the solid, lasting and three-dimensional qualities of sculpted objects, but he rarely saw them as completely static.[76] What interested him almost always was the movement they suggest, be it that of a stone figure half-stepping out of a mediaeval church portal (1: 500), the backward turning of Orpheus toward Eurydice on an ancient stone relief (1: 545), or the wind-swept garment of a sculpted Artemis dashing to the hunt with her retinue of nymphs (1: 557). In Rodin's sculptures, the interplay of light between the various surfaces creates for Rilke the sense of something that continues to shape itself before the eye of the beholder.[77]

'Archaic Torso of Apollo' is full of such imagined movement, concentrated in the slight turning of the statue's loins toward its absent centre. As in the work of Rodin, the play of light accentuates this dynamic. Glowing at first within the torso, light finally bursts forth from it, blinding the viewer and making it seem as if the sculpture is no longer contained within its boundaries. This presentation emphasises not the solidity of the object, but its imagined explosiveness. The aesthetic Rilke proposes in 'Archaic Torso of Apollo' – the preference for fragmentariness over wholeness, the fascination with paradox, and the dissolution of subject-object boundaries – is moving in the direction of modernism.

This is not to say, however, that Rilke actually makes the leap into modernism here. Even in the second volume of the *New Poems* he is still concerned to extend and criticise aestheticism from within. Nonetheless, there are increasing signs that the imaginary is located in rifts that open in the material world: the crack in a cup (1: 590), the cleft of a mountain (1: 638), the silence in the midst of a narrative (1: 560). These gaps are reflected in startling jumps between images and in discrepancies between the object described and the images with which it is linked. 'Archaic Torso of Apollo' is a contradiction in terms: the announcement of a new and radically subversive aesthetic couched in the rhetorical tones of an era more self-complacent about the hortatory power of poetry.

ENCRUSTED STYLE

'San Marco' (1908), another sonnet from the second volume of *New Poems*, approaches the question of fragmentation and wholeness from a different perspective than that of 'Archaic Torso of Apollo'. Both poems belong to a productive phase in Rilke's work during the late summer of 1908; the order in which he wrote them is not known. Where 'Archaic Torso of Apollo' wrestles with the problem of a fragment that radiates aesthetic energy more powerfully than if it had remained whole, 'San Marco' puzzles over a single structure that is composed of many separate elements. As its title indicates, the poem is a description of Saint Mark's cathedral in Venice.

In late November 1907, after a lecture tour to Prague, Breslau and Vienna, Rilke spent ten days in Venice, staying with the art dealer Piero Romanelli, whom he had met at the Salon d'Automne in Paris. It was his third trip to the city of canals, and it gave rise – after a delay of over half a year – to two of his best-known poems about Venice: 'Venezianischer Morgen' [Venetian Morning] (1: 609) and 'Spätherbst in Venedig' [Late Autumn in Venice] (1: 609–610).[78]

It also gave rise to the less frequently studied 'San Marco', an important document for Rilke's reflection on the aesthetic he had inherited and on the relation between poetry and history. Unlike August von Platen's series of Venetian sonnets (1834), nostalgic meditations on the city's past glories and present shadowy subsistence, Rilke's 'San Marco' pays close attention to its architectural object:

> In diesem Innern, das wie ausgehöhlt
> sich wölbt und wendet in den goldnen Smalten,
> rundkantig, glatt, mit Köstlichkeit geölt,
> ward dieses Staates Dunkelheit gehalten
>
> und heimlich aufgehäuft, als Gleichgewicht
> des Lichtes, das in allen seinen Dingen
> sich so vermehrte, daß sie fast vergingen – .
> Und plötzlich zweifelst du: vergehn sie nicht?
>
> und drängst zurück die harte Galerie,
> die, wie ein Gang im Bergwerk, nah am Glanz
> der Wölbung hängt; und du erkennst die heile
>
> Helle des Ausblicks: aber irgendwie
> wehmütig messend ihre müde Weile
> am nahen Überstehn des Viergespanns.   (1: 610)

In this inside, that, hollowed ring by ring,
is curved and convoluted in its golden glaze,
round-cornered, smooth, and salved with precious things,
the state's dark treasures kept from people's gaze,

secretly heaped on heap, to counterweigh
that blinding light that grew so much to lie
in objects that they almost passed away – .
And suddenly you doubt: do they not die?

and then you thrust the rigid gallery back,
which hangs suspended, like a mineshaft, there
close to the dome; and you can see the grand

brightness of prospect: yet, somehow at lack,
measuring, mournful, its tired moment where
it is outlasted by the nearby four-in-hand.

We know that Rilke prepared for his journeys by reading travel
guides and other literature about the places he was to visit. On his first
tour of Venice he used Baedeker's famous guidebook and Goethe's
Italienische Reise [Italian Journey].[79] He was fond of Philippe Monnier's
book on Venice, which he owned during his Paris period.[80] In 1906, just
a year before Rilke's third trip to Venice, a book that had already
become a standard guide for English-speaking tourists was translated for
the first time into French: the two-volume 'Traveller's Edition' of
Ruskin's *Stones of Venice*. Inspired by Robert de la Sizeranne's translation
of *The Religion of Beauty* and Marcel Proust's rendering of *The Bible of
Amiens*, Mathilde P. Crémieux had begun her translation of *The Stones of
Venice* in 1905, and it appeared, with a preface by Sizeranne, in a single
volume in 1906.[81] Sizeranne's preface situates Ruskin's aesthetic as an
attempt to re-evaluate pre-Renaissance art and emphasise the artisanal
aspect of art and the sanctity of work;[82] he also presents Ruskin as a kind
of magician able to revivify the vestiges of a former culture and to evoke
'invisible things' through a confrontation with things visible (p. xix).
Above all, Sizeranne presents Ruskin as an adversary of the art for art's
sake movement and a proponent of the notion that art is useful and
meaningful. Though Sizeranne's preface does not overtly attempt to
'modernise' Ruskin, he presents him as a 'precursor, prophet, and
guide' who will lead us into the future (p. xxiii). His reading of Ruskin's
The Stones of Venice (1851–53) reveals with particular persuasiveness those
features of his thought that made Ruskin's aesthetic still relevant in the
early years of the twentieth century.

Rilke's cult of vision, especially his exploration of the nexus between seeing, memory, and imagination in the *New Poems* and *Malte Laurids Brigge*, owes a good deal to the Ruskinian model. 'Be your own master', advised Ruskin in 1869, 'and see with your own eyes'.[83] Recent studies of Ruskin have shown how sophisticated Ruskin's theory of the 'art of seeing' actually was.[84] For Ruskin, man was essentially a *'seeing* creature'[85] and perception was a combination of seeing and feeling. By the same token, imagination was for him inextricably intertwined with both sight and recollection. Like Ruskin, Rilke was also interested in the way the eye moves as it observes an object, the 'constant shifts in focus as eye and mind travel through three-dimensional space'.[86]

Rilke had become acquainted with Ruskin's work at least several years before Sizeranne's preface to the French translation of *The Stones of Venice*. He appears to have read the German translation in the Eugen Diederichs edition, to which he refers in his 1902 review of Walter Pater's *Studies in the Renaissance*, composed in July 1901 (5: 600). He refers again to Ruskin in an essay on Heinrich Vogeler written just a few months earlier (April 1901), and discusses him at length in two letters to the German translator of Pater and Ruskin, Wilhelm Schölermann (6: 1421). Nonetheless, the French translation of Ruskin's *The Stones of Venice*, published shortly before Rilke's third trip to Venice, seems to have inspired him to take yet another look at the work in preparation for his journey.

Rilke's poem, 'San Marco', provides vivid testimony to his involvement with Ruskin's views on the nature of the cathedral's architecture. In a crucial passage in *The Stones of Venice*, Ruskin discusses what he terms 'the encrusted style'.[87] Exemplified in Saint Mark's cathedral, this style involves embedding fragments taken from elsewhere into a new and different aesthetic whole. From Ruskin's account of Saint Mark's, Rilke adopts several features: the conception of the basilica as a mine or quarry, and the notion that its inside has been hollowed out beneath the domes; the emphasis on its gold and azure decorations and its function as a treasury for booty brought from afar to increase the fortunes of state; the vision of the four horses above the portal as a source of strength counterbalancing the visual confusion of the architectural complex; and the valorisation of the Gothic at the expense of the Renaissance.

Unlike Ruskin, who begins his discussion of the basilica with a detailed description of its facade, Rilke's viewer is already inside the church at the beginning of the poem. Even when stationed inside, the viewer is acutely aware that ugly secrets are hidden, not just in the treasury itself, but in the dazzling surfaces of the cathedral walls themselves. Brilliant as they are, the costly decorations are in fact a sign of the dark underside of the Venetian state, whose riches had been obtained in part by plundering other nations. In *The Stones of Venice*, Ruskin had explained that Venetians' slow and expensive method of using oar-propelled boats to transport building materials made it advantageous to convey ready-cut pieces, especially precious stones taken from the ruins of older structures. These precious 'fragments' became quite literally building blocks for the monuments of Venice (p. 77).

The gilded objects form a 'Gleichgewicht' (counterweight) to the light that enters through the windows in the cupola and magnifies the glitter of the beautiful surfaces. Thus although the monument seems to have survived in all its radiance into our own age, the fragments of which it is composed bear witness to the destruction of earlier monuments.

The poem suggests that light, the traditional symbol of the Renaissance, is actually a degrading element, an agent of the beautiful objects' decay. The gilt decorations seem to have accumulated light to the point where it destroys them from within, rather than from without. This vision of architectural decadence owes much to Ruskin's view that Venetian culture began its downward course with excessive acquisition of riches.

Rilke's mention of glazed surfaces (the word he uses, 'Smalten', refers simultaneously to the shining blue and gold colours of the dome's interior) suggests his interest in what Ruskin had called the 'superficies' of the cathedral's ceiling. Yet Rilke's poem hesitates between this interest in surface and a more conventional fascination with depth: the speaker sees the domed ceilings both as dazzling concave surfaces and as spaces hollowed out of some originally more substantial material.

The poem hesitates between two architectural models: a Ruskinian preference for Gothic asymmetry, represented by the cupolas, and a classical model of beauty, represented by the Greek horses. As long as Rilke's viewer is inside the basilica, he emphasises the smooth, round shapes that seem imbued with a special dynamism, as if they were actually in motion, turning and twisting their brilliant surfaces. Indeed, the precious oil seems to have been poured on a little too thickly. Even so, the viewer is anxious to obliterate everything that goes against these undulating effects, mentally abolishing the horizontal lines of the gallery below the upper vaults.

The speaker of the poem imagines this gallery as a mineshaft. Applied to Saint Mark's, this idea is eminently Ruskinian: Ruskin writes, in *The*

Stones of Venice, that the Venetians used the ruins of older monuments as 'quarries' from which to mine the stones for their cathedral. At the same time, the cathedral is for Ruskin a quarry for the modern viewer, whom he exhorts to 'read the sculpture' as 'that great symbolic language of past ages, which has now so long been unspoken'. Rilke's observer, by contrast, does not 'read' the sculpture. Instead, he reverts at the end to a more conventional view that finds meaning in the unifying vision of an epiphanic moment, the healing wholeness of the light that meets him as he leaves the cathedral through its vast central portal. Two different mine images have been conflated here: one in which individual frag-ments are extracted for recomposition into a new whole; the other in which a journey into the bowels of the earth facilitates an ultimate emergence into light and knowledge. The Ruskinian conception of the basilica as a composite structure characterised by complex light and colour effects and properly viewed by a moving, rather than a still, eye dominates the better part of Rilke's sonnet. But in the final tercet it gives way to a more conventional perspectivism: the view through the portal, a wholeness of vision, and an emphasis on the bright light outside. By the same token, the poem's opening fascination with the basilica's dynamic interior yields in the last line to a new appreciation of the horse statues above the portal. The focus is on their solidity, their endurance, and the strangely transfixed way in which they project above the entrance.

This image is evocative in many ways. The crucial word is 'über-stehen' (outlast). The German word means to survive or endure; as an extension of this meaning, the word can also mean to last or become permanent. Rilke uses the same word at the end of his requiem for Wolf Graf von Kalckreuth, written only a few months after 'San Marco': 'Wer spricht von Siegen? Überstehn ist alles' (Who speaks of conquer-ing? Survival is everything; 1: 664). Applied to the bronze horses, 'überstehn' suggests that they have become an enduring art work, 'more lasting than bronze', to use Horace's famous phrase. At the same time, however, 'überstehn' also has the more literal meaning 'stand out over': the horses in fact protrude beyond the edges of the gallery at the spot where it is interrupted by the arch of the central portal. The rising arch of the portal suppresses the gallery for a brief portion of its length, allowing its curved line to obliterate momentarily the straight lines of the gallery. Whereas the gallery forces the viewer's eye to move horizontally across the facade, the horses seem to burst out of the building as if they were about to thunder forward right above the viewer's head. The emphasis here is on the tension between the two sets of lines – the lateral gallery and the frontally charging horses – that interrupt the convoluted shapes of the edifice.

This architectural contradiction is paralleled by another paradox. Emerging from the dark interior of the basilica, the speaker has a kind of epiphany, a sudden sense of illumination. The intricate variety of the decorative elements inside the cathedral had created a rich and complex chiaroscuro effect; but now this gives way to an unrelieved burst of light as the speaker passes through the central portal into the square outside. He is well aware, however, of the fleeting nature of this effect. In the final tercet, thought seems to go adrift. Vagueness and abstraction pervade this part of the poem, and the limp interpolation 'irgendwie' (somehow) suggests a sudden loss of explicative power. Rather than simply telling us that the viewer's bedazzlement by the light from outside is merely a momentary effect, Rilke gives us a periphrastic sentence that the reader is barely able to decode. The poem's ending subverts the expectations its opening sections create. Instead of tying everything together in a moment of closure, the poem finishes fitfully and inconclusively. Anyone who has not seen Saint Mark's cathedral will feel quite confused. What it says about the monument and its history is extremely allusive: it assumes that the reader has already seen the basilica and read the guide book.

The poem presents some of the same contradictions that characterise the building it describes. Are we to admire the bizarre beauty of this heteroclite structure, or to find it excessively mannered and over-wrought? Are the curvilinear shapes beautiful or contorted, the rectilinear shapes reassuring or tedious? Is light degrading, as it seems to be when it illuminates the decorations, or refreshing, as it appears when the visitor emerges into the open? Does the basilica represent the pinnacle of a cultural achievement or the beginning of a cultural decline? Do the elements from elsewhere that have gone into its making bespeak transience, like the gilded mosaics, or endurance, like the bronze horses? How solid are the horses anyway, with their prancing feet pawing the empty air, forever going nowhere?

Reflecting on Ruskin's discussion of Saint Mark's was, for Rilke, not merely a way of remembering an architectural monument that he had seen several times in actuality, most recently six months before. It was also a way of thinking about the history of style. Ruskin's theory about the transition from Gothic to Renaissance architecture had interesting resonances for a poet who was attempting to move beyond his own earlier manner. Ruskin's presentation, furthermore, of an architectural style put together from disparate elements recalled a work Rilke had already studied: Rodin's *Gate of Hell*, a work of art composed of many different individual pieces (each of them made, to be sure, by Rodin himself). Rilke described it in a note to his 1907 lecture on Rodin as 'dieses größte Gebirg seiner Schöpfung, das dem Meister jahrzehntelang als Steinbruch von Ideen gedient hat' (that greatest mountain of his creation, which has served the master for decades as a quarry for ideas; 5: 246). Different though they were in fundamental respects, the aesthetic theories of Ruskin and Rodin had a number of common features: their emphasis on 'seeing', especially on the eye as it travels over or around the object, their fascination with surfaces and with effects of light, and their insistence on the value of 'work' or craftsmanship. Re-reading Ruskin's *Stones of Venice* to prepare for his trip of November 1907, Rilke would inevitably have compared it to Rodin, the most important influence on his conception of art during that period.

Of course, 'Archaic Torso of Apollo' is more clearly affiliated with Rodin's aesthetics. But the meaningful fragment, as represented in 'Archaic Torso of Apollo', and the composite art work, as represented in 'San Marco', are but two sides of the one coin. Just as the beauty of the Apollo is enhanced by its viewer's imagination, so the Venetian basilica depends on an almost visionary capacity on the part of the observer. Rilke accepts Ruskin's premise that active participation on the part of the beholder is necessary to make visual and figurative sense of this complex work of art.

He also accepts Ruskin's notion that viewing a structure like Saint Mark's is the best way of reflecting on cultural history. Ruskin saw the 'stones of Venice' as archives, full of fragmentary 'documents' in need of piecing together. Architecture was for Ruskin the trace that history leaves, evidence from which the modern viewer can 'read' the history of an earlier culture.[88] Ruskin's book, *The Stones of Venice* was to be read, similarly, as a narrative in which the present-day viewer is repeatedly confronted with the historical past of which the stones speak. The moving eye that apprehends the architectural objects corresponds to the 'travel' undertaken by the mind as it attempts to follow the development of cultural history.[89]

In Rilke, as in Ruskin, history is really a kind of geology or archeology. He sees the city of Venice as a set of multiple layerings and a meeting-place of differing cultural styles. History is less an excursion into the past than a vision of the way in which disparate elements have been combined. The precious objects heaped up in its innermost chamber are a visual record of its past glories. History is not a linear narrative, but a conglomeration of elements present to the eye.

What Ruskin calls the 'encrusted style' of Venetian architecture is recreated by Rilke in his poem, with its disparate collection of images, and its lack of a single coherent perspective. The poem takes an ambivalent stance toward the phenomenon of pillaged accretion, which is admired, but ultimately put into question by the comparison with the dazzling light from outdoors and the classical beauty of the antique horses. Several different aesthetic ideals, Gothic, Romantic and Classicist, jostle in Rilke's sonnet. The structure of the poem emphasises this conflict by its shifts from past to present, from the object to its viewer, and by the dash and the question that follows it at the end of the second quatrain. The smooth flow is disquietingly interrupted by such disjunctures.

These features are common to much of Rilke's prodigious output of early summer 1908, which displays a heightened self-questioning tendency. The doubts, ambiguities, and confusions of 'San Marco' tell us much about the status of Rilke's meditation on his own aesthetic theory and practice at this point. In fact, we see early signs of the crisis that was to beset him during the completion of his novel, *Malte Laurids Brigge* (1910), itself a series of fragments, set together to make a whole like the stones of Saint Mark's. *Malte Laurids Brigge* is one of Rilke's most pronounced ventures into modernism, but it emerges, as does so much early modernist writing, from the ruins of a cultural world visible only in fragmentary and often incoherent form. Thinking about the eclectic style of Saint Mark's had provided Rilke with a model for a kind of art that is composed of fragments, fearing to be found decadent but striving to create something new. And yet, unlike the novel, Rilke's sonnet 'San Marco' partially glosses over what the novel reveals more frankly as disjunctures. These rifts are traces of conflicting aesthetic systems, a reflection of an ambivalence about the nature, value and possibility of originality. Nonetheless, Rilke's sonnet 'San Marco' is a remarkable attempt to come to terms with the problem of eclectic borrowing and, by extension, the ambiguous nature of the creative impulse.

CHAPTER 3

Writing troubles

Rilke's Paris period was punctuated by doubts about whether sheer hard work could resolve deeper questions about creativity and originality. Eclectic borrowing, already at issue in a poem like 'San Marco', is negatively presented in Rilke's novel, *The Notebooks of Malte Laurids Brigge*, a project that preceded the *New Poems* and continued beyond them. Malte's retelling of family stories and Danish history does not coalesce to create the luminous unity that Ruskin had observed in Saint Mark's cathedral. As Malte's desperation over his lack of narrative ability increases, he borrows more extensively from other sources. Even the novel's final segment, a reworking of the prodigal son story, is presented as a hypothesis, not as a narrative in its own right.

The textual mosaic of the novel itself is a creative achievement that continues to dazzle readers today. Yet Rilke was not so sure that he had succeeded. He terminated his work on the novel only while dictating its final version to a stenographer, and fell into a severe depression immediately after its publication in 1910. Rilke saw his protagonist's attempt to become a full-fledged writer as a failure, and he advised his readers to interpret the work 'gegen den Strom' (against the current).[1] In spite of these admonitions, however, he himself felt exhausted and directionless once the novel had gone to press. A long period of creative troubles began.

Rilke's poetry during the second decade of the century gives voice to several concerns. What was the nature of the creative impulse? Was craftsmanship really everything, as Rodin had claimed, or was there also such a thing as inspiration? For the first time, no doubt because he was no longer being guided by Rodin's ideal of persistent workmanship, we see Rilke struggling with questions about the sources of creativity. In contrast to the period when Rilke had imitated the practices of visual artists – observing animals at the zoo or representing a familiar passage from the Bible – he now begins to recall more specifically lyric traditions in which the creative impulse descends upon the poet unbidden. Repeatedly, he felt he was approaching the experience of inspiration; but repeatedly, it seemed to withhold itself from him. Much of his poetry from the period around 1912–14 revolves around paradoxical explorations of whether inspiration, elusive though it be, can somehow be summoned.

During this period, Rilke immersed himself in reading from the German tradition. His friendship with Norbert von Hellinggrath led him to the works of Friedrich Hölderlin, whose powerful articulation of the function of poetry in a time of intellectual and social upheaval seemed to presage a renewal of Rilke's own creative ability. In Hölderlin's writing, creativity was intimately connected with death, loss and suffering; the great poet knew how to turn moments of parting into 'heilig erschrockene Landschaft' (sacredly startled landscape; 2: 94). Could Hölderlin become a model for Rilke in his attempt to create poetic constructs in the face of what he saw as a collapse of cohesion in the external world and a loss of direction in his own life?

Rilke's writing had always been highly self-reflexive. But during these troubled years, its self-reflexivity is heightened and given more explicit expression. Rilke's poems cast about for ways to articulate this obsession with the nature and origin of poetry. No longer satisfied with craftsmanship, they call for inspiration; but inspiration repeatedly proves elusive. The poems locate its source variously in angels, the vastness of night, or a muse-like future beloved. For a brief moment, the outbreak of war seems to inspire the poet to become a mouthpiece for his nation. But the agonies of war overwhelm him and increase his despair. The mundane clerical duties Rilke performed while in the army, turning disastrous battles into official reports of victorious engagements, were extremely disturbing to him. More and more, Rilke's poems of this period register doubts about inspired expression and, indeed, the possibility of writing at all.

Rilke's selectiveness about what he was willing to publish during these years is rather puzzling, since some of his poems from the period are very fine. Yet Rilke was increasingly troubled about questions of originality. Again and again, the poems testify to a sense of belatedness, as if the true well-springs of poetry had long since dried up. Many of these poems speak too obviously with the voices of distinguished precursors from the German canon – Klopstock, Hölderlin, and Goethe.

Rilke's turn toward the canon in these years, though aimed at recapturing tradition, seems to have had the effect of obscuring from himself the actual path his work was taking. By contrast with the great poems of the eighteenth and early nineteenth centuries, his own production appeared fragmentary and disunified. The classical template gave him a negative perspective on the poems he was writing. What today's reader sees as exciting moves toward modernist innovation appeared to Rilke himself as symptoms of creative inadequacy.

Despite moments of achievement, Rilke was depressed throughout most of this period. He desperately feared mental illness. More generally, he wondered whether the creative mind was also in some sense a psychologically diseased mind. In an attempt to inform himself, he explored the nature of neurasthenia, hysteria, and sexual pathology in contemporary psychoanalytic theory. Convinced that writing rather than psychoanalysis was the best method of saving his sanity, he worried why the self-cure did not seem to be working. Suffering, loss, and death – themes intensified by his response to the 1914–18 war – were recurrent concerns in his poetry.

SEXUAL PATHOLOGY

Clear marks of Rilke's post-*Malte* depression are evident in his 1911 prose poem 'Judith's Rückkehr' [Judith's Return] (2: 38). In an earlier project for a poem on the Biblical figure of Judith, Rilke had seen her more positively. Rilke's 1909 jottings explore her transformation from a weak but pious widow to a heroine who succeeds in saving her people from destruction. A brief verse fragment depicts Judith's abandonment of her widow's weeds and her assumption of courage as God bestows strength upon her. A prose outline continues by sketching her triumphant presentation of Holofernes' head to her people in the torchlit marketplace (2:373). There are few precedents for Rilke's shift of emphasis from this glorious moment to the scenario of Judith's walk homeward in his 1911 prose poem. Most works of visual art that Rilke may have known depict the moments surrounding Judith's beheading of Holofernes.[2] Judith triumphant, holding up the head of Holofernes for the people of Bethulia to see, was occasionally, but less frequently, presented.[3] There is scarcely any pictorial tradition of Judith's departure from Holofernes' tent following her courageous act. A notable exception is Gustav Klimt's 'Judith II/Salomé' (1909), which shows the Jewish heroine hastening away after her deed, her bosom still bared, clutching the hair of Holofernes' head in the claw-like fingers of her left hand.[4]

Rilke's 'Judith's Return' builds on a sexualised conception of Judith not unlike that expressed in Klimt's painting. Rilke intensifies the effect by probing his protagonist's consciousness:

Schläfer, schwarz ist das Naß noch an meinen Füßen, ungenau. Tau sagen sie./ Ach, daß ich Judith bin, herkomme von ihm, aus dem Zelt aus dem Bett, austriefend sein Haupt, dreifach trunkenes Blut. Weintrunken, trunken vom Räucherwerk, trunken von mir – und jetzt nüchtern wie Tau./ Niedrig gehaltenes Haupt über dem Morgengras; ich aber oben auf meinem Gang, ich Erhobene./ Plötzlich leeres Gehirn, abfließende Bilder ins Erdreich; mir aber quillend ins Herz alle Breite der Nach-Tat./ Liebende, die ich bin./ Schrecken trieben in mir alle Wonnen zusamm, an mir sind alle Stellen./ Herz, mein berühmtes Herz, schlag an den Gegenwind:
wie ich geh, wie ich geh/ und schneller die Stimme in mir, meine, die rufen wird, Vogelruf, vor der Notstadt. (2: 38)

Sleepers, black is the moisture still on my feet, uncertain, dew they say./ Oh that I am Judith, coming from him, from the tent from the bed, dripping his head, triply drunken blood. Drunken with wine, drunken from incense, drunken from me – and now sober as dew./ Head held low over the morning grass; but I, above, walking, I, exalted./ Suddenly empty brain, images flowing into the earthly sphere; but spurting into my heart all the breadth of the after-deed./ Lover that I am./ Horrors drove all delights together in me, all places are on me./ Heart, my famous heart, beat into the oncoming wind:
as I walk, as I walk/ and faster the voice in me, mine, that will call, bird call, outside the city of need.

Rilke's immediate impulse for this poem was a performance of *Le Spectre de la Rose* [The Spectre of the Rose] with the title role danced by Nijinsky, in June 1911. Shortly afterward, on July 4, 1911, Rilke wrote to his friend and patron the princess Marie von Thurn and Taxis:

Ich glaube ich muß etwas für Nijinskij machen, den russischen Tänzer (ich schrieb Ihnen neulich über ihn), es geht mir nach, es ruft hinter mir her: ich soll, ich soll . . . Ein Gedicht, das sich sozusagen verschlucken läßt und dann tanzen. (6: 1472)

'I think I must create something for Nijinsky, the Russian dancer (I wrote to you about him recently), it's on my mind, it's calling out to me: I should, I should . . . A poem that can be swallowed, so to speak, and then danced.

In formulating this idea, Rilke was presumably recalling the fact that *The Spectre of the Rose* had been based on a poem: in this case, a text by Théophile Gautier. The second decade of the century was a period of balletomania, and Rilke was eager to exploit its possibilities for his own work. Unlike Hofmannsthal, however, who completed a ballet for Nijinsky the following year (*Die Josephslegende* [The Legend of Joseph], 1912), Rilke's ballet project did not go beyond a list of characters in French under the heading 'Figurines pour un ballet' [Figurines for a ballet] and two pages of dialogue in German that seem more like a scene from a symbolist play than a scenario for a dance.

The dialogue opens with a text that differs only in minor respects from the prose poem 'Judith's Return'. The speaker is not identified as Judith, but simply as 'la folle' (the madwoman); her interlocutor is 'le juif errant' (the wandering Jew). Other characters from the list of figures do not appear in this snatch of dialogue, but in Rilke's diary notes Nijinsky's name is written in Russian script against 'the wandering Jew', as well as against the name of another character, 'the indifferent one', a figure based on Watteau's 1717 painting by the same name. The picture shows a male figure in balletic pose. Rilke associated the painting with the idea of balance (6: 1028); and indeed, the elegant figure in the picture is a study in balance despite asymmetry. The man's left arm is held out horizontally, the right down beside his body; a rose-coloured cape is draped over his right shoulder, but has slid off his left shoulder to reveal a white satin jacket; his hat is decorated with a pink rose on the left side; and his white satin shoes, each decorated with pink rosettes, are arranged so that one foot is in front of the other and pointing toward the spectator. With its predominance of rose and white colouring, together with the rose-shaped decorations on hat and shoes, one can readily imagine how Rilke came to link this painting with *The Spectre of the Rose*, in which Nijinsky had danced the role of a young girl's male lover who appears to her in her dreams as the spirit of the rose she had worn in her hair while dancing. The ballet's exploration of the girl's romantic fantasies may have been one factor in Rilke's decision to centre his own ballet on the inner life of his principal figure, Judith. Yet the Biblical story of Judith is far removed from the dream-world of *The Spectre of the Rose*. Why did Rilke take up the gruesome topic of the woman who had slain a tyrant?

His designation of Judith, in the ballet project, as 'the madwoman' provides an important clue. After all, Oscar Wilde's text *Salomé* (1894) and its opera version by Richard Strauss (first performed in 1905), revolve around the figure of a woman who goes insane after her desire to receive the head of John the Baptist on a platter has been fulfilled.[5] As Klimt's 1909 'Judith' painting indicates, the figures of Judith and Salomé were often conflated,[6] since both tales involved a beheading.

The central figures of the two stories had been increasingly sexualised in the history of their representation. As the daughter of Herod's wife Herodiade, Salomé was customarily represented as a young woman; Oscar Wilde capitalised on this tradition by making her only partially aware of the force of her own powerful sexual impulses. Pictorial representations of Judith vary greatly with respect to her age, although even some of the early paintings show her as youthful. Most paintings from the earlier period show her as heroic, rather than erotically charged.

A turning-point in the depiction of Judith occurred with Hebbel's drama *Judith* (1839/40), which makes the Biblical figure a virginal widow, driven as much by thwarted sexual desire as by her wish to save her people from tyranny. Traumatised by her conflicting emotions, Hebbel's Judith loses her mind. She tells her maidservant that she will proclaim her murder of Holofernes to the sleeping camp so that his people rise up by the thousands and tear her into pieces (Act V, scene 1). Around the turn of the century Hebbel's *Judith* was increasingly identified with a certain kind of sexual pathology. At the same time, the figure of the femme fatale, frequently represented by Salomé, proliferated in literature and the visual arts. Both women, Judith and Salomé, were regarded as motivated by perverse eroticism and teetering on the brink of insanity.[7]

The notorious Otto Weininger, in his book *Geschlecht und Charakter* [Sex and Character] (1903), saw Hebbel's Judith as a prototype of female sexuality, especially in its hysteric mode. He wrote:

Ihre Sexualität, die sie stets knechten wird, zu überwinden, sind die Frauen unvermögend. Die Hysterie war eine solche ohnmächtige Abwehrbewegung gegen die Geschlechtlichkeit. Wäre der Kampf gegen die eigene Begier redlich und echt, wäre deren Niederlage *aufrichtig gewollt*, so wäre, sie ihr zu bereiten, dem Weibe auch möglich. Die Hysterie aber ist selbst das, was von den Hysterikerinnen angestrebt wird; sie suchen nicht wirklich zu genesen. [...] Die vornehmsten Exemplare des Geschlechts mögen fühlen, daß Knechtschaft ihnen nur eben darum ein Muß ist, weil sie sie wünschen – man denke an *Hebbels Judith* und *Wagners Kundry* – aber auch dies gibt ihnen keine Kraft, sich in Wahrheit gegen den Zwang zur Wehr zu setzen: im letzten Augenblicke küssen sie dennoch den Mann, der sie notzüchtigt, und suchen den zu ihrem Herrn zu machen, der sie zu vergewaltigen zögert. *Das Weib steht wie unter einem Fluche.*[8]

Women are incapable of overcoming their sexuality, which will always enslave them. Hysteria was a powerless defence against sexuality. If their struggle against their own desire were honest and authentic, if they *sincerely wished* to defeat desire, it would be possible for women to do so. Hysteria, however, is itself that which hysterics desire; they do not really seek to recover from it. [. . .] The most noble members of the sex may feel that slavery is only necessary because they wish it – think of *Hebbel's Judith* and *Wagner's Kundry* – but even this gives them no power genuinely to resist force: at the last moment they still kiss the man who violates them, and try to turn him who hesitates to ravish them into their master. *Woman is, as it were, under a curse.* (Weininger's italics.)

Rilke's prose poem, 'Judith's Return', is clearly indebted to this perspective on female sexual pathology.[9] Indeed, we can even link his idea to embody this kind of pathology in a ballet with Sigmund Freud's theory of the 'hysterische Konversion' (hysterical conversion) of affects into motor activity.[10] Many psychologists of the period focussed on the gestural language of patients suffering from hysteria, and of course Charcot's dramatic presentations of hysterics in various poses before an amphitheatre full of medical students were well known.[11]

As for the figure of the 'wandering Jew' in Rilke's ballet project, we may link it with a contemporary concern for pathology that drew connections between Jewishness and hysteria.[12] By the same token, Richard Wagner compares the figure of Kundry, in his opera *Parsifal*, with the 'eternal Jew':

Kundry lebt ein unermeßliches Leben unter stets wechselnden Wiedergeburten, infolge einer uralten Verwünschung, die sie, ähnlich dem 'ewigen Juden', dazu verdammt, in neuen Gestalten das Leiden der Liebesverführung über die Männer zu bringen; Erlösung, Auflösung, gänzliches Erlöschen ist ihr nur verheißen, wenn einst ein reinster, blühendster Mann ihrer machtvollsten Verführung widerstehen würde. Noch keiner hat ihr widerstanden.[13]

Kundry lives an immeasurable life with constantly changing rebirths, as a result of an ancient curse which condemns her, like the 'eternal Jew,' to inflict upon men the suffering of erotic seduction in ever-new forms; salvation, dissolution, total annihilation is promised her only if the purest, most blossoming man resists her most powerful seduction. No one has yet resisted her.

In Wagner's wake, Weininger links women and Jews in *Sex and Character*. Reviews of the Viennese performance of Oscar Wilde's *Salomé* in 1903 also hotly debated the representation of Jews in the play, especially the use of a Jewish accent by the actors playing the role of the Pharisees who dispute John's right to perform baptisms.[14]

Rilke's interest in sexual pathology is typical of the period: Kafka, too, read Freud at about the same time – 1912 – and drew on Freud's insights, sometimes parodying them, in his fiction. Rilke knew about psychoanalysis largely through Lou Andreas-Salomé; he had also discussed psychoanalytical theories with Victor Emil von Gebsattel during winter 1908/9. When Rilke asked Lou Andreas-Salomé whether he should consider undergoing analysis with Gebsattel, she answered – as he doubtless hoped she would – in the negative. Lou anticipated Rilke's fears that psychoanalysis might put an end to his creative ability.

At the time when Rilke wrote 'Judith's Return', in July 1911, he had just begun to emerge from his mysterious collapse during a trip to Egypt in early 1911. Partway through his voyage down the Nile Rilke had fallen ill; he had been forced to return to Cairo and take refuge with old friends of his wife's, John and May Knoop. He seems to have been feeling extremely depressed. In a letter from Cairo to his publisher Anton Kippenberg, Rilke described his sense of being overwhelmed by too many new impressions, confronted by 'diese Übertreibung im Äußeren, die viel zu viel ist für uns' (that excessive aspect of external reality that is much too much for us).[15] He can no longer understand the person he was when he set out on the journey, eager to get away from home at any price.

Rilke's description of his own state of mind accords with contemporary theories about hysteria, which was said to be induced when the subject was bombarded by excessive impressions. Weir Mitchell's famous 'rest cure' was a direct response to this conception: it kept the patient quiet and isolated, away from the bustle of family life and protected from what was seen as the overstimulation of reading material. The *Encyclopedia Britannica* of the time quotes Pierre Janet's theory of hysteria, according to which

(t)he hysterical subject [. . .] is incapable of taking into the field of consciousness all the impressions of which the normal individual is conscious. Strong momentary impressions are no longer controlled so efficiently because of the defective simultaneous impressions of previous memories. Hence the readiness with which the impulse of the moment is obeyed, the loss of emotional control and the increased susceptibility to external suggestion, which are so characteristic.[16]

This idea reappears in a somewhat different form in Rilke's prose poem 'Judith's Return'.

In relating Rilke's psychological condition in July 1911 to contemporary theories about hysteria, we must not forget what he had learned from Lou Andreas-Salomé. Despite her subsequent apprenticeship with Freud, she criticised his conception of the feminine and had a very different view of sexuality. Her 63-page essay *Die Erotik* [Eroticism], published in 1910 as a separate issue of Martin Buber's series of psycho-social monographs, devotes an entire chapter to the connection between sexuality and delusion or madness.[17] Here she takes up an issue that she feels has been neglected (pp. 21–22):

Allerdings enthält diese Geistesbeteiligung am Liebesrausch so viel – Rausch, so deutliche Symptome der Trunkenheit, daß kein Ausweg zu bleiben scheint, als sie auf romantisches Terrain abzuschieben, oder als einigermaßen pathologisch zu beargwohnen. Dieser wunde Punkt an der ganzen Geschichte wird meistens nur so berührt, wie wenn die Narrenkappe, die unser Verstand hier zeitweilig aufsetzt, davon abhielte, seinen Zustand selber ernst zu nehmen.

To be sure, this mental participation in the intoxication of love contains so much – intoxication, such clear symptoms of drunkenness, that there seems to be no way out other than to relegate it to romantic terrain or to suspect it of being somewhat pathological. This sore point in the whole story is usually treated as if the fool's cap that our reason puts on from time to time were to refrain from taking its own condition seriously.

Her picture of the hysteric subject was more positive than Freud's. She felt that Freud underestimated the strength of the ego and the positive nature of the unconscious; she argued that narcissistic and feminine impulses had a productive part to play in resisting the domination of reason over pleasure.[18]

Lou Andreas-Salomé's views of the erotic emerge in the theme of intoxication in 'Judith's Return'. Not only does Judith describe Holofernes as 'weintrunken, trunken vom Räucherwerk, trunken von mir' (drunken with wine, drunken from incense, drunken from me), her own speech pours forth in an only barely controlled manner, as if she, too, were intoxicated by the experience of seducing him and the act of murdering him. As his severed head, which she carries back with her as proof of her deed, drips blood onto the grass where she walks, she imagines the moment of his death, when his brain is suddenly emptied and its mental images flow out and away. Like the hysterics in Janet's theory, she loses sense of her identity and of the boundaries between herself and the outside world: 'an mir sind alle Stellen' (all places are on me). Imagery of depth versus surface ('an mir' suggests surface; 'in mir' depth) invoke the Freudian contrast between consciousness and the unconscious. Horror and desire coalesce in 'Judith's Return' in accordance with Weininger's ideas of hysteria as a manifestation of women's wish to be enslaved by sexuality. Judith's self-description as a 'Liebende' (lover) refers both to her love for her people, which has motivated her

act against Holofernes, and her sexual awakening, which (in the interpretation derived from Hebbel's play) has paradoxically coupled hatred
with desire.

In addition to working out this elaborate and, to modern sensibilities,
offensive reading of female sexuality, the poem appropriates a number
of other features from turn-of-the-century culture. The motif of moisture that is at once dew and blood recalls the moment at the beginning of
Wilde's *Salomé* where the guard slips on what at first appears to be spilled
wine but turns out to be blood – an omen of the bloody deed that will
occur later in the play. The contrast between the exalted figure of
Judith, holding the severed head down low in the grass, echoes the
iconography of Klimt's 'Judith II/Salomé' where Holofernes' head
appears in the lower right-hand corner of the painting.[19]

The poem explores the problem of identity in a subtle and highly
sophisticated fashion. The image of moisture, in its triple function as
dew, blood and semen, suggests the complicated entanglement of different but related phenomena. Judith's cry of despair over her own role,
'Ach, daß ich Judith bin' (Oh that I am Judith) expresses at once her
awareness of her unique function in the deliverance of her people and
her desire to be anyone other than the person she has become through
her deed. Her notion that Holofernes' intoxication has yielded, in death,
to sobriety, transfers to him her own shift from the intoxication of erotic
desire and thirst for vengeance to a sobriety in which she recognises
more clearly the full extent of what she has done and the complicated
motivation that underlies her deed. While she contrasts the severed
head with her own exaltation, the emptied-out brain with the emotions
spurting into her own heart, she also partially identifies with her de-
capitated enemy, imagining what it must be like to feel one's consciousness draining away. She can scarcely distinguish between her own body
and the 'places' that seem to be affixed to its surface; she exhorts her
own heart to beat 'an den Gegenwind' (into the oncoming wind) as if it
were in danger of stopping, as Holofernes' heart has done just moments
before.

Though the poem begins with an imagined address to the people of
Bethulia, sleeping in the embattled city while Judith returns from her
slaying of Holofernes, the speaker of this poem is much more alone than
any Judith in the cultural tradition. The maidservant of the Apocrypha,
who continues to appear in most of the visual representations as well as
in Hebbel's drama, is omitted in Rilke's poem. Once Rilke withdraws
the speech from the sketch for his ballet, where Judith's words are

followed by a conversation with the 'wandering Jew', her utterance becomes a monologue.

Rilke positions this monologue in what he perceives as a gap in the traditional narrative, which transports Judith almost immediately from Holofernes' tent to the walls of Bethulia. The Biblical text, for example, reads as follows:

> She rolled the body off the bed and removed the mosquito-net from its posts; quickly she came out and gave Holofernes' head to her maid, who put it in the food-bag. Then the two of them went out together as they always did when they went to pray. They passed through the camp, went round the valley and up the hill to Bethulia till they approached its gates.
>
> From a distance Judith called to the guards: 'Open up! Open the gate! God, our God, is with us, still showing his strength in Israel and his might against our enemies. Today he has shown it!' (*Judith* 13: 9–11).[20]

Rilke expands the return to Bethulia round the valley and up the hill, represented by a single sentence in the *Book of Judith*, by exploring the consciousness of his protagonist as she struggles with contradictory and only barely articulable feelings. His empathetic vision of a female hysteric, confused and virtually traumatised by sexual emotions she had not anticipated, brings his poem into the domain of contemporary psychoanalytic discourse.

At the same time, however, as he appropriates these elements of the culture around him, Rilke also adapts and ultimately resists them. To the exploration of sexual pathology he adds his own private theory of 'intransitive Liebe' (intransitive love), worked out in part through conversations and correspondence with Lou Andreas-Salomé, but developed and elaborated in his novel *Malte Laurids Brigge* in a way that goes well beyond anything that Lou had envisaged. Rilke associates 'intransitive love' with a series of famous women whose love had been unrequited: he mentions Héloise, Gaspara Stampa, Marianna Alcoforado, Louise Labbé, Marceline Desbordes, Mechthild von Magdeburg, Bettina von Arnim and a number of others. By disconnecting their love from its original human object, Rilke (and his fictional stand-in, Malte) claimed that these women were able to transcend earthly love and turn it into creative energy. In *Malte* he writes:

> Schlecht leben die Geliebten und in Gefahr. Ach, daß sie sich überstünden und Liebende würden. Um die Liebenden ist lauter Sicherheit. Niemand verdächtigt sie mehr, und sie selbst sind nicht imstande, sich zu verraten. In ihnen ist das Geheimnis heil geworden, sie schreien es im Ganzen aus wie Nachtigallen,

es hat keine Teile. Sie klagen um einen; aber die ganze Natur stimmt in sie ein: es ist die Klage um einen Ewigen. Sie stürzen sich dem Verlorenen nach, aber schon mit den ersten Schritten überholen sie ihn, und *vor* ihnen ist nur noch Gott. (6: 924)

Loved ones live poorly and in danger. Oh, that they might transcend themselves and become lovers. Around lovers there is nothing but security. No one suspects them any more, and they themselves are not capable of betraying themselves. The secret has become whole in them, they cry it out as a whole like nightingales, it has no parts. They lament a single person; but the whole of nature chimes in: it is a lament for an eternal one. They hasten to follow the lost one, but with their first steps they have already overtaken him, and *ahead of them* is only God.

By having his Judith declare herself a 'Liebende' (lover), Rilke places her in this series of women who transcend human emotions and thus unite themselves with the whole of nature.

It is no surprise, then, that Judith speaks of the voice inside her as a 'Vogelruf' (bird call). This image links her with the metaphor of nightingales with which the transcending lovers are compared in *Malte*. We will see how this motif of 'bird call' recurs as a figure for poetic inspiration in Rilke's poem 'Du im Voraus verlorne Geliebte' [Lost from the Outset] of 1913/14; and in Rilke's late works the image of a bird is associated with his concept of an imaginary space that is at once inside and outside, enfolded in the human psyche and projected into outer space – the world, in other words, of the creative imagination.

Independently of this special usage to which Rilke puts the metaphor of 'bird call' before and after 1911, the sudden emergence of the motif in the last section of the poem suggests that Judith is moving toward a new and unconventional understanding of herself. The abrupt, unmediated character of the poem's last lines captures something of her frenzied sense of no longer really quite knowing who or what she is, how and if she is distinct from the voice within her, to what extent she is responsible for her own speech and actions, and finally, whether she is separate from nature or part of it. Is she a heroine and saviour, or a person who has committed an 'unnatural' deed? By assimilating her voice to the call of a bird, she aligns herself with the natural world. Yet it is hard to imagine that her people, however relieved to find themselves freed from tyranny, might hear her triumphant announcement as if it were birdsong. The thoughts that rush together here in these final lines of the poem gloss over the character of her deed by re-appropriating and re-interpreting the nature imagery of the opening. If the moisture on her feet is in fact dew, then this continuation of the nature imagery would be appropriate; but, on another level, both we and she know that the moisture is in fact blood. Traditional metaphors from the mediaeval dawn song, in which lovers who have spent the night part at the break of day, here repress full consciousness of the way Judith has in fact spent her night.[21] By framing the poem in terms of nature (grass, dew, birdsong), complete awareness of Holofernes' murder and her part in it is kept, if only momentarily, at bay.

The hesitation, furthermore, that Judith expresses between thinking of the 'voice' as disembodied and speaking, as it were, through her, and as her own voice that is only belatedly recognisable as such, suggests an ambivalence about the nature of individual utterance as a prophetic vehicle. In these final lines of the poem, Rilke returns to an earlier notion of poetic creativity. In the Romantic period, birdsong had been identified with the voice of nature and simultaneously with the voice of the poet, the only human capable of 'translating' the voice of nature into human language. It is as if Judith's heroism lies less in her killing of Holofernes and more in her exhortation to the sleeping city, which takes the implicit form of a visionary utterance.

Rilke thus redefines Judith's madness as creativity. In doing so, he extends both a Romantic topos, that of the mad poet as poet-prophet, and Lou Andreas-Salomé's view that the manifestations of illness were often signs of great strength and power of resistance.[22] Taking up Judith's position and speaking in her voice allows Rilke to resist accepting entirely the theories of Charcot, Janet, Weininger and Freud, and to substitute for them the view that those moments when one bursts the bounds of rationality are also the moments that give rise to exceptional articulation. At the same time, Rilke's text concludes, not with ecstatic expression, but with the negative reference to Judith's home town as a 'Not-Stadt' (city of need).

The question of unity and disunity is acute in this text. The fact that Rilke copied it into Marie von Thurn und Taxis's 'little blue book' (6: 1472) speaks in favour of our regarding the poem as complete; yet at the same time, it is curiously fragmented and awkward in its conclusion. These discrepancies and ambivalences may account for much of the fascination the text exerts. It sets the stage for Rilke's often quite remarkable free verse poems of 1912 to 1914, in which he explores more probingly the links between inspiration, creativity, loss and suffering.

SUMMONING ANGELS

Upon first reading, Rilke's *Duineser Elegien* [Duino Elegies] seem new and strange; the imagery they develop is astonishing and almost surrealistic; their metrical forms and their general tenor give them a disturbingly fractured appearance. The opening passages of *Die Zweite Elegie* [The Second Elegy] (1912) display this innovative style at its most striking, describing the angels in a series of remarkable images drawn from natural and architectural space:

> Frühe Geglückte, ihr Verwöhnten der Schöpfung,
> Höhenzüge, morgenrötliche Grate
> aller Erschaffung, – Pollen der blühenden Gottheit,
> Gelenke des Lichtes, Gänge, Treppen, Throne.
> Räume aus Wesen, Schilde aus Wonne, Tumulte
> stürmisch entzückten Gefühls und plötzlich, einzeln,
> *Spiegel*: die die entströmte eigene Schönheit
> wiederschöpfen zurück in das eigene Antlitz.　　　(I: 689)

> Blessed early on, you favoured ones of creation,
> ranges of mountains, dawn-flushed ridges
> of all creation, – pollen of blossoming godhead,
> hinges of light, corridors, stairways, thrones,
> rooms made of being, shields of delight, tumults
> of stormy enraptured emotion and suddenly, singly,
> *mirrors*: reflecting your own outflowing beauty
> back into your own faces.

In Rudolf Kassner's *Die Mystik, die Künstler und das Leben* [Mysticism, Artists, and Life], there is a characterisation of Blake's prophetic books that could almost pass for a description of Rilke's *Duino Elegies*. Kassner writes of the impression they create of 'etwas ganz Neuem, Unnatürlichem' (something quite new and unnatural); they seem like fragments of ancient epics; and they develop spatial and visual imagery that resists ordinary logical modes of understanding.[23] The similarities between Kassner's description of Blake's poetry and certain innovative features of Rilke's *Elegies* are not entirely coincidental. Rilke and Kassner, who had known each other since 1899, had been together among the guests at Marie von Thurn und Taxis's Castle Duino in 1910, two years before Rilke wrote the first two elegies in his series. Kassner was a presence in the gestation of the *Duino Elegies* from the very beginning. Shortly after composing *The First Elegy*, Rilke sent his text to Marie von Thurn und Taxis, who read it, at Rilke's instigation, to Kassner and Hofmannsthal; *The Eighth Elegy* is dedicated to Kassner.

Rilke appears to have studied Kassner's works intensively; from 1911 on, he frequently recommended books by Kassner to various correspondents. In addition to his description of Blake's remarkable imagery and the 'fragment'-like nature of his epics, several other passages in Kassner's book may have suggested some major elements in Rilke's *Duino Elegies*. Rilke's English, learned hastily at commercial school in Linz, was not strong; still, with the guidance of Kassner's commentary, he could doubtless make out something of the quotations from Blake included in the book. One of these is a nine-line passage expounding Blake's unorthodox system of ethics in which the only sin is that of 'self-pollution' – the topic of Rilke's *Third Elegy*. Rilke's statement at the beginning of *The Second Elegy* that 'jeder Engel ist schrecklich' (every angel is terrible; 1:689) extends and generalises Blake's description of the 'fiery angels'. Kassner's book also includes a long discussion of mirrors in its chapter on William Morris and Edward Burne-Jones,[24] much of which Rilke seems to have incorporated in his reconfiguration of the angels as self-reflecting mirrors.

A number of other texts combined with Kassner in Rilke's imagination to crystallise in the angel motif of the *Duino Elegies*. The motif also draws heavily on the Pre-Raphaelites' obsession with angels. In Edward Burne-Jones's paintings 'The Annunciation', 'The Prioress' Tale', and 'The Flower of God', angels, architecture, and the aesthetic are linked. Rilke's readers, above all his current patron, Marie von Thurn und Taxis (who called him 'Dottor Serafico'), were still susceptible to the seductions of angelology, the special art of calling on one's guardian angel.[25] The opening passage of *The Second Elegy* addresses the problem of summoning angels in a world far removed from that of Biblical antiquity:

> Jeder Engel ist schrecklich. Und dennoch, weh mir,
> ansing ich euch, fast tödliche Vögel der Seele,
> wissend um euch. Wohin sind die Tage Tobiae,
> da der Strahlendsten einer stand an der einfachen Haustür,
> zur Reise ein wenig verkleidet und schon nicht mehr furchtbar;
> (Jüngling dem Jüngling, wie er neugierig hinaussah).   (1: 689)

> Every angel is terrible. Yet, alas,
> I sing of you, almost deadly birds of the soul,
> knowing of you. Where are the days of Tobias,
> when one of the radiant ones stood at the simple house door,
> a little disguised for his journey, already no longer terrifying;
> (a youth for the youth, as he curiously looked outside).

Despite their apparent celebration of inspiration, Rilke's *Duino Elegies* are in fact the result of an intense exercise of the will, a desire to break a writing block and keep a poetic career alive. The first two elegies, written rapidly one after the other, along with some other elegiac fragments, in late January and early February 1912, predate the completion of the sequence by ten years. These first two do not relate to each other in quite the same way as the eight elegies that follow. In some ways, the second elegy is simply a reworking of the first. They might be two halves of a folding screen on which similar images appear in varying arrangements. The motifs they share include: the angel, night, spring, lovers, classical antiquity, and the relation between human beings and the divine. Of all the *Duino Elegies*, these two are probably the best known – there are still many readers who can recite them by heart. While taking the freedom to look at some parts of both elegies together, I shall focus mainly on the second elegy, to my mind conceptually more daring and poetically more accomplished.

Critical discussion about the figure of the angel in the *Duino Elegies* has concentrated on the ways in which Rilke adapts traditional iconography to his own purposes. Far less consideration has been given to the question why the angel appears in this context at all. Kassner's chapter on Blake does not fully account for the emergence of the angel motif in Rilke's work at this point.[26]

Rilke's writing during the post-*Malte* period circles around his desperate hope for inspiration, a state of mind he describes in a multiplicity of different metaphors involving waiting for something or someone that never quite arrives. In a famous poem that opens *Der Teppich des Lebens* [The Carpet of Life] (1899), Stefan George describes a similar search for a way out of emotional distress and an attendant writing block, a search terminated by the appearance of a naked angel.[27] George's angel is extravagantly decorated with flowers and announces himself as an emissary of the life beautiful; he instructs the poet not to praise precipitous cliffs by the perilous tide, but instead to learn his art from the simpler and more straitened lines of gentler landscapes. Many of the most significant elements in Rilke's *Elegies* are already present here: the agonised search for a way to express despair; a hope for renewal of the poetic faculty; and the angel as a figure for the aesthetic.

Even the precipitous cliffs that appear in George's poem seem to have found a parallel in the topography of the landscape where Rilke first conceived his *Elegies*. While staying at Castle Duino, Rilke had spent several hours climbing up and down the steep rock face on which it is built. Marie von Thurn und Taxis describes the circumstances under which the *Elegies* came into being. A violent wind was blowing, and Rilke climbed about on the steep rocky cliffs below castle Duino. Suddenly, he seemed to hear a voice calling out what would become the opening words of *The First Elegy*: 'Wer, wenn ich schriee, hörte mich denn, aus der Engel Ordnungen?' (who, from the orders of angels would hear me if I cried out?; 1: 685).[28] That night he wrote the whole of the first elegy.

To read Rilke's *Duino Elegies* as, among other things, a – conscious or unconscious – response to George's angel poem from *The Carpet of Life* is to add an extra dimension to the poetic credo they present. In essence, the *Duino Elegies* turn George's poem inside out, countermanding the notion of a divine resolution to the problem of poetic expression and arguing against a simplistic conception of the beautiful. Like the young writer in *Malte Laurids Brigge*, who discovers that great art must also take account of all that is ugly, unpleasant, and horrifying, the speaker of Rilke's *Elegies* regards the beautiful as 'des Schrecklichen Anfang' (the beginning of terror) as he puts it in *The First Elegy* (1: 685).

What Rilke chooses to view as inspiration – or even more specifically, as writing to the dictation of a power outside himself – is actually a confluence of several different factors: the strong wind (the very emblem of inspiration) on the cliffs at Duino, dim recollections of George's angel poem, and thoughts about Kassner's discussion of Blake and other English poets.

Also critical for the genesis of the *Elegies* was a less ambitious project that Rilke had completed in mid- to late January 1912, just before the composition of the first two elegies. This was *Das Marien-Leben* [The Life of Mary], a sequence of poems originally intended to accompany illustrations by Heinrich Vogeler but finally detached from them (to Vogeler's great annoyance).

Two poems in *The Life of Mary* are of importance in connection with the angel motif in the *Duino Elegies*: 'Mariae Verkündigung' [The Annunciation to Mary] (1: 669–670) and 'Vom Tode Mariae' [On Mary's Death] (1: 678–681). Certain unusual vocabulary[29] predates similar usages in the *Elegies*, as do some extraordinary descriptions of real and psychological space. Missing from *The Life of Mary* (though present in *The Second Elegy*) is the figure of Tobias being led by the angel Raphael. Legends of the Madonna frequently included depictions of this episode, which had come to represent protection, especially of the young; by the same token, Raphael had come to be regarded as a guardian spirit of all humanity.[30] When the speaker of *The Second Elegy* asks where the 'Tage Tobiae' (days of Tobias) have gone, he is thus not merely wondering why angels no longer simply appear on our doorstep to guide us on our way, but also referring to the passage in *The First Elegy* about those who have died young. The motif of early death will be taken up once again in *The Tenth Elegy*.

Much of the spatial imagery of *The Second Elegy* has its origins in mediaeval mysticism. Rilke had, in effect, already performed a preliminary exercise for this passage in his poem 'Die Darstellung Mariae im Tempel' [The Presentation of Mary in the Temple] from *The Life of Mary* (I, 667–668). The subject was frequently represented in the visual arts, notably by Dürer (1520), Carpaccio, and Titian (ca. 1550). Drawing upon this pictorial tradition, which derives from an apocryphal text, the *Protevangelium Jacobi* of around the eighth century, Rilke shows the Virgin climbing the steps to the altar all alone. In contrast to both the written and the pictorial traditions, however, Rilke presents the episode from Mary's perspective. Inviting us to share her awestruck vision of the holy place, the speaker of the poem asks us to turn ourselves imaginatively into architectural space, as if our own most secret spaces were made of stone columns and staircases, dizzying outlooks, multiple bannisters, with palace built upon palace. The effect of this interior architecture resembles a picture by Piranesi much more than any traditional representation of the Virgin in the temple.

In the *Duino Elegies*, Rilke reworks this evocation of imaginary space with a stroke of syncretic brilliance. The dawn-flushed mountain ranges recall Schiller's elegy 'Der Spaziergang' [The Walk], the divine pollen picks up Novalis's title for some of his fragments, 'Blütenstaub' [Pollen]; the mirror image derives from Kassner; the image of overwhelming light recalls Mechthild of Magdeburg's late thirteenth-century mystical text 'Das Fließende Licht der Gottheit' [The Flowing Light of the Godhead]. This eclectic combination of ideas and images from different authors and traditions creates a startling effect. The great spaces of natural landscape and architectural design remove the angels from any connection with human form – the shape they are said to have taken in scriptural times ('the days of Tobias'). In dramatic contrast to Pre-Raphaelite depictions of angels, for example, Rilke's angel is disembodied and almost unrepresentable, an abstract figure of imagination, creativity and the aesthetic.

Human beings at first seem more solid than the angels. But in spite of our physical bodies, we are constantly in a state of change, evaporating like the scent given off by smoking amber,[31] dew rising from morning grass, or steam from a dish of food:

> Schmeckt denn der Weltraum,
> in den wir uns lösen, nach uns? Fangen die Engel
> wirklich nur Ihriges auf, ihnen Entströmtes,
> oder ist manchmal, wie aus Versehen, ein wenig
> unseres Wesens dabei? Sind wir in ihre
> Züge soviel nur gemischt wie das Vage in die Gesichter
> schwangerer Frauen? Sie merken es nicht in dem Wirbel
> ihrer Rückkehr zu sich. (Wie sollten sie's merken.)   (1: 689–690)

> Does outer space, then,
> in which we dissolve, taste of us? Do the angels really
> only capture their own, what has streamed forth from them,
> or is sometimes, as if by mistake, a little
> of our being in it too? Are we in their features
> only as little mingled as vagueness in faces
> of pregnant women? They do not notice it in the whirling
> of their return to themselves. (How would they notice it?)

The continual interchange postulated here between one human being and another, between human beings and nature, human beings and the space in which angels move, highlights the fleeting nature of our lives. Much of this passage seems like a modification of Walter Pater's contention: 'That clear, perpetual outline of face and limb is but an image of ours' (*Renaissance*, p. 150). But whereas Pater emphasises both 'continual vanishing away' (p. 152) and 'renew[al] from moment to moment' (p. 150), the speaker of *The Second Elegy* is overwhelmed by a sense of continual self-dissolution. He wonders if some small part of our dissolving being might be captured by the angels.

Lovers, he says, have a stronger sense of existence. The way has been prepared for the emergence of this idea by the image of the smile, a fleeting expression that, in Rilke's private language, is at the same time a talisman of the eternal. The act of love seems to promise the couple that their feelings will last forever: the spot where they lie appears to them like 'pure duration'. Yet even these happy lovers in their moment of ecstasy are in fact, the speaker tells us, caught up in the constant transience of being. The imagery here derives from the poetic tradition of the 'eternal moment', most familiar from its articulation during the Romantic period, where it became an emblem for the nature of poetry itself. In other words, even at this point in the elegy, where Rilke appears to address some of the most fundamental questions about human existence – love, death and our relation to the divine –, he also explores issues of language and aesthetic expression:

Liebende könnten, verstünden sie's, in der Nachtluft
wunderlich reden. Denn es scheint, daß uns alles
verheimlicht. Siehe, die Bäume *sind*; die Häuser,
die wir bewohnen, bestehn noch. Wir nur
ziehen allem vorbei wie ein luftiger Austausch.   (1: 690)

Lovers could, if they knew how, speak wondrously
in the night air. For it seems that everything
hides us. Look, the trees *are*; the houses
that we inhabit, stand yet. We alone
drift past everything like an airy exchange.

In a long passage that follows, the speaker attempts to find equivalents
for what can scarcely be expressed in human language (1:691). This part
of *The Second Elegy* forms a counterpoint to a similar passage about lovers
in *The First Elegy*. But there is an important difference. The lovers in *The
First Elegy* are those mentioned in *Malte Laurids Brigge* who have lost their
loved one or whose love remains unrequited. The lovers of *The Second
Elegy*, by contrast, are couples whose love is fulfilled and who, if they had
the capacity to speak, would 'speak wondrously in the night air'. Yet
speech is denied them, and even their most tender embrace is an
illusion. Furthermore, as we have seen, even the metaphors used to
characterise the angel, that figure most recalcitrant to representation in
human language, are derived in large measure from the text of a mystic
lover, Mechthild von Magdeburg, who formulates her devotion to God
in terms of a search for the ideal beloved. The allusion to her text forms
a kind of hinge between the passage on unrequited love in *The First Elegy*
and the meditation on erotic fulfilment in *The Second Elegy*.[32]

In what appears at first glance to be a rather sudden shift, motivated
though it may be by the reflections on the tender and almost tentative
embrace of the loving couple, the speaker calls to mind characteristic
gestures from classical antiquity:

Erstaunte euch nicht auf attischen Stelen die Vorsicht
menschlicher Geste? war nicht Liebe und Abschied
so leicht auf die Schultern gelegt, als wär es aus anderm
Stoffe gemacht als bei uns? Gedenkt euch der Hände,
wie sie drucklos beruhen, obwohl in den Torsen die Kraft steht.
                                                        (1: 691–92)

Weren't you amazed at the caution of human gesture
on Attic gravestones? were not love and parting
so lightly laid on the shoulders as if they were made
of other fabric than we? Think of the hands,
of the way they touch without pressure, although strength
remains in the torsos.

To the English-speaking reader, the image recalls Keats's 'On a Grecian Urn'. Did Rilke know this poem? Several indications suggest that
he may have;[33] he certainly would have known something about Keats
from Rudolf Kassner's book on the English poets. Indeed, Kassner
comments particularly on the ode 'On a Grecian Urn', noting that
'the words here are as light as the limbs of young Greeks on old
vases'.[34] The similarity between this remark and Rilke's lines about the
gestures of figures on Attic gravestones suggests that Rilke is indeed
alluding to Keats's poem which, like *The Second Elegy*, is also a meditation on the transience of human existence and the more enduring
character of artistic representation. The contrast between Attic grave
markers, as survivors of a long-past age, and the fleeting nature of the
human emotional relations they depict, frail gestures carved into solid
stone, continues the elegy's line of thought about permanence and the
aesthetic. Human problems are addressed here, but they are continually subordinated to, or framed by, issues concerning the nature of
art.

For this reason, *The Second Elegy* concludes with reflections on the
problem of representation and the positioning of human existence
between the earthly and the divine. The final section opens by express-
ing a desire for a narrow strip of fertile land that would provide firm
footing for human beings:

> Fänden auch wir ein reines, verhaltenes, schmales
> Menschliches, einen unseren Streifen Fruchtlands
> zwischen Strom und Gestein.   (1: 692)

> If we could only find a pure, restrained, narrow
> human thing, our own strip of fertile land
> between river and stone.

Rilke may have been climbing the rock face at Duino when the first lines
of his *Elegies* occurred to him, but the imagery here evokes a different
kind of landscape. It is precisely between river and rock that the centaur
in Maurice de Guérin's story of the same title, which Rilke had just been
translating, spends his life. Human beings play no part in the centaur's
story, except for one passage where the centaur recounts his thoughts
upon first seeing a man walking beside a river on the other side of the
gorge. The centaur imagines that the man is a former centaur who, as a
punishment by the gods, has been pushed down from the heights and
condemned to live out his life reduced to one half of his being. The idea
of humans as under 'pressure' from the gods, articulated in the preced-

ing section of Rilke's *Second Elegy*, provides the secret link between the two passages.

The desire for a strip of purely human territory is motivated by the consciousness, on one hand, of the precarious nature of human life, and, on the other, of the ability of human emotions to transcend the limitations placed on bodily existence. But, the elegy concludes, we cannot follow this movement of the heart all the way, either through visual representations or through the divine. The language Rilke uses here to express this idea picks up once again the image of the lovers' parting that had been evoked in the passage on Attic grave markers:

> Denn das eigene Herz übersteigt uns
> noch immer wie jene. Und wir können ihm nicht mehr
> nachschaun in Bilder, die es besänftigen, noch in
> göttliche Körper, in denen es größer sich mäßigt.   (1: 692)

> For our own heart transcends us
> still, as do the gods. And we can no longer follow it
> with our eyes into images that console or into
> divine bodies where it is more grandly tempered.

This passage is difficult, both syntactically and conceptually. Its argument depends on a division between the physical and the emotional sides of our being. As it transcends human existence, our heart takes leave of our body, as it were, so that the two halves become like parting lovers. We find ourselves frustrated in our attempt to follow this movement with our eyes as our heart moves farther and farther away. Images, like those on Attic gravestones or those in our mind's eye (the word for images, 'Bilder', can mean both actual pictures and mental representations), may be able to console us, but they also lie beyond our full comprehension. Similarly, the divine is a more moderated or balanced version of overwhelming human feeling. In that direction, too, we cannot go all the way.

Rilke's word 'nachschaun' (to follow with one's eyes) is an interesting choice here. It recalls Rilke's long-standing interest in the story of Orpheus, about which he had written as early as 1904, in one of the few longer poems included in the *New Poems*, 'Orpheus. Eurydice. Hermes'. Orpheus here follows the receding Eurydice with his eyes as she sinks back into the underworld after his fateful glance back at her. *The First Elegy* had ended, furthermore, with five lines about Linos, the singer who had been Orpheus's teacher. In the ancient tradition Rilke alludes to, a dirge on Linos' death is the originating point of all elegiac song. In

The First Elegy, the vibrations made by this original music remain for ever in nature, and it is this continuing resonance that 'hinreißt und tröstet und hilft' (transports and consoles and helps) us in the form of poetry today (1: 688). We can discern here a first version of the concept of Orpheus that Rilke was soon to develop in the *Sonnets*.

In keeping with the complex relationship between the first two elegies, the second partially retracts the conclusion of the first, no longer affirming that song performs a cathartic function; instead, it puts into question the consoling power of both aesthetic representation and religious belief. The first elegy poses the question of inspiration, claiming that, although no heavenly figure will come at our beck and call in this post-classical age, the poet would do well to listen to the voices that still resonate in nature and vouchsafe an impression of what it would be like to have transcended bodily existence. The second elegy addresses the problem of transience, which involves not only the transience of human life but also that of cultural tradition. The 'days of Tobias' are past, when contact between heavenly and earthly beings was an almost everyday affair, as are also the days of classical antiquity, when the depiction of a lovers' parting could take the viewer some of the way toward the divine. We have no terrain that we can call uniquely human, nor does the world of aesthetic representation as we know it provide an adequate substitute.

Little attention has been paid to the piecework structure of the first two *Elegies*. Rhetorical devices – apostrophe, questions, exclamations and a not altogether logical use of conjunctions – create transitions from topic to topic; but the 'seams' joining the pieces are still very much in evidence. Only on closer reading do connections begin to emerge out of the chaotic movement from motif to motif – angels, night, lovers, dead youths, Greek memorials and overwhelming gods. This composition in largish blocks is different from the fine mosaic technique of earlier works like 'San Marco'. The effect is precisely not that of a unified whole made up of myriad borrowed fragments; in the *Elegies* Rilke draws attention to the jumps and rifts in human consciousness, its understanding of the universe, and its ability to represent that understanding in poetry.

The world Rilke depicts in the *Elegies* is a collection of fragments that remain in human consciousness like broken columns from an earlier age. From time to time, a complete elegiac distich, or at least a complete hexameter or pentameter line (in the sense of classical German metrics), emerges from verses that recall, but do not completely enact, these classical forms.[35] Traditional poetic themes, love and death for example, are addressed in ways far removed from the imagery in which they have usually been embodied. And the dominating figure of the angel, though recalling Biblical tradition, seems to have undergone some strange and inexplicable transformation. Bodily parts – hands and torsos – seem oddly disconnected, and facial expressions – a smile, an upward glance – appear independent of the body to which they belong. The sheer abstraction of their language brings these elegies close to allegory, and yet it resists any kind of simplistic decoding that would yield an easily articulated message. It seems to speak to the deepest and most primitive layers of our consciousness, and yet to go beyond any merely human conception of reality.

In their reflection on problems of tradition and the modern world, Rilke's *Elegies* rightfully take a place next to T.S. Eliot's *Wasteland*. What is the role of poetry in a world that has abandoned religion and in which even the cult of the aesthetic is no longer unquestioningly accepted? Is there any way to leave this cult behind us without giving up all hope for the future of aesthetic representation?

THE POETICS OF RUIN

For Rilke as for Eliot, fragmentation was a danger that constantly threatened. In the *New Poems* assemblages of often quite disparate metaphoric material stand in for objects, but rifts, gaps and silences are read as images for the creative impulse. In *Malte Laurids Brigge* fragmentation is more explicitly disturbing. Torn-down buildings seem to reveal the raw underside of the city, people's faces seem to come away in their hands, and tramcars seem to break through the walls of the protagonist's lodgings. Malte's notebook jottings are fragmentary and discontinuous, and he complains that he has lost the ability to narrate coherently. During the psychological crisis that followed completion of the novel, Rilke felt beset by a sense that things were falling apart. *The Duino Elegies* gave expression to his feelings of disempowerment and alienation and to his search for a unified vision. Much of the poetry he wrote in 1912–14 belongs in this context.

Despite major studies by Ulrich Fülleborn and Anthony Stephens,[36] Rilke's poems from this period remain in the shadow of the works he published during his lifetime. Some of these texts began as sketches for or spin-offs from the *Duino Elegies*, whose early genesis overlaps with them. Smaller sequences also emerged – the 'Spanische Trilogie' [Spanish Trilogy] and the 'Gedichte an die Nacht' [Poems to Night]. Even the great poems from this period that Rilke retained as isolated texts frankly display their character as fragments from an uncompleted project.

The poem to which I now turn was begun in Venice, the site of Rilke's earlier reflections on the problem of fragmentation. Unlike poems he had written during his previous trips to Venice, 'Perlen entrollen' [Pearls roll away] (1912) does not focus on a view of the city or its architectural monuments. Although the poem is addressed to an unnamed loved one, neither she nor anything else is physically present to the speaker of the poem. Like the *Duino Elegies*, the poem is a meditative piece. It registers the movement of the poet's thoughts about ageing and creativity, fragmentation and wholeness. Its conclusion breaks off as if to suggest that this meditation is destined to remain forever in suspension:

> Perlen entrollen. Weh, riß eine der Schnüre?
> Aber was hülf es, reih ich sie wieder: du fehlst mir,
> starke Schließe, die sie verhielte, Geliebte.
>
> War es nicht Zeit? Wie der Vormorgen den Aufgang,
> wart ich dich an, blaß von geleisteter Nacht;
> wie ein volles Theater, bild ich ein großes Gesicht,
> daß deines hohen mittleren Auftritts
> nichts mir entginge. O wie ein Golf hofft ins Offne
> und vom gestreckten Leuchtturm
> scheinende Räume wirft; wie ein Flußbett der Wüste,
> daß es vom reinen Gebirg bestürze, noch himmlisch,
> der Regen, –
> wie der Gefangne, aufrecht, die Antwort des einen
> Sternes ersehnt, herein in sein schuldloses Fenster;
> wie einer die warmen
> Krücken sich wegreißt, daß man sie hin an den Altar
> hänge, und daliegt und ohne Wunder nicht aufkann:
> siehe, so wälz ich, wenn du nicht kommst, mich zu Ende.
>
> Dich nur begehr ich. Muß nicht die Spalte im Pflaster,
> wenn sie armsälig, Grasdrang verspürt: muß sie den ganzen
> Frühling nicht wollen? Siehe, den Frühling der Erde.
> Braucht nicht der Mond, damit sich sein Abbild im Dorfteich
> fände, des fremden Gestirns große Erscheinung? Wie kann
> das Geringste geschehn, wenn nicht die Fülle der Zukunft,
> alle vollzählige Zeit, sich uns entgegenbewegt?
>
> Bist du nicht endlich in ihr, Unsägliche? Noch eine Weile,
> und ich besteh dich nicht mehr. Ich altere oder dahin
> bin ich von Kindern verdrängt...   (2:42–43)

Pearls roll away. Alas, did one of the threads break?
But how would it help if I strung them together: I've lost
                                          you,
sturdy clasp to retain them, beloved.

Was it not time? As the foredawn longs for the sunrise,
I wait toward you, pale from the business of night;
like a full theatre I wear an expectant face
so that your splendid centre-stage entrance
will not escape me. Oh as a gulf hopes into the open sea
and casts from its outstretched lighthouse
shining space; as a river-bed hopes in the desert
for rain to pour, still heavenly, down from pure
mountains, –
as a prisoner, upright, longs for the answer of one single
star, in through his innocent window;
as a cripple tosses the still warm
crutches away, that they be hung at the altar,
and lies there and, void of a miracle, cannot arise:
look, so I'll fling myself, if you don't come, to my end.

You alone I desire. Must not the crack in the pavement,
when it, impoverished, senses the thrust of the grass: must
                                          it not
wish for the springtime, full and entire? Look, the spring
                                          of the earth.
Does not the moon, so that its image may show
in the village pond, depend on the alien star's grand
                                          arrival? How can
the slightest thing happen, unless the whole sum of the
                                          future,
all of accountable time, is moving toward us?

Are you not, finally, there, my ineffable love? Just a while,
and I won't hold out any more. I'm ageing or else I'm
being supplanted by children . . .

The body of the poem is composed of a long series of similes, none of them closely related to the others. It is as if the poet were trying out different ideas but not finding any single one of them compelling enough to develop at greater length. The analogies become increasingly dissociated and the voice that proposes them increasingly desperate. In 'Pearls roll away', the Symbolist world of correspondences is, in essence, tried and found wanting. Even the opening image of the broken necklace is abandoned as the poem proceeds. The world of this poem is one in which no element fits neatly with another; everything is slipping out of one's grasp; things are cracking apart and breaking into pieces.

The images of 'Pearls roll away' are taken from different conceptual domains. The broken necklace, the early dawn, the expectant theatre audience, the gulf with its lighthouse, the dry riverbed, the prisoner at his window, the cripple hoping for a miracle, the lover who does not appear, the crack in the pavement, the sun and the moon: these images move between hope and hopelessness. Only one phrase is an actual borrowing: 'die Fülle der Zukunft' (the whole sum of the future), a direct quotation from the Romantic poet-philosopher Novalis (*Fragmente*; 2: 2313). The metaphor of rain coming down from the mountain to fertilise a desert is modelled on Hölderlin, as are the rhythms and language of the poem;[37] and the notion of a future beloved derives from Hölderlin's predecessor, Klopstock. Other images in the sequence have vaguer origins in poetic tradition: the association of pearls with poetry, especially with poetry born from suffering,[38] and the imagery of sun and moon in their complementary relationship.[39] But the sequence is deliberately fractured and the connections between its elements remain elusive.

Some of the similes are subtly ironic, such as the description of the waiting poet as 'blaß von geleisteter Nacht' (pale from the business of night), when – unlike the parting lovers of a mediaeval dawn song to which this phrase alludes – he has not actually accomplished anything during his night of waiting. The description of the prisoner as 'aufrecht' (upright), a word with the double meaning of 'standing' and 'honest', and of his window as 'schuldlos' (innocent), which begs to be read as a displaced epithet, makes us wonder whether the prisoner is rightfully imprisoned. The speaker's attempt to blackmail the inspiring muse, who persistently withholds her arrival, by threatening suicide ('so wälz ich, wenn du nicht kommst, mich zu Ende', I'll fling myself, if you don't come, to my end) is undercut by his final recognition that death will arrive sooner or later anyway: 'Ich altere oder dahin/ bin ich von Kindern verdrängt' (I'm ageing or else I'm / being supplanted by children...). We are in a world where nothing quite fits. Despite these puzzling discrepancies, the poem has a compelling quality. It is a desperate search for descriptive powers that expresses itself as a string of not quite appropriate analogies.

The analogical technique was much loved by the late nineteenth-century Symbolists. The opening poem of Maurice Maeterlinck's volume *Hothouses* (1889) is similarly constructed. The hothouse is compared in rapid succession with the thoughts of a starving princess, the boredom of a sailor in the desert, a woman who has fainted on a harvest day, a madwoman in a court of law, a sailing boat on a canal, night birds resting on lilies, a bell tolling at midday, sick people resting on their way through a meadow, the smell of ether on a sunny day. The hothouse, Maeterlinck suggests, is a breeder of analogies that feed the poet's imagination.

Although Rilke shares with Maeterlinck a tendency to construct extravagant images, he is more aware than Maeterlinck of the difficulty of making these images into a coherent unity. In 'Pearls roll away', the tension borne by the series of forced analogies expresses the speaker's subconscious recognition that his hopes cannot be fulfilled. Rilke's sequence of images proceeds from examples of reasonable expectations – the sunrise that follows the last hours of the night, the actor who will step onto the stage as soon as the curtain rises – before shifting to images that are irrational or impossible: the gulf is said to cast beams from its lighthouse in order to attract, rather than to ward off, ships approaching from the open sea; the dried-out river bed in the desert longs for rain, and expects it still to be 'heavenly' after it has passed down the mountainside, accumulating silt along the way; the prisoner longs for an answer from a star he sees through the window of his cell; and the cripple anticipates a miracle that will enable him to walk away from the altar without his crutches.

The analogies of 'Pearls roll away' are desperate attempts to put things back into their place. They aim to replace emptiness with fullness, isolation and abandonment with the satisfaction of requited love. But a series of subjunctive verbs (in the original German) dominates the first half of 'Pearls roll away' and suggests the improbability of the various hopes articulated. These subjunctive forms undermine the analogies proposed by drawing attention to their speculative or hypothetical character. The analogical principle, in Maeterlinck a sign of the poet's unusual imaginative fecundity, becomes quite the opposite in 'Pearls roll away': a creative strategy of desperation.

In the context of Rilke's meditation on the nature of poetic creativity, 'Pearls roll away' can be read as an expression of disillusion about allegory. If allegory is an image-making technique designed to repair the ruptures of modern existence, then Rilke's limping analogies foreground these ruptures rather than smoothing them over.

The third section of the poem attempts to re-establish the sense of wholeness absent from the preceding sections. The first emerging blade of grass is seen as heralding the full arrival of spring; the moon's reflection in the pond as a sign of the wholeness of the cosmic system, in which the moon depends on the light of the sun; and the slightest event as a function of a predetermined and undisturbable wholeness of time. Rilke's use of these images returns to a pre-symbolist consciousness that emphasises universals and unity over more idiosyncratic metaphor-making.

In its emphasis on the moon as the crucial link between sun and earth, Rilke's metaphor betrays an essentially Romantic origin. The Romantic underpinnings of the speaker's ultimately unsuccessful attempt to create a world whose unity depends on reflection becomes even clearer when we look more closely at the formulation Rilke borrows from Novalis: the 'Fülle der Zukunft' (sum of the future).[40] The Romantics saw poetry as an adumbration of a future wholeness that was also a kind of transcendence. For Novalis, as for his contemporary Friedrich Schlegel, the fragment is not so much a truncated form as a figure that points forward to a totality that will only be realised in infinity but that is already immanent in the fragment itself.

The final section of Rilke's poem begins with a question that is more than a mere effusion: 'Bist du nicht endlich in ihr, Unsägliche?' (Are you not, finally, there, my ineffable love?). In effect, the beloved is really a figure for the transcendent, and the transcendent is that which, by its very nature, cannot be articulated in human language. In this context, the world 'endlich' (finally) acquires a double meaning: 'at long last', but also 'finite'. The speaker hopes, paradoxically, to be able to meet his longed-for beloved as an embodied, finite entity within the infinite fullness of time as a totality. Since she cannot be encountered in finite reality, her coming must be deferred to the infinite, to which, as an 'ineffable' being, she belongs. The speaker's hope against hope finds partial expression in his curious suggestion that the 'sum of the future' is somehow 'moving toward us'. By the same token, the expression 'alle vollzählige Zeit' ('all of accountable time' or 'time in its entirety') implies that the completeness of time (infinity, in other words), can somehow also be counted. The dilemma of the Romantic vision becomes acutely apparent in Rilke's rendering. His poem breaks off with dots of suspension, but the effect is wistful, possibly even depressed. Unlike the fragments of Novalis and Schlegel, this fragmentary poem does not anticipate a transcendent whole.

In rethinking the Romantics' conception of the fragment, Rilke also rethinks their conception of organic wholeness. In 'Pearls roll away', individual, unsustained images are embedded in a longer, meditative text, but they do not combine to form a unity. Instead, the images threaten to break apart from one another. The image of the crack in the pavement makes this problem evident. Here, nature's attempt to reconstitute itself as a whole is blocked by the resistant concrete that refuses to yield entirely to the pressure of spring grass. At the same time, the man-made object, the pavement, is also broken and disunified. The speaker's invocations of wholeness cannot cover over this fissure. What conclusion can we draw about that other man-made object, the one whose construction we are observing, the poem?

In the *New Poems* Rilke had presented a number of cracked or fissured objects. In a poem of 1907, for example, a blind man is visualised as interrupting the city's continuity, 'wie ein dunkler Sprung durch eine helle Tasse geht' (as a dark crack runs through a light cup; 1: 590). In an unexpected moment of transfiguration, however, the blind man, holding out his hand to beg for money from a passerby, suddenly seems as if he were engaged in a solemn rite like the ceremony of marriage. Another 1907 poem describes the many attempts made by the painter Hokusai to paint Mount Fuji, until the point where the mountain seems to raise itself like an apparition behind the split formed by the crater at its peak (1: 639). In contrast to these earlier poems, 'Pearls roll away' withholds the transfiguration that emanates from such ruptures in Rilke's earlier poetry.

One might almost say that 'Pearls roll away' is constituted as much by the rifts between its various images as by the connecting power of analogy. The poem is marked by interruptions, hesitations, sudden stops and starts: words or clauses interpolated in other clauses or between appositional phrases, logical sequences that are not consistently sustained, startling enjambements, unexpected short lines, rhetorical questions, exclamations, a dash, and the concluding dots of suspension that, astonishingly, allow this intense and emotional poem simply to fade away.

By constructing this string of analogies, Rilke reflects on the problematic relation of allegory and ruin. If, in the Symbolists' poetry of correspondences, allegory was the way in which a broken universe could be put back together, analogy, in Rilke's poem, is a constant testimony to the inadequacy of this remedy. Rather than showing a hidden similarity, or correspondence, among the various images he adduces, the speaker of 'Pearls roll away' seems to weigh his similes one after another and discard them as not quite sufficient. Chronology and logic have come adrift: hope for a future love is cast in terms of regret over something lost, and even the future itself seems to be moving backward toward the speaker. Similarly, the speaker himself, a latecomer unable to collect and restring the escaping poetic pearls, feels that he is about to be edged out by the younger generation that follows him. Born too late to make the allegoric method fully functional, he is nonetheless too early to develop a viable alternative momentum.

The poem is also a reconsideration of poetic subjectivity. Its imagery reveals how intensely Rilke desires to mediate between an inner and an outer world: the auditorium and the stage, the gulf and the open sea, the lighthouse and its extended beam, the rain and the riverbed, the prisoner and the star outside his window are all attempts to render the speaker's longing to communicate with something or someone outside himself. Yet the poem is haunted by the fear that there may be nothing other than subjectivity, that the 'other', be it transcendent or simply out of our immediate range of vision, may be nothing more than a figment of our imagination. The poem constantly gestures toward an outside world which it also implicitly denies.

'Pearls roll away' is in every sense a poem of transition. More clearly than the early *Duino Elegies*, it articulates a movement from Rilke's encrusted style to his poetry of ruins, his carefully crafted and tightly 'closed' *New Poems* and the more open forms of his late work, his engagement with symbolism and his first steps toward modernism.

FAINT STRENGTH

In 1911 Katharina Kippenberg, shocked at Rilke's ignorance of canonical texts, persuaded him to read Shakespeare's *Tempest* with her.[41] As she expected, he was charmed; but he also had some reservations. The poetic result of this ambivalent response is one of Rilke's few attempts at dramatic monologue and one of his most brilliant stylistic imitations. Written in early 1913 and not published until eight years later, 'Der Geist Ariel' [The Spirit Ariel] is not merely an exercise in Shakespearean verse, but also an important document from the period of Rilke's poetic crisis:

Man hat ihn einmal irgendwo befreit
mit jenem Ruck, mit dem man sich als Jüngling
ans Große hinriß, weg von jeder Rücksicht.
Da ward er willens, sieh: und seither dient er,
nach jeder Tat gefaßt auf seine Freiheit.
Und halb sehr herrisch, halb beinah verschämt,
bringt mans ihm vor, daß man für dies und dies
ihn weiter brauche, ach, und muß es sagen,
was man ihm half. Und dennoch fühlt man selbst,
wie alles das, was man mit ihm zurückhält,
fehlt in der Luft. Verführend fast und süß:
ihn hinzulassen – , um dann, nicht mehr zaubernd,
ins Schicksal eingelassen wie die andern,
zu wissen, daß sich seine leichte Freundschaft,
jetzt ohne Spannung, nirgends mehr verpflichtet,
ein Überschuß zu dieses Atmens Raum,
gedankenlos im Element beschäftigt.
Abhängig fürder, länger nicht begabt,
den dumpfen Mund zu jenem Ruf zu formen,
auf den er stürzte. Machtlos, alternd, arm
und doch *ihn* atmend wie unfaßlich weit
verteilten Duft, der erst das Unsichtbare
vollzählig macht. Auflächelnd, daß man dem
so winken durfte, in so großen Umgang
so leicht gewöhnt. Aufweinend vielleicht auch,
wenn man bedenkt, wie's einen liebte und
fortwollte, beides, immer ganz in Einem.

(Ließ ich es schon? Nun schreckt mich dieser Mann,
der wieder Herzog wird. Wie er sich sanft
den Draht ins Haupt zieht und sich zu den andern
Figuren hängt und künftighin das Spiel
um Milde bittet ... Welcher Epilog
vollbrachter Herrschaft. Abtun, bloßes Dastehn
mit nichts als eigner Kraft: 'und das ist wenig.')   (2:50–51)

One set him free some time, some place, and with
the force with which one's youth impelled itself
toward the whole, gave up all things beside.
Then he was willing, look: since then he's served,
in every deed intent upon his freedom.
And half a master, half almost ashamed,
one lets him know that one will need him still
for this and that – and has to tell him then
why one had helped him. Yet one feels oneself

How everything that one retains with him
is absent from the air. Tempting almost, and sweet,
to let him go – ; and working spells no more,
subordinate with other men to fate,
to know that now his easy friendship, bound
to nothing more, and freed of every stress,
a superfluity to this span of breath,
is self-absorbed, unthinking, in the elements.
Henceforth dependent, I shall lack the gift
to shape the lifeless mouth to form that cry
which caused his fall. And strengthless, ageing, poor,
yet breathing *him* like scent intangibly
scattered afar, which only now completes
invisibility. And smiling, that
one could so beckon it, that is so used
to intercourse so great. And weeping too,
perhaps, when one recalls the way it loved
and fled one, both: and all of this as one.

(Have I let go already? Turning duke
again, this man alarms me now. How gently he
pulls upon the string, and packs himself
away with other puppets, and implores
the play for grace ... O what an epilogue
to mastery. To cast off, stand there merely,
no strength but one's own: 'which is most faint.')

A meditation on Prospero's dismissal of Ariel and abjuration of magic at the end of the play, the poem is a clue to some of the problems that haunt the *Duino Elegies*. By the time he wrote 'The Spirit Ariel', Rilke had already written the first two elegies and parts of the third, sixth and tenth; in 1913–14 he continued to write verse closely related to the elegies in theme and style. In many ways 'The Spirit Ariel' belongs with these texts, many of which also employ iambic pentameter.

Rilke's choice of dramatic monologue is significant. As generally understood, the form has three principal characteristics: it fixes a critical moment in a time-sequence that is otherwise only implied, it renders from within the character of a person who is presented as clearly distinct from the author, and it addresses an unseen audience whose tacit responses direct the course of the speaker's argument. In an important article of 1976, Ralph Rader distinguishes the dramatic monologue from other related forms. In the mask lyric, 'the poet speaks through an actor who is registered almost overtly as an artificial self'; in the dramatic monologue, by contrast, 'the poet simulates an activity of a person imagined as virtually real whom we understand as we would an 'other' natural person, inferring from outward act and expression to inward purpose'.[42]

In the German tradition, mask lyric (the 'Rollengedicht') is more familiar than dramatic monologue, and Hofmannsthal is its most brilliant practitioner. Rilke knew Hofmannsthal's work well, but 'The Spirit Ariel' scarcely resembles any of Hofmannsthal's mask lyrics.

In English, the dramatic monologue was perfected by Robert Browning. Evidence that Rilke knew Browning's poetry is tenuous, although two of his contemporaries quote him as saying that he had learned English at one point 'in order to read Browning' or 'in order to be able to read Keats and Browning'.[43] We know he read Rudolf Kassner's book on the English poets, which includes substantial chapters on Keats and Browning. Nonetheless, the tone of Rilke's 'Ariel' is very different from the snarling voices in which Browning specialised.

An important characteristic of dramatic monologue is its ambiguous relation to the reader, a relation Robert Langbaum sees as a suspension 'between sympathy and judgment'.[44] This ambiguity is fully exploited in Rilke's adaptation of the form. Rilke heightens the effect by his use of pastiche, a form that may also be seen as suspended between sympathy and judgment, identification and critique.

Unlike most dramatic monologues, 'The Spirit Ariel' makes little use of the first person. In fact, the first-person pronoun occurs only in the parenthetical ending which steps away from Prospero and looks at him, at least partially, from without. The body of the poem is cast in the impersonal form using the pronoun 'man' (one). The impersonal pronoun had already been a crucial instrument in *Malte Laurids Brigge* (1910), the novel that had been both the earliest expression and the proximate cause of Rilke's poetic crisis. The pronoun 'one' has a curious quality of being suspended between speaker and audience: it enables self-reference while at the same time calling forth empathy on the part of the listener. Rilke not only imitates the voice of Prospero, he makes us become Prospero along with him. One effect of this technique is to heighten the tensions inherent in the dramatic monologue form by highlighting the suspension between speaker and audience. It also contributes to the peculiar sense of vagueness this poem projects, its pervasive refusal to identify clearly who and what it refers to and when and where the soliloquy takes place. This may have something to do with the indefinite location of the island in Shakespeare's play. But as the poem proceeds, the pronoun 'one' becomes part of a more general-ised indeterminacy that attaches to this text. Rilke's choice of the impersonal pronoun is in part a strategy for defusing what might otherwise be seen as derivative writing in 'The Spirit Ariel'. By casting the poem in this form Rilke makes us collude with him, as it were, in his production of a Shakespeare imitation.[45]

While the poem alludes most directly to the epilogue of *The Tempest*, several other moments in the play are captured in Rilke's text. These include Prospero's repeated promises to Ariel that he will set him free (I,ii,246; I,ii,501–2; IV,i,265–6; V,i,96); his commentary at the end of the masque: 'These our actors,/ As I foretold you, were all spirits and/ Are melted into air, into thin air' (IV,i,148–50); Prospero's description of the elves on the island as 'demi-puppets' (V,i,36); his last words to Ariel, 'then to the elements!/ Be free and fare thou well!' (V,i,318–19); and finally, of course, the lines from the end of the play to which we have already alluded: 'And what strength I have's mine own;/ Which is most faint' (Epilogue, 2–3).

Although the dramatic moment at which we must suppose Rilke's version of Prospero's monologue to be situated corresponds to that of Shakespeare's epilogue, Rilke casts his poem in the verse form of the play as a whole, rather than in the trochaic tetrameter that Shakespeare uses for the play's final lines. Although Rilke's speaker is clearly looking back on an action that has already taken place, 'The Spirit Ariel' does not partake of the sense of closure conveyed by Shakespeare's more formal-sounding epilogue. Rather, the poem simultaneously looks back and looks on. It looks back at Prospero's acquisition of Ariel as his servant and his ultimate dismissal of him; it looks on as Prospero gives up his magic and becomes an ordinary mortal once again. And even though it steps briefly out of the Prospero persona to view him from an external perspective, its penultimate gesture is collusive as it returns to the impersonal form 'nichts als eigner Kraft' (no strength but one's own) before finally introducing the direct quotation with which it concludes.

The identification with Prospero called for by this text has its prehis-tory, in Rilke's development, in a series of poems that see the poet as a kind of magician, holy man or alchemist. Toward the end of his life, Rilke continued to work out the motif of the magician (2: 150). But Rilke's poems on magician figures make it clear that he saw the concept as highly problematic. However much power he appears to have, the magician is revealed in the last analysis as subject to forces beyond his own control. 'The Spirit Ariel' explores this problem more probingly than any of the poems that precede or follow it. By problematising the creative process in this way, 'The Spirit Ariel' questions the sacralised view of poetry promulgated by Stefan George and other members of the art for art's sake movement.

In a larger sense, however, the poem is also a questioning of creativity as such. It is ironic that Katharina Kippenberg chose *The Tempest* as part of her attempt to re-inspire Rilke during his poetic crisis, since he appears to have understood Prospero's epilogue (like many readers before and after him) as Shakespeare's farewell to poetry. This reading made *The Tempest* less a new inspiration for poetry than a confirmation of Rilke's sense that he had now embarked on what was to be, if not a permanent inability to write, at the very least a prolonged poetic silence.

Shakespeare's depiction of Ariel's spirit existence meshed well with the impressionist or empiriocritical views that had played such a prominent role in *Malte* and contributed to Rilke's sense that reality had become too disseminated to be grasped in language.[46] In April 1913, just a few months after composing 'The Spirit Ariel', Rilke wrote two poems about Narcissus that attempt to capture this despair over an elusive reality. The second poem takes the form of a monologue in the voice of Narcissus; it is more a conventional mask lyric, however, than a dramatic monologue. In Rilke's first Narcissus poem, the essence of the youth is 'verdichtet wie der Duft vom Heliotrop' (concentrated like the scent of a heliotrope; 2: 56) and in his second Narcissus poem it is transmuted into an undefined something that emanates from Narcissus and 'löst/ sich in der Luft und im Gefühl der Haine' (dissolves/ in the air and in the ambience of the groves; 2: 56). Similarly, in 'The Spirit Ariel', the released sprite becomes like 'unfaßlich weit/ verteilten Duft' (scent intangibly scattered afar). Rilke's Narcissus dissolves 'im offnen Wind' (in the open wind; 2: 56) or 'in dem teilnahmslosen/ zerstreuten Wasser' (in the impassive, dissipated water; 2: 57); his Ariel returns, like Shakespeare's, to the 'elements' and is diffused into the air. The two figures have become assimilated to the deliquescent aesthete of the late nineteenth century. Yet, as Kassner had rather tartly commented in his book on English poetry, 'it makes a difference whether it is an aesthete or Prospero who says that all the world's a stage' (*Mysticism*, p. 219).

'The Spirit Ariel' is significant in Rilke's poetic development because of the way it dissolves, not only individuals into aerial particles, but also the hierarchy of master and servant. The poem begins with the moment of Ariel's first 'freeing' by Prospero; but he is freed into a second subservient relation. But the dependency, as the poem goes on to show, works both ways: Prospero is also dependent on Ariel. At the same time, by binding Ariel to servitude, he alienates the spirit creature from his intrinsic connection with nature. For it is Ariel's essence to be everywhere and nowhere at once, to be simultaneously the voice of nature and the expression of human fantasies. When Prospero releases Ariel, his own voice is dulled and he is no longer able to utter the commands that have created his magic spells.

The cry that cannot be uttered recalls the unanswered cry of Rilke's *First Elegy*: 'Wer, wenn ich schriee, hörte mich denn aus der Engel/ Ordnungen?' (Who, if I cried, would hear me then from the angels'/ hierarchies?; 1: 685). The angels have their hierarchies, but these are not permeable to the world of the human speaker. Given the impossibility of an angelic response, the speaker of the first elegy decides to hold back his cry. This renunciation is echoed in 'The Spirit Ariel'. But the notion of hierarchy still lingers: Prospero's return to his dukedom places him high in the hierarchies of contemporary society but demotes him from the sovereign role he had played on the island. True 'mastery', this poem implies, is the mastery of the creative genius, for whom the magician Prospero, able to call forth storms and cause shipwrecks, becomes an allegory.

'The Spirit Ariel' is compelling because of the way in which the poem feels its way into Shakespeare's text and attempts to reproduce its spirit. Only the parenthetical concluding section, itself a kind of epilogue, takes issue with Prospero's epilogue in *The Tempest*, but even this it does with a certain mournful admiration. The 'Epilog/ vollbrachter Herrschaft' (epilogue/ to mastery) is at once an anticlimax and a more powerful turning – more powerful because the work which is now to be done will be undertaken from the vantage-point of a mere mortal and will hence demand more heroic efforts, in effect a different kind of mastery.

Now although the poem refers explicitly to one master, Shakespeare, it also contains traces of another: Goethe. Rilke had long been antipathetic to Goethe; as in the case of Shakespeare, it was Katharina Kippenberg who introduced him to Goethe's works. The Kippenbergs presented him with the Insel edition of Goethe, and Rilke seems to have read more of his German predecessor than he did of Shakespeare. The most obvious Goethean element in 'The Spirit Ariel' is the reference to breathing: 'ein Überschuß zu dieses Atmens Raum' (a superfluity to this span of breath). Goethe's use of this term is particularly prominent in the *West-östlicher Divan* [West-eastern Divan], which Rilke read during the period when he composed 'The Spirit Ariel'. But instead of Goethe's notion of a mutual exchange between self and world, represented by his concept of 'systole' and 'diastole' (breathing in and breathing out), Rilke sees breath and air as something common to self and world but thoroughly disseminated throughout both of them such that the two become indistinguishable. While Ariel is Prospero's servant, he seems to be missing from the air; once he is freed, Prospero takes in his essence with the air he breathes. Goethe's system of regular interchange has become assimilated to the atomist conception of reality. From Goethe, Rilke also adopted several items of vocabulary at this time, notably the word 'Übermaß' (excess, in the sense of something splendidly overwhelming); here this word becomes 'Überschuß' (superfluity), and once again it is assimilated to an atomistic conception in which Ariel is seen as part of a universe made up of free-floating particles.

In the German tradition, the atomistic world was most clearly represented in the works of the early Hofmannsthal. In the third of his terza rima poems on the theme of transience, Hofmannsthal quotes the famous line from Shakespeare's *Tempest*: 'we are such stuff as dreams are made on'. Hofmannsthal emphasises the unitary nature of reality in the last line of this poem: 'und drei sind Eins: ein Mensch, ein Ding, ein Traum' (and three are one: a man, a thing, a dream).[47] An echo of this idea can be heard in the line that concludes the first section of Rilke's Ariel poem: 'immer ganz in Einem' ('and all of this as one').

Rilke's Ariel has much in common with the central figure of another text by Hofmannsthal, 'Der Jüngling in der Landschaft' [The Youth in the Landscape]. The titular figure of this poem walks among the spring flowerbeds preparing (one assumes) to become a gardener. The porous nature of the youth's relationship to the external world is very similar to that of Rilke's Ariel, though the young gardener makes no efforts to secure his independence.

The excessively porous quality of empiricist atomism had lain at the root of the crisis depicted in Hofmannsthal's fictive letter from Lord Chandos to Francis Bacon (1902). The silenced mouth of Rilke's Prospero, no longer able to conjure up fantasies because he has become indistinguishable from the disseminated particles that make up the world around him, recalls Chandos's inability to use ordinary language. The poem thus brings together two different poetic crises: Shakespeare's alleged farewell to dramatic creativity and Hofmannsthal's depiction of an empiricist-aestheticist crisis that puts all literary writing into question.

But the poem does not end here. The seven-line epilogue expresses dismay at Prospero's final decision to abjure magic. Structurally, this final, parenthetical section of Rilke's poem is puzzling. The poem pivots uneasily on the opening line of this part with its ambiguous identification of the speaking self: 'Have I let go already?' Is this 'I' Prospero? If so, why was the preceding monologue conducted in the impersonal form, instead of in the first person? The speaker who claims to be 'alarmed' by the man who is turning back into a duke must stand outside Prospero. What accounts for this shift in perspective?

If Rilke had read Browning, this feature of 'The Spirit Ariel' might be traceable to 'Caliban upon Setebos', another poem inspired by Shakespeare's *Tempest*.[48] Browning frames Caliban's lengthy monologue with two passages in parentheses. The first parenthesis looks at Caliban from without, the second, while still in Caliban's voice, shows him reflecting on the validity of his meditation. 'Caliban upon Setebos' also uses pronouns in an unconventional way. Trapped in the body of a monster, Caliban sees himself only occasionally as 'I' and more frequently as 'he'. His reflections are simultaneously primitive and astute, 'natural theology' and sophisticated psychology.

In her discussion of dramatic monologue, Adena Rosmarin remarks that 'the reader of a dramatic monologue [...] struggles out of the speaker's struggle by taking a perspective on it even as he paradoxically continues to dwell within it'.[49] She sees dramatic monologues as exemplifying a 'strange loop', which she defines as 'not simply a suggestively incomplete series, but one that explicitly turns back on itself, remarking its own incompletion' (p. 44). Browning's dramatic monologues are good examples of this 'strange loop'.

Unfortunately, there is no way of knowing whether Rilke knew Browning's 'Caliban' or any other of his dramatic monologues. Still, the parenthetical conclusion of 'The Spirit Ariel' vividly enacts the hermeneutic position of a reader at once sympathetic to and distant from the poetic soliloquy. Like many of Browning's monologues, Rilke's Shakespeare poem is incompletely aware and at the same time curiously self-reflexive. Although the poem invites us at the beginning to accept the convention of the dramatic monologue, innocently taking the speaker for Prospero, the conclusion of the poem looks back knowingly at this strategy and asks us to call it into question. But in another paradoxical loop, the reader who has now recognised Prospero as a mere marionette, suddenly hears his voice speaking directly once more with all its old magic. The 'strange loop' is put here to stunning effect.

'The Spirit Ariel' occupies an intriguing space in Rilke's work. Pastiche is frequently a sign of a transitional moment in literary history, an acknowledgment that the forms it employs and the attitudes it embodies are on the brink of passing into disuse. Sustained Renaissance imitations in the manner of Hofmannsthal's early verse dramas were certainly no longer thinkable in 1913. Also disappearing in this period was the concept of the creative genius and, most particularly, the notion of the poet as prophet.

'The Spirit Ariel' stands as a first open acknowledgment of Rilke's sense that the idea of the poet-'magician' was no longer timely. Casting off the magic cloak would mean writing a different kind of poetry. In the *Duino Elegies*, the speaker will ultimately turn away from the angel and toward the things of this earth. In 'The Spirit Ariel', this move is still regarded with some degree of dismay.

Nonetheless, the poem is remarkable for the way in which it subverts its own position. Presented as a critique of Shakespeare's conclusion to *The Tempest* – a critique of both the demotion of Prospero and the artificial device of the epilogue – , the last part of Rilke's poem is also a critique of his own desire to imitate the master Prospero and, by implication, the series of 'masters' who are assimilated to him. 'The Spirit Ariel' precedes by a year and a half the poem 'Wendung' [Turning Point], a text that looks forward to a fresh beginning based on a new way of integrating the images stored within the poet's imagination. 'The Spirit Ariel' does not yet take this step. But in many ways it is a more effective, and certainly a more moving poem. The poet-magician is disseminated into the air, then all but obliterated by the final parenthesis. Pastiche disappears at the very end of the poem to be replaced by citation, a citation that paradoxically locates the greatest strength of Shakespeare's *Tempest* in its concluding admission of weakness.

Rilke did not publish 'The Spirit Ariel' until many years after he wrote it. In mid-December 1921, Rilke sent the poem to the Kippenbergs to be included in the periodical *Inselschiff*; at the same time he ordered himself a volume of Shakespeare in the new Insel edition.[50] Releasing the poem for publication, he may have seen himself as making an admission of poetic defeat. Yet less than eight weeks later, he experienced the sudden burst of energy that enabled him to complete the *Duino Elegies*. The despairing epilogue had become a reconciliation with the 'faint strength' of the merely human.

BORROWED VOICES

One of Rilke's most intriguing poems is an untitled piece written in Paris in the winter of 1913/14. Extraordinarily syncretic and curiously fragmented, the poem includes echoes of and allusions to several poetic precursors. The problematic relationship between influence and inspiration is broached by means of an address to a muse-like 'beloved' whose paradoxical nature allows the speaker to see himself as simultaneously backward- and forward-looking, a receiver of past traditions and an initiator of new ones. But is not the muse by nature a paradoxical figure, an artificial shunt between original genius, arising from within the subject, and inspiration, an inexplicable influence from outside the subject?

In 'Du im Voraus/verlorne Geliebte' [Lost from the Outset], the voices of poetic predecessors can be heard at every turn. The German tradition, to which Rilke had turned anew during this period, is recalled by echoes of Klopstock, Hölty, Goethe and Hölderlin; the French tradition, in which he had long been steeped, is represented by Mallarmé; and the English, which he knew only imperfectly, by Keats.[51]

In a moment, we shall listen more closely to the way these poets speak in Rilke's text; for the time being, I would like merely to summarise some of the different positions they represent. Three regard poetry as divinely inspired (Klopstock, Hölty and Hölderlin), one regards it as a reflex of external reality (Goethe), and two see it as a response to previous poetic texts (Mallarmé and Keats). Two locate the muse-like beloved in the future (Klopstock and Hölty), one in the present (Goethe), and one in the past (Hölderlin); three invoke the theme of loss and restoration (Klopstock, Hölderlin, Mallarmé), and three present themselves as latecomers in a distinguished poetic lineage (Hölderlin, Mallarmé, Keats). Against this complexly shifting set of previous poems, Rilke's 'Lost from the Outset' exhibits an equally complex set of responses, diverging from them in distinctive ways but ultimately blending their voices into a single lament.

The poem passes rapidly through a series of images that seem only loosely connected:

> Du im Voraus
> verlorne Geliebte, Nimmergekommene,
> nicht weiß ich, welche Töne dir lieb sind.
> Nicht mehr versuch ich, dich, wenn das Kommende wogt,

zu erkennen. Alle die großen
Bilder in mir, im Fernen erfahrene Landschaft,
Städte und Türme und Brücken und un-
vermutete Wendung der Wege
und das Gewaltige jener von Göttern
einst durchwachsenen Länder:
steigt zur Bedeutung in mir
deiner, Entgehende, an.

Ach, die Gärten bist du,
ach, ich sah sie mit solcher
Hoffnung. Ein offenes Fenster
im Landhaus –, und du tratest beinahe
mir nachdenklich heran. Gassen fand ich, –
du warst sie gerade gegangen,
und die Spiegel manchmal der Läden der Händler
waren noch schwindlich von dir und gaben erschrocken
mein zu plötzliches Bild. – Wer weiß, ob derselbe
Vogel nicht hinklang durch uns
gestern, einzeln, im Abend?   (2:79)

Lost from the outset,
beloved, never arriving:
I know not what tones you delight in.
No more, when the future portends, do I try
to discern you. All of the splendid
images in me, landscape perceived at a distance,
cities and towers and bridges and unexpected turns in the roadway,
the grandeur of lands
deep-rooted once with gods:
swells to significance in me,
betokening you, as you vanish.

You are the gardens,
I saw them, oh, with such
hope. A window ajar
in the country house – and you almost stepped
pensively in toward me. I found narrow streets –
you just had gone down them,
and shopkeepers' mirroring windows still were
dizzy at times with you and gave back, startled,
my too sudden reflection. – Who knows if it wasn't the same
bird that rang through us both,
yesterday, each alone, in the evening?

Beginning with a highly rhetorical address to the beloved, the poem proceeds to evoke a series of grandiose but relatively abstract land-scapes, some of them defined by the manifold constructions of human civilisation, others marked by traces of ancient but now forgotten gods, and concludes with another invocation of the beloved. The second section of the poem opens with images of gardens and a country house, moves to narrow streets and shop windows in what is evidently the old town of some European city, and ends by recalling a bird singing in the evening, a motif that seems to belong more properly to the suburban and rural settings of this section's opening lines. Disparate though this sequence of images appears, we can nonetheless trace the poem's intertextual origins by focussing on each of the main motifs in turn: the lost love, the landscape and garden imagery, the stroll through the old town, and the birdsong heard by the lovers.

The principal motif, the beloved 'im Voraus verloren' (lost from the outset), is usually seen as an adaptation of the curious concept of 'intransitive Liebe' (intransitive love) developed in *Malte Laurids Brigge* (1910). Customarily, the idea of intransitive love has been traced to a biographical origin, Rilke's problematic relationship with women and in particular with his wife, Clara. Yet the narrator of *Malte* justifies his ideas about love by an appeal to previous texts: the letters of great lovers such as Héloise, Marianna Alcoforado, Bettina von Arnim, and Gas-para Stampa. The beloved apostrophised in 'Lost from the Outset' is similarly intertextual, and her intertextual origin, not some quirk in Rilke's personal psychology, is the principal reason why she is – inevi-tably – lost before she has even arrived.

She is derived from two of Rilke's German predecessors, Klopstock and Hölty, both of whom wrote poems addressed to a muse-like figure whose appearance the poet still only anticipates. Klopstock's elegy 'Die künftige Geliebte' [The Future Beloved], written in 1747, belongs to the German elegiac tradition in which Rilke had immersed himself when he began work on the *Duino Elegies* in 1912. Traces of elegiac meters, in particular a preponderance of dactyls and some very ingenious spon-dees, are apparent in 'Lost from the Outset', if somewhat less obviously than in the *Duino Elegies*. Its elegiac cast, the motif of the unknown beloved and the idea that nature can communicate between the poet and the beloved, all mark 'Lost from the Outset' as a poem in the tradition initiated by Klopstock's elegy.

Klopstock's 'The Future Beloved' is not so much a poem of personal experience as a reworking of the myth of Persephone. In Klopstock's elegy, the future beloved is pictured as the daughter of a cruel mother nature to whom the poet addresses his plea for her release into the world of springtime flowers. Just as Demeter herself had begged for Persephone's release from the underworld, now the poet's tears appear to be answered by a sigh or breath of wind that calls to him as one shade to another. The winds that communicate between the two are seen as analogous to those which in the Golden Age communicated, via the gods, between the shepherd and his shepherdess; thus by implication they link the poet's song with the divinely inspired song of the ancients. We shall see later how Rilke adapts the motifs of the underworld, ancient song and poetic inspiration.

Hölty's two poems titled, like Klopstock's, 'Die künftige Geliebte' [The Future Beloved] (both 1775), are more conventional, but they share with Rilke's poem their garden settings, as well as the motif of birdsong. In one of the poems the woman's floral dress blends with the colours of the flowers around her so that they seem to be part of a single continuum, a fancy Rilke develops further when he claims that his beloved is identical with the gardens.

This conflation of the poem's object with the world of nature is matched by a tranposition of external reality into the poet's subjectivity. The internalised images of Rilke's poem, 'the splendid/ images in me' recall Hölderlin's elegy 'Menons Klagen um Diotima' [Menon's Lament for Diotima], in which 'Bilder aus hellerer Zeit' (images from a brighter time) maintain the speaker's link with his beloved after he has lost her. What Menon remembers are the gardens, mountains and paths where he and Diotima were together, the stars that seemed to witness their happiness, and the roses and lilies that seemed like objective correlatives of their love. But the natural settings shared by Hölderlin's lovers become, in Rilke's poem, something far less intimately experienced ('im Fernen erfahrene Landschaft', landscape perceived at a distance) and the phenomena of the external world are compressed into a sparse list of unmodified nouns ('Städte und Türme und Brücken', cities and towers and bridges). Similarly, though clearly drawing on Hölderlin's ideas and even imitating his style, Rilke's image of 'lands/ once dwelt in by gods' also remains abstract. Though both poets postulate that the gods of antiquity have left no more than traces inscribed in human memory, the moments of intimation that provide, for Hölderlin's Menon, a transitional, anticipatory vision validating poetic utterance in the present, remain inaccessible to the speaker of Rilke's poem.

In adapting images from Klopstock, Hölty and Hölderlin, Rilke implicitly takes issue with an entire tradition of poems addressed to the absent beloved. He does so because of what he sees as a dysfunctionality in the elegiac form itself. The German elegiac tradition had been a metapoetic tradition dealing not merely with individual loss but also with the loss and possible recuperation of poetic utterance altogether. Can poetic inspiration be recaptured in modern times? This is a central question for Rilke during his transitional period.

'Lost from the Outset' also revokes a more optimistic and far from elegiac text, Goethe's love lyric 'Gegenwart' [Presence] (1812). Inimical toward Goethe and indeed largely ignorant of his works for a good deal of his creative life, Rilke had begun to read his poetry quite intensively in 1910–12. Most of this reading had been urged upon him by his publishers, Anton and Katharina Kippenberg; but 'Presence' was a poem he discovered for himself and carefully copied for future reference during a visit to the Weimar archives in 1911. Goethe's 'Presence' neither projects a future beloved nor bemoans a lost one; rather, it evokes that tantalising moment when a lover is about to be reunited with his mistress.

'Presence' opens confidently: 'Alles kündet dich an!' (Everything announces your coming!). Unquestioningly, if not entirely unambiguously, the speaker locates intimations of the loved one's imminent arrival in natural phenomena such as the rising sun and the garden flowers, and claims that when she steps into the garden she herself will become 'die Rose der Rosen, Lilie der Lilien' (the rose of all roses, lily of all lilies). Rilke internalises these elements, placing the indicators of her arrival less in the external world than in the poet's consciousness, and asserting a more than merely metaphorical identity between the beloved and the gardens.

Where Goethe invokes the presence of the beloved, Rilke deplores her absence; where in Goethe's poem nature announces the imminent arrival of the beloved, Rilke sees only traces, perhaps even deceptive traces, of her previous existence.[52] Where Goethe ends his poem with an affirmative coupling of life and eternity, Rilke's poem ends with a question, and his lovers remain separated even at the moment when some kind of shared experience is most urgently desired and implicitly postulated. Most importantly, Goethe's 'Presence' is the expression of a way of seeing in which the absolute is regarded as immanent in the individual. By reworking this text, Rilke aims, among other things, to revoke its basic presupposition, Goethe's conception of poetry as the reflex of a concrete, present situation.

Combined with Rilke's reversal of Goethe's lyric is also a reversal of the myth of Orpheus and his transformation of nature into song. Who is, after all, the beloved 'lost from the outset' if not a latter-day Eurydice? A Eurydice, paradoxically, who has gathered up into herself the functions of Pluto as well, since it is she for whom the poet must find strains sufficiently charming to ensure her emergence: 'nicht weiß ich, welche Töne dir lieb sind' (I know not what tones you delight in). In keeping with Rilke's ambivalence about originality and influence, he all but suppresses this allusion to Orpheus and Eurydice.

In a poem written almost ten years earlier, 'Orpheus. Eurydice. Hermes' (1904), Rilke had already developed a version of the interior landscape that figures, in a more compressed form, in the first section of 'Lost from the Outset'. The earlier poem conceives of the journey out of the underworld as a passage through the mineshafts of the travellers' souls, a subterranean landscape full of imaginary cliffs, forests, bridges, ponds and meadows (1: 542). In 'Lost from the Outset' the landscape imagery is more frankly located in the realm of the imaginary: 'alle die großen/ Bilder in mir' (all of the splendid/ images in me). The modern Eurydice has been reduced to the traces of her previous existence. No longer does she follow Orpheus on his upward climb, but her traces, incorporated into the poet's inner world, mount in his consciousness as if to meet her. The modern Orpheus, for his part, has lost the extraordinary power of song that permitted his mythic forbear not only to win the hoped-for release of Eurydice from the underworld but also to transform the world around him after her second loss. And at the end of the poem it is not, as in the classical tradition, Orpheus who charms nature with his lament for Eurydice. Instead, nature itself – but only perhaps – links the perennially separated lovers through the song of a bird heard by both of them at once.

Yet there is a strange clash between the Orphic landscape, defined largely by imagery from nature, and the speaker's sudden confrontation with his own reflection in the shop windows, which suggests a more urban setting. To be sure, cities, bridges and towers are also mentioned in the first part of the poem, but they remain abstract; the shop-window image is more concrete. Indeed, when Rilke gave Harriet Cohen a copy of the poem twelve years after its composition, she thought it had been written specially for her and alluded to how they had looked at the windows of antique shops in the old town of Geneva.[53] Despite the personal effect it creates, however, the shop-window passage is not directly attributable to Rilke's own experience.

The remarkable image derives, rather, from Mallarmé's prose poem 'Le Démon de l'analogie' [The Demon of Analogy], in which the speaker suddenly sees his hand reflected in the window of a shop specialising in antique musical instruments and decorated with the feathers of birds from ancient times. 'The Demon of Analogy' directly treats the problem of inspiration. The text suggests that words are sometimes given to the poet as if by dictation, an experience Rilke felt he had had with the opening lines of the *Duino Elegies*.[54] From the point of view of intertextual relations, dictation is an interesting concept, since it bridges the gap, as it were, between inspiration and influence.

'The Demon of Analogy' claims that the poet is essentially an elegist, condemned to mourn the death of a mysterious figure it calls the 'Pénultième' (Penultimate). I have shown elsewhere that the 'Penultimate' can be understood as an allusion both to the classical hexameter and to Eurydice, whose loss gave rise to Orpheus' all-transforming song.[55] Whatever Rilke may have made of the 'Penultimate' – and it was well known for having created a public furor when Mallarmé's text first appeared – he would certainly have recognised the Orphic dimension of Mallarmé's 'Demon of Analogy'. Obsessed with the problems of originality and epigonality raised by his concern with German poetic tradition, Rilke was naturally attracted by the idea of Orpheus as a poetic predecessor at once disabling and enabling.

In Mallarmé's 'Demon of Analogy' the modern poet, wandering through the city, is haunted by a mysterious phrase that he manages to capture in its entirety by recovering the voice from the past that seems to be dictating the words (273). Several elements of this otherwise obscure text are relatively accessible: the phrase dictated by a voice not the poet's own; the scene where the poet suddenly sees his hand reflected in the shop window; the imagery of birds and feathers that recurs throughout the text; and the concluding claim that the speaker is condemned to bear the burden of mourning. These aspects alone would suffice to motivate the appearance of the shop-window reflection, coupled with the image of a bird, in the concluding section of Rilke's poem.[56]

Mallarmé's phrase 'une chute antérieure de plume ou de rameau' (a previous fall of feather or palm; p. 273) links the fall of Icarus to the Fall of Man. Through the double meaning of 'plume' ('feather' and 'pen'), these two falls become the precondition of poetic utterance. Hölderlin, perhaps the most daring of all German poets in his attempt to recuperate a classical heritage, had engaged in similar kinds of conflations, notably by creating analogies between Dionysos and Christ. Thus Rilke could assimilate Mallarmé to the poetic tradition that had preoccupied him during the period when he was writing 'Lost from the Outset'.

Most importantly, however, it is Orpheus that Rilke and Mallarmé both see as the precursor of the modern poet, although they also have doubts about their role as successors to Orpheus. In Rilke, doubt expresses itself in the question 'who knows?' with which he ends his poem 'Lost from the Outset'. The Orphic tradition cannot be unquestioningly continued by these two poets of a later age.

The birdsong motif with which the poem concludes is a final desperate attempt on Rilke's part to align himself, despite these difficulties, with poetic tradition. In both of Hölty's poems on the 'future beloved', birds are an important element of the garden scene, singing a bridesong for the poet and his loved one (177) or serenading the sleeping girl outside her window at evening (188). In one poem, the beloved herself becomes a kind of great bird or angel in a winged dress, a figure emerging from the spirit world and an emanation of nature itself. Dizzy with expectation in the red glow of evening, the garden takes on the colour of the flowers on her dress and the air resounds with the beat of wings as she descends to earth. Rilke's conflation of the loved one with her setting is displaced from the gardens into the old town setting of the shop-window episode, but the dizziness that accompanies this conflation, a hidden vestige of Hölty's poem, secretly unifies the otherwise disparate imagery in this section.

Rilke's bird, resounding (perhaps) through the poet and his imaginary loved one, also recalls Keats's nightingale, the 'immortal bird' heard by succeeding generations from ancient days to the present: 'Perhaps the self-same song that found a path/ Through the sad heart of Ruth, when, sick for home,/ She stood in tears amid the alien corn.'[57] Rilke can scarcely have been aware of the full intricacies of Keats's ode; he certainly would not have recognised its multiple allusions to Milton, Shakespeare, Wordsworth and Coleridge.[58] But even without this more specialised knowledge, it is hard to ignore the way in which Keats's poem treats the relation between present and past. In taking up Keats's idea of a song that remains identical across space and time, Rilke places himself decisively within poetic tradition, conceiving inspiration as a voice from the past, disembodied and displaced into nature.

But embodiment and its opposite are by no means simple in Rilke. Rilke insists that hearing is a kind of disembodied seeing. Thus at the same time as he seeks the right 'Töne' (tones) for his poem, he conjures up internalised images of landscape, and at the end of a sequence preoccupied with sight – the gardens, the open window, the mirroring shop fronts – he suddenly returns to hearing by evoking the song of the bird. Nonetheless, Rilke does speak of the bird itself. By resisting the word 'Vogelruf' (birdcall), which he does use elsewhere, in favour of 'Vogel' (bird), Rilke creates a curious effect. It is as if the bird were more corporeal than its listeners. In this way, the speaker of the poem is virtually disembodied and placed on the same insubstantial plane as his imaginary beloved. If the 'tones' Rilke seeks at the beginning of the poem for his address to the beloved are never found, they are somehow replaced or even usurped at the end by an auditory experience of an extremely abstract kind. Rilke is on the way to developing the concept of a realm of pure hearing that will be invoked at the beginning of his *Sonnets to Orpheus*.

More important for our present context, however, is that this process of disembodiment is a way of reaching back into the past. Rilke's 'Lost from the Outset' is a poem about the difficult coming-into-being of poetry and its complex relationship to the present of sensory experience and the past of myth and memory. In suggesting a possible mental meeting of the lovers through the medium of birdsong, Rilke points toward, but at the same time just stops short of, a conception of poetry as a vehicle for poetic synthesis. 'Lost from the Outset' repeatedly lets the dead poets speak, but the dashes that punctuate the text are signs of discontinuity, symptoms of a need to break off the syntactic structures initiated and to keep on beginning again. The anguish of the poem is that of an impossible decision between originality and influence, between the expression of an individual self and that of a past poetic tradition.

It would be too simplistic to read Rilke's dialogue with tradition as merely an expression of his own sense of enfeeblement and belatedness. In 'Lost from the Outset', several different ways of thinking about creativity jostle each other but never quite become integrated into a single coherent theory. Does poetry come from inside (from the poet's subjectivity or stored-up experience) or from outside (from the muse, from divine inspiration, from triggering elements in external reality)? The poet seems to understand authenticity not as an act of speaking in one's own voice, but as a search for those 'tones' that will motivate the release of creative power, a search that involves imitation and appropriation as much as it involves invention. The landscape of Rilke's poem is void of inspiration, abandoned by the gods, but it is still so full of the past that the present seems almost crowded out. This past, however, is in another sense inaccessible, like someone who has just disappeared around a corner. The poem's genuine innovation, its elliptical rendition of classical elegiac metres, serves not to breathe new life into the 'tones' of past poetry, but to thwart the complete recuperation of the poetic tradition, however much the poem's speaker thinks he desires it.

At the same time, 'Lost from the Outset' is also a decisive break with Goethe – despite the fact that Rilke was charmed by his poem 'Presence'. Goethe was, after all, the canonical German poet who had most insistently argued for the existence of original genius. In Rilke's day and beyond, Goethe's lyrics set the standard for what readers recognised as the 'authentic' voice of poetry. Along with his emphasis on 'originality' and 'authenticity', Goethe also believed in the solid reality of the external world and of the immanence of the divine within this reality. 'Presence' is eloquent testimony to this whole cluster of views. Indeed, its very title insists on them, since 'Gegenwart' means both 'presence' and 'the present'. For Goethe, the future is firmly anchored in the present moment of which it forms an immanent part. In 'Lost from the Outset', Rilke refuses to accept Goethe's notion of immanence; he has given up hope of 'discerning' the beloved in actual reality and the present moment. Whatever differences Rilke has with Klopstock, Hölty, and Hölderlin, they are minor compared to this more radical argument with Goethe. 'Lost from the Outset' is above all a revocation of Goethe's views on reality, poetry and the possibility of original expression.

Rilke's poem is situated on the brink of a new understanding of poetic creativity. Aware that 'originality' is an effect, not an essence, 'Lost from the Outset' still cannot quite free itself from the ambition to be original; conscious that its images have been gathered from elsewhere, that its 'tones' must be sought, that the inspiring 'bird' is also the voice of tradition, it nonetheless claims to speak in the voice of a single individual and to articulate that individual's experiences. Torn by these ambiguities, it reflects poignantly on the paradoxical nature of the originality effect.

WAR AND MOURNING

Rilke's relation to loss was intensified by the arrival of the First World War. To be sure, his *Fünf Gesänge* [Five Cantos] (1914) are generally thought of as a hymn to war, an enthusiastic welcome to an ancient god who has returned to shake the earth once more. This impression, derived mainly from the first cantos, is superficially supported by the fact that the sequence appeared in *Kriegsalmanach für das Jahr 1914* [War Almanach for the Year 1914] put out by the Insel publishing house. Yet the *Five Cantos'* publication in the company of a collection of patriotic poems inspired by the outbreak of war has led to a serious misapprehension about them. They are in fact constructed as an attack on the notion that war might revive a flagging sense of national identity and restore lost cultural vigour: 'Auf, und schreckt den schrecklichen Gott! Bestürzt ihn' (Arise, and startle the terrible god! Topple him; 2: 91). Like the *Duino Elegies*, the *Cantos* consist in a meditation that unfolds an argument gradually, ultimately turning away from its own initial assumptions. The *Five Cantos* articulate the public mood while arguing against the war enthusiasm that held many in its grip.

The *Five Cantos* were composed in August 1914 on a flyleaf of the final volume in the new Hölderlin edition that had just been brought out by Norbert Hellingrath. The rhythms, vocabulary, syntax and imagery of Hölderlin's late hymns pervade the *Cantos*. Rilke re-interprets Hölderlin's scheme, however, by claiming that the god of war has emerged only because we have too long ignored the gods of peace. As the speaker recognises the full destructive powers of war, the ancient god is seen as a volcano which, after years of quietude, has suddenly begun to spew forth flame (2: 88). The god of war destroys us even as he awakens us. The fifth canto exhorts readers to leave hatred behind and join forces under the mutual banner of pain rather than under national flags. In the final analysis, the *Five Cantos* do not celebrate war at all. They see war as an inevitable result of our alienation from the peaceful forces immanent in nature and hail it as a terrible event designed to awaken us from ignorance and neglect of all that is good.

Taken as a whole, the *Five Cantos* are a piece of special pleading. They mount an argument designed to persuade those attracted by the excitement of war that it is not an enthusiasm that should be cultivated. Rather, the *Cantos* exhort readers to recall the loss and suffering war brings and to mobilise mourning in the service of a new 'insight' that will burn away error.[59]

In choosing Hölderlin as his stylistic model for the *Five Cantos*, Rilke implies more than he states explicitly in the poems. The relationship between Rilke and Hölderlin does not rest solely upon a cluster of borrowed images and an imitation of rhythmic and linguistic mannerisms. More importantly, it is Rilke's bid to situate himself in a distinctly German poetic lineage. Hölderlin saw himself as a poet for a time of need, a voice that articulated a vision of his nation as the natural heir to the great traditions of classical antiquity while finding its deepest wellsprings in its native landscape and, metaphorically, the river Rhine. He insists on the 'Germanness' of countryside, language, and his own poetry. Hölderlin's contemporaries thought of him as a precursor of a cultural rebirth still to come; and Hölderlin himself regarded poetry as a prophetic anticipation of future harmony. Rilke implicitly positions himself in Hölderlin's wake as a singer of 'deutscher Gesang' (German song), even though he no longer believes that 'alles ist gut' (all is good). By giving his poems on war the title *Fünf Gesänge* Rilke harks back to, but also criticises Hölderlin's notion of patriotic poetry.

Rilke seems to have 'heard' Hölderlin's voice in two ways. In the *Five Cantos*, the more expansive voice of Hölderlin's elegies dominates. But there is also the sparer, more elliptical, hermetic mode of Hölderlin's late hymns. I will conclude this chapter by taking a brief look at Rilke's first attempt to develop a more cryptic manner in his only published poem of the late war years, 'Seele im Raum' [Soul in Space] (1917).

Few specialist studies refer to 'Soul in Space'; it has received no extended critical attention. The poem is reproduced in the six-volume edition of Rilke's works (2: 109–110) without any indication that it had been published during the poet's lifetime (2: 891). 'Soul in Space' first appeared in a collection of texts produced to celebrate the fiftieth anniversary of the 'Alice Frauenverein' [Alice Women's Society].[60] Rilke's poem took pride of place as the first text in the collection.[61] What was this organisation and why did Rilke contribute to their anniversary volume?

The Alice Women's Society had been formed by Queen Victoria's daughter, Alice Maud Mary, after her marriage to Prince Louis of Hesse. Brought up from early childhood to visit the poor, she retained her charitable impulses in her new home, taking a special interest in women with new babies, the mentally handicapped and the blind.[62] Her Women's Society, founded in 1867, had two branches, one designed to train nurses for wartime service, the other working to improve the education of women in general. When Alice died of typhoid in 1878, the work of the Women's Society was carried on by her daughter-in-law, Grand Duchess Eleonore of Hesse, who expanded the guild's interests to cover adoption services, welfare of mothers and infants, and rest cures for women with tuberculosis.[63] Eleonore also continued Alice's work in training nurses for war duty. Under the name 'Sister Marie', she herself nursed wounded soldiers in field hospitals during World War I. She had trained in England under Florence Nightingale, and she became something of a Florence Nightingale figure on the German front. By this time, too, the Alice Society had developed formal links with the Red Cross; in 1937, its name would be officially changed to 'Das Deutsche Rote Kreuz' (The German Red Cross). Several photographs exist of 'Sister Marie' in Red Cross uniform with other nurses, with her husband the Grand Duke at the front, and, in one instance, as a solitary female figure surrounded by dozens of convalescent soldiers.[64] Her organisation not only did good works, it also had to raise money to support its charitable ventures. One of its most original fund-raising ideas was the first airmail service in Germany (1912), the proceeds of which went toward the Alice Society's mother-and-baby welfare organisation. For the price of a special postage stamp, one could send a postcard to its destination via biplane; a photograph of one of these aeroplanes, appealingly named 'Yellow Dog', is reproduced in a biography of the Grand Duchess.[65] The volume to which Rilke contributed 'Soul in Space' was published in 1917 to raise money for the Alice Society's war effort. A number of other poets had been invited to contribute, and those who were not themselves at the front did so: the volume includes texts by Stefan Zweig, Peter Altenberg, Alfred Kerr and several other writers who had already gained a literary reputation. With few exceptions, most of the contributions address the themes of war, loss and death quite directly.

Rilke's poem initiates the collection. The volume is handsomely printed in a decisive Gothic typeface on good paper; its grey wrappers bear a restrained graphic design. In this context, along with other war poems, Rilke's poem becomes more powerful and also more poignant. Above all, its formal and syntactical daring becomes much more apparent in the company of relatively traditional verses about death and destruction.

Rilke's poem speaks in the voice of a soul taking leave of the body in which it has been housed. In this way, the poem puts the anthology's subscribers imaginatively into the position of those dying at the front: the reader no longer considers the war from a distance, but actually visualises what it might be like to experience physical mortality. Strained syntax, agonised questions, hesitation and fear confront the reader with the profound disorientation of a newly dead soul:

> Hier bin ich, hier bin ich, Entrungene,
> taumelnd.
> Wag ichs denn? Werf ich mich?

Fähige waren schon viel
dort, wo ich drängte. Nun wo
auch noch die Mindesten restlos Macht vollziehn,
schweigend vor Meisterschaft –:
Wag ichs denn? Werf ich mich?

Zwar ich ertrug, vom befangenen Körper aus,
Nächte; ja ich befreundete
ihn, den irdenen, mit der Unendlichkeit;
schluchzend
überfloß, das ich hob,
sein schmuckloses Herz.

Aber nun, wem zeig ichs,
daß ich die Seele bin? Wen
wunderts?
Plötzlich soll ich die Ewige sein,
nicht mehr am Gegensatz haftend, nicht mehr
Trösterin; fühlend mit nichts als
Himmeln.

Kaum noch geheim;
denn unter den offenen
allen Geheimnissen eines,
ein ängstliches.

O wie durchgehn sich die großen Umarmungen. Welche
wird mich umfangen, welche mich weiter
geben, mich, linkisch
Umarmende?

Oder vergaß ich und kanns?
Vergaß den erschöpflichen Aufruhr
jener Schwerliebenden? Staun,
stürze aufwärts und kanns?   (2: 109–111)

Here I am, here I am, wrested away,
staggering.
Dare I? Shall I take off?

Many, before, have been capable
there, where I forced my way. Now where
even the lowliest accomplish full power,
silent with mastery –:
Dare I? Shall I take off?

Yes, I endured, from within my awkward body,
nights; indeed, I acquainted
him, that earthen one, with infinity;
sobbing,
overflowed what I raised,
his unornamented heart.

Now, though, whom shall I show that
I am the soul? Who is
astonished?
Suddenly, I am to be the eternal one,
no longer clutching my opposite, no longer
consoling; feeling at one with nothing but
heavens.

Barely still secret; for
among all the open
secrets, one,
an anxious one.

O how the great embraces interpenetrate. Which
will enfold me, which will hand me
on, me, awkwardly
embracing?

Or did I forget and am able to do it?
Forgot the exhaustible uproar of
those who love ponderously? Stare in amazement,
plunge upward, and am able to do it?

'Soul in Space' is a telling document of Rilke's war experience. He
had been called up by the Austrian army in late November 1915, but his
health had not proved equal after the first weeks of basic training. He
was then given clerical tasks at the war archives and finally released from
service in May 1916. During 1915, he wrote very little poetry; in 1916, he
only wrote a few pages of drafts; and in 1917 this trickle almost dried up
completely. 'Soul in Space' is the only text from 1917 that Rilke regarded
as finished; his incomplete poetic sketches from this period are minimal.
No wonder he felt so desperate. Does his monologue of the soul also
express more personal feelings? Does it suggest a desire for death,
perhaps even a suicide wish?

The irregular ebb and flow of the lines recalls Hölderlin's late hymns,
expressions of a profound sense of despair at living in a 'dürftige Zeit'
(needy time). The poem's syntactic structures also recall peculiarities of
Hölderlin's poetry: adjectives placed after their noun, interpolated

phrases that interrupt straightforward sentence structure, participial phrases and gerundives, deictics whose reference is only gradually revealed.

There is also another and more specific link between the two poets. 'Soul in Space' bears a warm dedication to the Grand Duchess of Hesse[-Darmstadt]; Hölderlin's 'Patmos' is dedicated to the Landgrave of Hesse-Homburg, and a dedicatory copy was presented to him in 1803. The positions of the two dedicatees are equivalent. Until Hesse-Darmstadt entered the North German Confederation 1866 it was ruled by a landgrave, as was Hesse-Homburg; after 1866, the landgrave of Hesse-Darmstadt was given the title of Grand Duke. The similarity in dedication between Hölderlin's and Rilke's poems suggests that 'Patmos' may have been in Rilke's mind when he composed 'Soul in Space'.

'Soul in Space' is in many ways a revocation of the claim articulated in 'Patmos' that 'wo [...] Gefahr ist, da wächst/ das Rettende auch' (where [...] there is danger, there salvation/ grows too). In 'Patmos', Hölderlin meditates on the question whether divine goodness is still present in turbulent times. The mystery of death is likened to the harvest which cuts down the grain but is not ultimately a negative thing. The speaker of 'Patmos' wishes for wings so that he can go over into the realm of death and return to life again. Hardly has he made this wish than a spirit steals him away and takes him to a new country – 'Asia', the source, in the Romantic mind, of poetry and prophecy. Later in the poem, the dead are awakened to their new world by the power of song, though many of them still shy away from the unaccustomed brilliance of heavenly light.

These motifs from 'Patmos' are reworked in 'Soul in Space'. The newly dead soul has been 'wrested away' from its bodily housing but is hesitant to enter its new domain. Rilke's use of 'werfen' (literally 'to throw'; rendered in my translation as 'take off') is part of Rilke's special vocabulary for bird flight. Birds 'werfen' (throw) themselves through the air (2: 167). The verb 'stürzen' (rendered 'plunge') in the poem's last line means to fall, to stumble, to hasten, or to startle. Any kind of sudden bodily motion is encompassed by this verb. In the language of aviation, a 'Sturzflug' is a sudden descent. Here, in accord with Rilke's tendency to reverse familiar metaphors, the soul hopes to plunge upwards.

This rather odd imagery suggests that Rilke is thinking of the Egyptian conception of the soul or spiritual aspect of a person, sometimes represented as a human-headed bird, called the 'ba'.[66] In some papyri, the soul is shown about to take flight from the dead body, represented as a black skeletal figure lying on a bier; numerous tomb carvings and papyrus illustrations show a feathered 'ba' with wings outspread, leaving an encased mummy or parting from the shadow of the deceased standing at the threshhold of his tomb.[67]

Furthermore, the poem's attribution to the soul – the way in which it speaks with the soul's voice – recalls an Egyptian text that particularly fascinated Rilke during his 1911 stay in Cairo and that he felt he understood better than specialist scholars who had worked on it.[68] This was 'The Man Who Was Tired of Life', a Middle Kingdom dialogue between a man and his 'ba'.[69] It is one of the earliest studies of the problem of suicide. Although the text has numerous gaps and lacunae, its general import is clear enough: both the disillusioned man and his soul hesitate between life and death. The man, claiming that the soul is 'too stupid to ease misery in life', urges it to go ahead to the Kingdom of the West; the soul argues that the man should not seek death prematurely. In the end, both the man and his soul decide in favour of life. The most moving part of the text, a passage somewhat reminiscent of Job's complaint to his creator, is a long verse sequence in which the desperate man addresses his soul. Feeling abandoned by friends and exposed to a world full of hatred and misery, the man asks repeatedly whether there is anyone in whom he can confide:

> To whom can I speak today?
> Hearts are rapacious
> And there is no man's heart in which one can trust. (p. 207)

For the man weighed down by care, his individual situation and the condition of the world around him are equally desperate; only his soul's response saves him from casting life aside.

Rilke's poem is a reworking and inversion of the Egyptian papyrus text. Here, the body is dead, and only the soul hesitates to take its leave and plunge into the unknown. The bird-like soul is not only uncertain what course to take, it also needs to gain control of its new form and learn to navigate in the new kind of space through which it will be moving. By means of this image, Rilke's poem also refers to a broader problem of achievement and success. In the final stanza, the soul asks if mastery may be possible for it, just as it has been for others before. It is surely not far-fetched to think of this achievement of mastery not only in terms of the afterlife, but also in terms of poetic creativity. Rilke's attempt to overcome the writing block that had become painfully exacerbated by his work in the Austrian War Archives forms a subterranean level of meaning in this poem ostensibly about confronting death.

Several elements in 'Soul in Space' anticipate images and ideas that Rilke works out more fully in the *Duino Elegies*. The 'großen Umarmungen' (great embraces) of 'Soul in Space' will become, in *The Fifth Elegy*, the metaphor of successful love-making as a correlative for creative achievement. The question, 'wem zeig ichs,/ daß ich die Seele bin?' (whom shall I show/ that I am the soul?) will become, in *The Seventh Elegy*, the idea of showing one's accomplishment to a transcendent being. Apart from specific images, 'Soul in Space' also moves decisively toward the abstract modes of expression characteristic of Rilke's later poetry.

Some of this abstraction may have to do with the esoteric approach the poem takes to the mystery of death, termed here an open secret. The underlying idea that the soul is female and the body male, in part determined by the gender of the German words 'Seele' and 'Körper', suggests a variety of esoteric beliefs, notably Orphism.[70] According to Orphic belief, the soul was imprisoned in the body as a punishment for an ancient sin committed by the Titans.[71] Initiation into the Orphic rites conferred escape from the 'cycle of rebirth' or metempsychosis that the soul would otherwise be condemned to endure. After drinking the water of a sacred spring, the dead person cast off his bodily form, and rose, purified, toward the heavens.

Rilke's poem develops several ideas that consider the soul's relation to the body in much this way. During life, the soul is constrained by the 'awkward body'; before death, it acquaints the body with eternity and in the moment of death, it raises the body's 'unornamented heart' onto a higher level. Once the soul leaves the body, it no longer clings to its 'opposite' or provides it with consolation; its only communion is with the heavens. The connection between body and soul before death is one kind of 'embrace', the soul's relation to the cosmos after death is another. Embraces that include the body are weighted or 'ponderous'; those that take place after death are light and aerial. The poem's posture as an interior monologue on the part of the newly dead soul is not only frightening, but, on another level, an attempt to effect a reconciliation with death.

'Soul in Space' reveals a great deal about Rilke's increasing despair about the war and the shadow it cast over the possibility of continuing to write poetry. But even as it confronts actual and metaphorical death, it also begins a daring plunge into an unaccustomed sphere beyond the reach of conventional poetic language. Rilke's poem 'An die Musik' [To Music], written the following year, moves more surely into the abstract modes that will characterise his poetry of the twenties.

CHAPTER 4

The modernist turn

Rilke's shift to abstraction is accompanied by continuing reflections on the nature of poetry. His modernism has two faces: it moves, on the one hand, toward a concept of poetry as essence that extends the Symbolist notion of 'pure poetry', and on the other, toward a revival of the classical German poets' elegiac invocation of more coherent traditions. The boldly compressed and elliptical effects that become increasingly evident in Rilke's poetry owe much to the spare, hermetic poetry of Mallarmé. In the early nineteen-twenties, Rilke discovered Paul Valéry, whose poetry he read and translated with profound admiration. The emphasis of both French poets on that which cannot be adequately rendered in language and on that which is not represented in visible, audible, or tangible reality held great appeal for Rilke. Rilke found new confirmations of his earlier concept of the 'leere Mitte' (empty centre) in the French poets' obsession with silence and absence. By the same token, his interest in the transformation of reality through the creative imagination found equivalents in the French poets' free transposition of one sensory impression into another.

As early as 1913, Rilke had read Wilhelm Worringer's book, *Abstraktion und Einfühlung* [Abstraction and Empathy] (1908).[1] For Worringer, the two terms of his title were polar opposites. Abstraction was not so much a modernist phenomenon as a tendency present in art of many periods. The earliest beginnings of art are marked by abstraction, Worringer wrote; but while some cultures continued to value abstraction highly throughout their development, occidental art shifted toward empathetic forms in which aesthetic pleasure is simultaneously a confirmation of individual subjective needs.[2] Worringer regarded abstraction in twentieth-century Western art as a response to cultural insecurity: abstract forms and the almost mathematical laws that underlie them provide a sense of repose within the monstrous confusion of the modern world view.[3]

Rilke's discovery of abstract art took a decisive turning during the war years, when external reality was collapsing in more than a merely metaphorical sense. During this period, he became acquainted with Paul Klee, who lent him between forty and sixty of his watercolours in 1915.[4] Rilke kept them for several months and evidently examined them quite closely; he had a more immediate response to these experiments in colour, especially the Tunisian paintings, than to Klee's graphic works. During the last year of the war, Rilke and Klee were next-door neighbours in Munich. In 1921, Rilke read Wilhelm Hausenstein's book *Kairuan* [Kairouan], a study of Paul Klee and twentieth-century art. Here he found ideas very close to his own way of thinking. Hausenstein saw Klee's work as a response to the disappearance of the object in the modern world. Instead of the concrete reality of objects, Klee, in Hausenstein's view, represented the extraordinary complexity of their relationship to one another; Klee's art manifests the 'Bezogenheit' (relatedness) of things, transforming it into an 'intersphärische Trigonometrie' (interspherical trigonometry) that makes his paintings 'inwendig lauter Figur' (inwardly nothing but figure).[5] In Rilke's late poetry, 'Bezug' (relation) and 'Figur' ('figure') are used in a similar sense.

In *The Tenth Elegy*, Rilke argues not so much against abstraction as against modern urban life when he insists on the value of concrete objects, holding up the work of the 'Töpfer am Nil' (potters on the Nile) as models of creativity. At the same time, he deplores the tasteless world of modern commerce, which prevents us from gaining access to our innermost selves. As an antidote to the flimsy proliferation of cheap objects, he proposes a poetically transformed world in which the 'figure' or structural reconception of concrete reality will rescue its alarming tendency toward degration. Rilke's disturbing experiences during the war years were, paradoxically, a crucible for the new kind of poetry he subsequently created.

Increasingly, Rilke began to understand the task of art not so much as that of representing reality, but of transforming it into what he termed 'das Unsichtbare' (the invisible). At the same time, he came to conceive of artistic form or 'Figur' (figure) as a way of retaining the object in a kind of structural metamorphosis. The early Picasso, whose work Rilke first seriously confronted in 1915 – specifically, 'La Mort d'Arlequin' [The Death of Harlequin] and 'La Famille de Saltimbanques' [The Family of Acrobats] (both 1905) – was close to what Rilke had in mind when he wrote, in *The Seventh Elegy*, of what he saw as the need for 'Bewahrung der noch erkannten Gestalt' (retention of still recognisable shape; 1: 712). In his own poetry, spatial metaphors became equivalents for the structures he wishes to retain in the process of transforming the tangible world into the imaginary. External reality, he believed, was in the process of vanishing away: the task of the poet was to rescue it by reconfiguring it as abstract structure.

Even before what Rilke himself saw as his poetic renewal in 1922, his 1918 poem 'An die Musik' [To Music] takes a decisive step toward modernism. When he read Hausenstein's book on Paul Klee three years later, he concurred that Klee's graphic work was 'oft Umschreibung von Musik' (often a transposition of music).[6] In a letter to Hausenstein in which he discusses his book at length, Rilke adds a note asking Hausenstein to give Klee a copy of 'Ur-Geräusch' [Primal Noise], an essay whose starting-point is the transformation of sound into spatial configurations on a wax recording.[7] Rilke's brilliant handling of metaphor and the innovative spatial figures he constructs in 'To Music' prepare for a move toward abstraction in his late elegies and the *Sonette an Orpheus* [Sonnets to Orpheus]. The 'figures' of dance and acrobatic performance correspond to the transformative power of poetry, which gives shape to that which is transitory and evanescent. Temples and monuments become objective correlatives for poetry and song – or rather, as these poems conceive it, poetry and song metamorphose into architecture. 'Mausoleum', a late poem that explicitly deals with the transformation of song into an architectural monument, is perhaps Rilke's most advanced foray into modernism. Elliptical, hermetic and idiosyncratic, it radically extends the innovative techniques of 'To Music'.

THE OTHER SIDE OF THE AIR

Although Rilke attended several house concerts during the war years, his poem 'An die Musik' [To Music] (1918) should not be taken as a sign of a new-found interest in an art form for which he had previously shown little appreciation. 'Music' is here merely another avatar of the metaphors Rilke had been seeking throughout his crisis period for the complex interaction of subject and object in the imaginative act. 'Die große Nacht' (great night), the 'im Voraus verlorne Geliebte' (beloved, lost from the outset), 'das innere Mädchen' (the inner maiden), 'die Berge des Herzens' (the heart's mountains), 'der Engel' (the angel), 'Weltinnenraum' (world-innerspace) – all these are metaphors for that almost ungraspable relationship. They are also, as we have seen, metaphors for the poet's engagement with literary tradition. In 'To Music' Rilke reworks several notions precious to the Symbolists, notably Verlaine's call for poetry to become closer to music in 'L'Art poétique' [The Art of Poetry], and Mallarmé's idea that pure poetry is really a type of silence. Both concepts emphasise form as opposed to content, and Rilke's pared-down poem, at once ecstatic and questioning, alerts us to the problematic relationship of form and content from the very beginning:

> Musik: Atem der Statuen. Vielleicht:
> Stille der Bilder. Du Sprache wo Sprachen
> enden. Du Zeit,
> die senkrecht steht auf der Richtung
> vergehender Herzen.

> Gefühle zu wem? O du der Gefühle
> Wandlung in was? –: in hörbare Landschaft.
> Du Fremde: Musik. Du uns entwachsener
> Herzraum. Innigstes unser,
> das, uns übersteigend, hinausdrängt, –
> heiliger Abschied:
> da uns das Innre umsteht
> als geübteste Ferne, als andre
> Seite der Luft:
> rein,
> riesig,
> nicht mehr bewohnbar.   (2: 111)

Music: breath of statues. Perhaps:
silence of pictures. You language where languages
end. You time,
standing upright upon the direction
  of vanishing hearts.

Feelings for whom? O you transformation
of feelings into what? –: into audible landscape.
You stranger: music. Grown out of us, you
heart-space. Innermost part of us,
which, in transcending us, thrusts its way outward, –
sacred taking of leave:
when space from inside surrounds us as
distance most practised, the other
side of the air:
pure,
gigantic,
no longer habitable.

Formally, Rilke extends the experiment he had begun in 'Soul in Space' in the more accomplished 'To Music'. It is a remarkable tour de force. Its predominantly dactylic meter suggests the free modulations of classical elegiacs Rilke had already been experimenting with in his *Duino Elegies*; but these elegiacs are more broken down, even more like ruins of the original verse form than the rhythms of the *Elegies*. Here and there, a complete classical hexameter can be discerned, but it crosses over two lines. Occasional spondees suggest the classical pentameter, but no sequence of syllables forms a complete pentameter line. The 'music' of ancient poetry is audible here, but only vestigially.

The opening lines of the poem shift disconcertingly from definition to apostrophe. Is the speaker describing music or addressing it? The hesitation between these two modes characterises the entire poem. Its opening statement is followed by a more doubtful 'vielleicht' (perhaps); questions that seem rhetorical are given an answer; what cannot be articulated is somehow expressed; colons propose identities that can only be paradoxical; the whole remains at once remote and strangely compelling.

Music is first defined by means of two metaphors. Parallel grammatical structures conceal the fact that these two metaphors are incommensurate: is 'Atem der Statuen' (breath of statues) the same kind of thing as 'Stille der Bilder' (silence of pictures)? Pictures may be silent, but statues don't breathe. Except, of course, in Romantic tales, where they are apt to come to life, as in Eichendorff's famous novella, *Das Marmorbild* [The Marble Statue] (1819). Or unless, more interestingly, the 'breath' of statues is to be understood as their aura – a word derived from the Latin word for a 'breath of air'. Air is also involved, etymologically as well as according to traditional poetics, in inspiration – a fact Rilke exploits in his sonnet, 'Früher Apollo' [Early Apollo]. In these opening lines of 'To Music', Rilke describes not only abstract form, but also inspiration, which gives radiance and life to form.

During Rilke's years of poetic crisis, a series of poems had begun to emerge in which music is the central metaphor: 'Bestürz mich, Musik' [Batter me, music] (1913; 2: 60–61), 'Strophen zu einer Fest-Musik' [Stanzas for Celebratory Music] (1915; 2: 98–99), 'Ode an Bellman' [Ode to Bellman] (1915; 2: 100–101). In all these poems, music is less sound than space, not just filling a cathedral with swelling notes, but actually becoming the vaulted ceilings and high pillars. 'To Music' enacts a similar transformation, but it is not merely a reworking of the

Symbolist idea of interchangeability: it is also a reworking of a Romantic conception of the relationship between poet and nature.

'To Music' must be seen in connection with three essays that Rilke wrote in the years before and after the poem. The first part of 'Erlebnis' [Experience] (1913; 6: 1036–1040) recounts a 'spot in time' experience (to adopt Wordsworth's phrase) in which the narrator feels as if he has slipped over onto the other side of reality. The second part (also 1913; 6: 1040–1042) recalls the sound of a bird call that seems to separate body and mind and continues to resonate in interior space. Finally, a short and rather bizarre essay called 'Ur-Geräusch' [Primal Noise] (1919; 6: 1085–1093) recalls a science experiment Rilke had witnessed at boarding school. A teacher had created a phonograph using simple materials that came to hand: a cardboard cone, a sheet of paper, a lump of wax, and a bristle from a hairbrush. Later, when Rilke began to read about human anatomy, he discovered that there is a set of spiral grooves on the cranium not unlike the grooves on a record. What would happen, he gruesomely wonders, if one were to 'play' the cranial grooves on a phonograph? The sound that would issue forth would be, he claims, 'primal noise', the elemental sound of the universe.

'Geräusch' (noise) is, of course, the opposite of music. Still, the underlying idea of 'Primal Noise' will help us to understand 'To Music'. The eccentric essay on the phonograph is in fact a reworking of a familiar Romantic trope: the idea of a latent music in nature. The Romantics liked to think of the Aeolian harp, as well as the larger wind harp that was also popular at the time, as ways of capturing this latent music and making it audible. The poet was also conceived as a kind of instrument that could 'hear' the secret voice of nature and translate it into human language. Rilke knew about this conception of the 'voice of nature' from Eichendorff, whom he had been reading since his school years, and Novalis, whom he was reading during his crisis period.

I believe, though, that Rilke must have also thought back to his early (summer 1898) reading of Emerson.[8] In a crucial passage, Emerson writes:

For poetry was all written before time was, and whenever we are so finely organized that we can penetrate into that region where the air is music, we hear those primal warblings and attempt to write them down...[9]

'To Music' can be read as an attempt to represent in words Emerson's 'region where the air is music'.

With this Emersonian idea in mind, the poem 'To Music' becomes more intelligible. Music transcends verbal language: it is a 'Sprache wo Sprachen/ enden' (language where languages/ end). As such, it provides a hope that had been absent from 'Ausgesetzt auf den Bergen des Herzens' [Exposed on the Heart's Mountains] (2: 94–95), written four years earlier. There, the poet climbing above the timberline toward the barren peak of a mountain can only hear the unconscious 'song' of simple vegetation; for himself, burdened by consciousness, there can be no release through either song or language: 'Ach, der zu wissen begann/ und schweigt nun, ausgesetzt auf den Bergen des Herzens' (Oh, he who began to know/ and falls silent now, exposed on the heart's mountains; 2: 94–95). 'To Music' hopes for a way of reaching beyond the point where 'languages end' by finding another form of expression in music.

Paradoxically, however, this poem draws attention to its own dependence on linguistic expression. The fundamental gesture of 'To Music' is naming: seldom has a poem been so determinedly nominal. Although there are in fact several finite verbs and a number of participial forms, nouns dominate. Nouns are linked with one another by colons, genitive constructions, and in one case simple compounding ('Herzraum', heart-space). In this respect, the poem enacts one of Rilke's favourite Emersonian principles: the idea that the poet was the 'Namer or Language-maker, naming things sometimes after their appearance, sometimes after their essence' (Emerson, 3: 21). Rilke was to use the same structure in his 'mirror' sonnet of 1922, once again beginning with the familiar name of the object to be defined and proceeding to describe its essence. What 'To Music' calls 'die andere Seite der Luft' (the other side of the air) is not unlike the virtual space of mirrors that Rilke explores in his later sonnet; and significantly, both poems situate their object with relation to temporality.

In the poem before us, music is correctly called time, since musical structure depends on temporality. But the speaker claims that music as time differs from our ordinary experience of time, in which everything tends toward its own decay. Endowed with the permanence – in other words, the infinite repeatability – of all artistic production, music 'stands upright' or vertically while human life ebbs away along a horizontal time line.

Rilke's conceit, that there are, as it were, two temporal axes, one vertical and the other horizontal, is reduplicated in several other sets of doublings and polarities in the poem. Visual art (statues and pictures) is envisaged as both dynamic (breathing) and static (silent). Later, when music is said to transform feelings into 'audible landscape', seeing and hearing are paradoxically brought into conjunction, as in Symbolist synaesthesia. Music is something that can be defined as well as something that can be addressed. A definition is more static than an apostrophe, since the latter involves directedness, a reaching out from the speaker to a 'you'. Both definitions and apostrophes, however, subsist in a kind of perennial present that differs fundamentally from the present time of actions and events. In general, we define things that are not actually present – otherwise, we could just point. When we define music, we include in our definition not only music we have heard in the past but also that which we may hear in the future. Apostrophe shifts the coordinates of the continual present somewhat. The addressee may be absent or present, but in either case apostrophe arrests time by dwelling on the relationality of speaker and addressee and by holding the addressee suspended for a moment in imagination. Repeated vocatives, when not simply the result of rapture (another kind of suspension), most often occur when the addressee cannot answer back – usually because it is inanimate. By calling the name of the thing addressed, apostrophic structures implicitly breathe life into it. If music is the 'Atem der Statuen' (breath of statues), it is in part because the speaker of this poem brings it to life by means of the vocative 'you'. Living hearts are always in the process of 'vanishing' as they inevitably proceed toward death; but anything summoned in a poem is called into existence and thus prevented from vanishing. At the same time, repeated apostrophe abolishes narrative temporality and thus suggests the existence of a different temporality that is the essence of lyric poetry.[10]

The second section of the poem reworks a motif that Rilke had already begun to develop some years earlier: the concept of 'Weltinnenraum' (worldinnerspace). This was essentially a way of representing the phenomenon of creative perception, or more specifically, the complicated process of reciprocal projection and appropriation that constitutes the creative act. In a poem from 1914, Rilke formulated it as follows:

> Durch alle Wesen reicht der *eine* Raum:
> Weltinnenraum. Die Vögel fliegen still
> durch uns hindurch. O, der ich wachsen will,
> ich seh hinaus, und *in* mir wächst der Baum.   (2: 93)

> Through every being goes a *single* space:
> worldinnerspace. The birds fly silently
> through us. O, if I wish to grow apace,
> I look outside, and *in* me grows the tree.

Rilke's term, 'worldinnerspace' actually combines 'cosmic' or 'outer space' ('Weltraum', where space ships travel) with the interior space of the human psyche. This space is identical with poetry and the imagination. In a 1924 poem on the same topic, Rilke disposes the terms somewhat differently, contrasting real space with poetic space: 'Durch den sich Vögel werfen ist nicht der/ vertraute Raum, der die Gestalt dir steigert' (The space birds fling themselves through is not that/ familiar space that makes your form enhanced; 2: 167).

In 'To Music', the most intimate human feelings ('Herzraum', heart-space) become projected outward into music, presenting the listener with an 'audible landscape' that gives objective shape to emotions that would otherwise remain subjective and murky. Emerson suggests that melodies are latent in landscapes:

The sea, the mountain-ridge, Niagara, and every flower-bed, pre-exist, or super-exist, in pre-cantations, which sail like odors in the air. (*Collected Works*, 3: 25)

Rilke's metaphor moves in the opposite direction: when we hear music, we can trace its structures with our ears just as we trace the shapes of a landscape with our eyes.

Given Rilke's inventive use of metaphor in 'To Music', it is odd to find him understanding the 'content', if one can put it that way, of music in conventional terms as the transposition of feelings into another medium. What interests him, however, is the way in which feelings, when translated into music, lose both their subjective moorings and their directionality. Feelings are no longer 'for' another person, nor do they belong to ourselves any more. They have 'grown out of us' in a double sense, emerging from the deepest regions of our psyche, but also transcending or outgrowing us, as a child might outgrow its clothes. The image that follows, of music forcing its way out, is a birth metaphor. When music 'outgrows' us, it comes fully into existence. As musical structures leave human emotions behind, they 'take leave' of us, in a reversal of the summoning vocatives deployed in the earlier part of the poem. Though originating in the human heart, music separates from us and becomes an autonomous art object. This happens precisely in those moments when we have most closely appropriated the music: our 'most practised' passages are those that soar beyond us.

The 'other side of the air' is perhaps the most captivating image in the entire poem. Although we can imagine 'the other side of the mirror', 'the other side of the air' is harder to conceptualise. This is precisely

Rilke's point. The other side of the air is a region so different from the natural world of human life that it cannot even be described in ordinary language. It is 'rein' (pure) because it is not contaminated, so to speak, by the substance and weight of bodies; it is 'riesig' (gigantic) because, unlike the real world, it has no constraining boundaries; but it is also 'nicht mehr bewohnbar' (no longer habitable), because it cannot sustain real bodies or even real breathing. This is the world of the imaginary that Rilke continued to evoke in one form or another throughout his works. It comes into being as a result of a sudden reversal or inversion in which solid objects appear to be transformed or transfigured. The flamingos of Rilke's *New Poems* step into this imaginary space, for example. Malte Laurids Brigge longs for the moment when a kind of atmospheric inversion will occur, turning him, the writer of impressions, into the one who will be 'geschrieben' (written), 'der Eindruck, der sich verwandeln wird' (the impression that will be transformed; 6: 756). In a later poem, 'Gong' (1926), that relies on a similar kind of naming, defining and calling structure to that of 'To Music', Rilke describes the sound of the gong as 'Umkehr der Räume. Entwurf/ innerer Welten im Frein...' (inversion of spaces. Projection/ of innermost worlds into the open air...; 2: 186).

The transference of sound into space takes place on an imaginary level in 'Gong' and 'To Music'. The metaphor has to do with the way in which art translates actuality into something simultaneously more ethereal and more permanent. This exchange is less peculiar than it seems, however. Rilke had actually experienced the transference of sound into space when he witnessed the teacher's demonstration of the home-made phonograph, or, as he called it, 'Sprechmaschine' (speaking machine). There, the transference moved in both directions: first, a boy spoke into a cardboard cone which passed the vibrations of his speech by means of a paper membrane and a primitive 'needle' into grooves on the wax cylinder. Sound became space. Then, when the wax 'record' was played, sound emerged again from the cone. Space became sound. A better example of the 'Umkehr der Räume' (inversion of space) could hardly be devised.

The phonograph provides a brilliant metaphor for the poet as conceived by Emerson and his intellectual relatives, the German Romantics. Unlike the wind harp, the phonograph Rilke saw in his high-school physics class not only produced sound, but also recorded it. Human poetry may never attain the unconscious beauty of birdsong, but it has a greater degree of permanence. The poet, 'finely organized' enough to 'penetrate that region where the air is music', is a highly sophisticated kind of phonograph that can record and transmit the finest nuances of nature's latent music.

Considering Rilke's general aversion to modern technology, it is astonishing to see him make use of the poet-as-phonograph metaphor. Even more astonishing is the fact that he liked to conclude his poetry readings with a rendition of 'Primal Noise'.[11] Evidently, he held the strange little essay in high regard.

How did his audience respond to it? One would love to know. Today's readers certainly find the speculations about 'playing' the cranial grooves on a phonograph thoroughly ghoulish. From the perspective of a world still fascinated by spiritism, however, the idea that the grooves on a skull could be made to 'speak' suggested that the human mind could be given a voice from beyond the grave. In German, the afterlife is commonly called 'das Jenseits' (the other side). Death, memorials and the function of poetry as a mode of remembrance are key themes for Rilke throughout his works.

These considerations throw new light on 'To Music'. Far from a rhapsody over the beauties of music, the poem is in fact another fragment of the vast elegiac project Rilke was engaged in during the war years and their aftermath. All the important figures in 'To Music' are sorrowful: hearts are vanishing away, our innermost space takes leave of us. Time stands still, speech ends, pictures are silent, and if statues breathe, what kind of breathing is that? Music gives feelings shape, but the shapes it forms are so abstract they can hardly be named or identified. The poem itself peters out at the end in vocables whose meaning can scarcely be understood. Music is that which is fundamentally alien, distant from us, uninhabitable.

'To Music' revokes precisely what it is usually thought to invoke: the notion of music as the highest form of poetry. It opens a frightening abyss in the Symbolist concept of silence as the supreme music. It also revokes Emersonian Romanticism by suggesting that, far from giving us access to 'primal warblings' and a chance to record them in writing, 'the region where the air is music' is a realm that cannot be inhabited by living beings. It suggests that the suspension of time that all lyric – especially apostrophic poetry[12] – aims to achieve may, from another perspective, really be a form of death.

THE ARCHITECT'S PARADOX

Rilke's *Sonnets to Orpheus* (1922) reconceive the conflation of music and space that he had already begun to develop in 'To Music'. Although the *Sonnets* are in many ways Rilke's most daring step into the modernist sphere, they in fact take their starting-point in a cluster of consciously classicising subtexts. The most obvious motivation for the *Sonnets* was a reproduction of a fourteenth-century pen drawing by Cima da Conegliano which had been given to Rilke by his friend Balladine Klossowska and which he had hung on the wall opposite his desk at Muzot. The picture, which shows Orpheus charming the animals of the woods with his song, recalled an aspect of classical mythology that had long interested Rilke, from the composition of his poem 'Orpheus. Eurydice. Hermes' (1904) to his fascination with the Orphism of Bachofen in 1913/14.[13] Here is the opening *Sonnet to Orpheus*:

> Da stieg ein Baum. O reine Übersteigung!
> O Orpheus singt! O hoher Baum im Ohr!
> Und alles schwieg. Doch selbst in der Verschweigung
> ging neuer Anfang, Wink und Wandlung vor.
>
> Tiere aus Stille   drangen aus dem klaren
> gelösten Wald   von Lager und Genist;
> und da ergab sich, daß sie nicht aus List
> und nicht aus Angst in sich so leise waren,
>
> sondern aus Hören. Brüllen, Schrei, Geröhr
> schien klein in ihren Herzen. Und wo eben
> kaum eine Hütte war, dies zu empfangen,
>
> ein Unterschlupf aus dunkelstem Verlangen
> mit einem Zugang, dessen Pfosten beben, –
> da schufst du ihnen Tempel im Gehör.   (1: 731)
>
> There rose a tree. O purest of transcending!
> O Orpheus sings! O tall tree in the ear!
> And all was still. And yet, as sound was ending,
> a new beginning, gesture, change appeared.
>
> Creatures of silence   crept forth from the clear
> lightening forest   from their lairs and nests;
> and so it happened that it wasn't fear
> or craftiness that kept all sound suppressed,

but listening. Bellows, howls, and roars
seemed small within their hearts. And where
there barely was a hut to penetrate,

a covert made of dark desire, a door,
an entryway whose very posts vibrate –
you made a temple for them in the ear.

The woodland animals, rapt in Orpheus' song, are taken by Conegliano from the classical tradition. Rilke would not have needed the
drawing to be familiar with this motif. But the single tree that opens the
Sonnets to Orpheus owes its presence more directly to Conegliano, who
depicts Orpheus leaning against a tree-trunk. The classical versions of
the Orpheus story (Rilke knew Ovid's but probably not Virgil's) speak of
trees in the plural, and they speak of them bowing down before the
power of Orpheus' song. Conegliano's tree is static; Rilke's tree is
dynamic, as it emerges dramatically at the beginning of his poem. In
effect, Rilke's sonnet reverses the bowing down of the trees in Ovid's
Metamorphoses. But Ovid and Conegliano do not account for the extraordinary imagery Rilke develops here. A more important ingredient in
the alchemy that precipitated the *Sonnets to Orpheus* is a set of texts by Paul
Valéry.

Wolfgang Leppmann suggests in his biography of Rilke that the *Sonnets
to Orpheus* contain echoes of three texts by Valéry: 'Orphée' [Orpheus],
'Le Cimetière marin' [Graveyard by the Sea] and 'L'âme et la danse'
[The Soul and the Dance].[14] Indeed, Rilke had translated 'Graveyard by
the Sea' the year before the conception of the *Sonnets to Orpheus*, and had
already been preoccupied with 'The Soul and the Dance', of which he
made himself a copy in 1922 and which he was to translate in 1926. But
the relation of Rilke's *Sonnets to Orpheus* to Valéry's sonnet 'Orpheus' is a
more complicated matter. The poem as we know it was not published
until 1926, when Valéry added it to the second edition of his *Album des vers
anciens* [Album of Early Verse].[15] In other words, it was not widely
disseminated until after the emergence of Rilke's *Sonnets*.[16] And yet there
are some striking similarities between Valéry's 'Orpheus' and the first
poem in Rilke's sequence, notably the image, common to both poems, of
a temple erected by the power of Orphic song.

There was, however, another possible source. This was an early prose
version of the poem. Valéry's essay 'Paradoxe sur l'architecte' [Paradox
Concerning the Architect], which had appeared in a well-known and
relatively widely distributed journal,[17] concludes with the first version of

'Orpheus', cunningly hidden in the last two paragraphs of prose. It seems to have been Pierre Louÿs who discovered that this final section of the essay was in fact an almost perfect sonnet; it was certainly Louÿs who encouraged Valéry to let him publish it in verse form.[18] Despite its early date, 'Paradox Concerning the Architect' bears a close relation to 'Eupalinos ou l'architecte' [Eupalinos or the Architect], which Rilke had read on its first appearance in 1921 and began to translate, at the request of the Insel Verlag, in 1922. Thus it is not unlikely that Rilke would have looked back at the earlier essay at this time. In view of a number of ideas and images common to Rilke's first sonnet and Valéry's first essay on the architect, elements not contained in the section that became 'Orpheus', we may surmise that Rilke was familiar with the 1891 essay.

In 'Paradox Concerning the Architect', civilisation is to be saved from decadence by an architect-musician who will restore art to its rightful place. Rilke's sonnet celebrates a similar revalorisation of art. By reconnecting with the nineteenth-century cult of art through Valéry's 1891 essay on the architect, Rilke laid aside the doubts about poetry that had beset him for over ten years. In Valéry's essay and in Rilke's sonnet, silence is the precondition for the triumphal emergence of Orphic song. Rilke liked to identify his own lengthy writing block with Valéry's period of poetic renunciation. Acordingly, in Rilke's sonnet, silence is read both as voluntary restraint from speech and as a way of concealing secrets: not 'Schweigen', but 'Verschweigung'.

Valéry's essay begins by imagining the birth of an architect who will renew the worn-out culture of a dying age by breathing into it the religious spirit of antiquity: 'autrefois, aux siècles orphiques, l'esprit soufflait sur le marbre; les murailles antiques ont vécu comme des hommes, et les architectures perpétuaient les songes' (once, in the Orphic centuries, the spirit breathed upon marble, ancient walls lived like human beings, and works of architecture perpetuated dreams; Valéry, 2: 1402). The architect who is to revive this spirit is one who has the soul of a musician, 'l'âme vibrante et résonnante de l'artiste' (the vibrant and resonant soul of the artist; Valéry, 2: 1403). The temple he erects will seem like an emanatation of music itself, the sounds of violins forming its stained-glass windows, church organs hollowing out its sapphire domes, the notes of flutes rising up as graceful columns. In a passage reminiscent of Huysmans' aestheticist flights of fancy, Valéry describes the decorations of the temple, its hieratic bands, its lotus flowers with pale calyxes and golden aureoles and its precious inlaid gems (2: 1404). The temple will imitate the forms of plant life, with graceful arches curved like stems and columns rising like the trunks of trees. 'Et c'est la forêt du silence...' (and it is the forest of silence...), a forest where one forgets all else and simply listens (Valéry, 2: 1404).

The idea of a temple created by sound transformed into space is central to Rilke's first *Sonnet to Orpheus*. The poem opens with the emergence of a tree, described in the second line as a 'hoher Baum im Ohr' (tall tree in the ear), and concludes with the erection of audible sanctuaries, 'Tempel im Gehör' (temples [the original is plural] in the ear). In accordance with Ovid's *Metamorphoses* and the drawing by Conegliano, it is animals, not human beings, who listen to Rilke's Orpheus. By including the animals Rilke eliminates part of the paradox represented by Valéry's architect, whose temple, shaped by music, is also a forest of silence. Valéry's 'forêt du silence' (forest of silence) becomes Rilke's 'Tiere aus Stille' (creatures [made] of silence), and the temple itself is the spatial embodiment of sound.

The last two paragraphs of Valéry's 'Paradox Concerning the Architect', those which comprise the original version of the sonnet 'Orpheus', describe the entrance of a visitor to the sanctuary who falls into a reverie as he observes its splendours:

Il évoque, en un bois thessalien, Orphée, sous les myrtes; et le soir antique descend. Le bois sacré s'emplit lentement de lumière, et le dieu tient la lyre entre ses doigts d'argent. Le dieu chante, et, selon le rythme tout-puissant, s'élèvent au soleil les fabuleuses pierres, et l'on voit grandir vers l'azur incandescent, les murs d'or harmonieux d'un sanctuaire.

Il chante! assis au bord du ciel splendide, Orphée! Son oeuvre se revêt d'un vespéral trophée, et sa lyre divine enchante les porphyres, car le temple érigé par ce *musicien* unit la sûreté des rythmes anciens, à l'âme immense du grand hymne sur la lyre!... (Valéry's italics and ellipses; Valéry, 2: 1405)

He evokes, in a Thessalian wood, Orpheus, beneath the myrtles; and evening falls. The sacred wood fills slowly with light, and the god holds the lyre between his silver fingers. The god sings, and, in accord with the all-powerful rhythm, fabulous stones rise up toward the sun, and one sees, growing toward the incandescent azure sky, the harmonious golden walls of a sanctuary.

He sings! seated at the edge of a splendid sky, Orpheus! His work is decked with a vesperal trophy, and his divine lyre casts a spell over the porphyry stones, for the temple erected by this *musician* combines the confidence of ancient rhythms with the expansive soul of the great hymn on the lyre! ...

The temple, whose erection had been projected by the narrator into the future, is now linked by the fantasy of its (imaginary) visitor with a mythic past.

In the first *Sonnet to Orpheus* Rilke adapts the paradox by which sound becomes space, but eliminates that by which future becomes past. Nonetheless, although Rilke's sonnet is cast in the past tense, it switches dramatically into the present at the moment when Orpheus sings. The ecstatic tone with its multiple exclamation marks, implying the presence of a wondering observer, forms another link between Rilke's sonnet and Valéry's Orphic reverie. And the dominant motif cluster – Orphic song, the luminous wood and the emerging temple – is common to both texts.

Valéry's 'Paradox Concerning the Architect' is essentially a Symbolist text. By contrast, his two long dialogues of March and December 1921, 'Eupalinos or the Architect' and 'The Soul and the Dance', attempt to recreate something of the classical spirit for modern times. A combination of Symbolist and classicising moments is characteristic of Rilke's *Sonnets to Orpheus*. Yet Rilke converts these ingredients into a sonnet sequence decisively modernist in character.

The poetic credo of the *Sonnets* urges the value of remaining close to direct experience (the taste of fruit, the sight of stars, the call of a bird) and early forms of human creative activity (an ancient sarcophagus, the temple in Karnak or the Roman aqueducts). Nonetheless, the poems are set at one remove from Orphic experience, since they presuppose that Orpheus has already gone before. The modern poet is a successor, not an originator.

Yet the opening sonnet also claims that Orphic song brings 'neuer Anfang, Wink und Wandlung' (new beginning, gesture and change). This effect applies not only to Orpheus' song in the past, but also to every recreation of it in the present. The three terms, 'new beginning', 'gesture', and 'change' (literally, transformation), easy to neglect under the pressure of the more powerful images that surround them, require closer examination.

In view of Rilke's long-standing concerns about origins and originality, the formulation 'new beginning' is important. It suggests, first of all, that Orpheus' song is not merely a lament for something lost, but also the creation of something new. A poet who treads in the footsteps of Orpheus is engaged in a project of revival and renewal. Toward the end of the *Sonnets to Orpheus*, Rilke once more invokes the idea of renewal in a passage about the human urge to start over again, seeing it as an act of building: 'O diese Lust, immer neu, aus gelockertem Lehm!' (O this desire, always new, from loosened clay! 1: 767).

The second term, 'gesture', had special significance for Rilke. The word he uses, 'Wink', means not only 'gesture', but 'wave of the hand', 'hint', or 'sign'. Sometimes Rilke uses the term in connection with the seductive nature of the wordly, in which all things tempt us to emotional response (2: 92). This response, however, is also a function of past experience, since present objects inevitably summon up personal memories and associations. Every turn in the road ahead is at once an enticement to the unseen landscape beyond and a reminder to look backward and remember. By the same token, Orpheus' song is an invitation to participate in both the loss it memorialises and the new tradition it initiates. As he entices the forest animals from their hiding-places, he also summons the reader to listen with them. To what is the reader listening? Not just to the present poem, but also to the whole tradition of Orphic poetry that underlies it. In this way, the word 'gesture' becomes a kind of code for the allusiveness of poetry.

'Change' or 'transformation', the third term in the series, refers to the metamorphosis undergone first by Orpheus' sorrow as it is turned into song. It also refers to Orpheus himself, whose singing head is transformed into the voice of nature itself after his dismemberment by the Maenads. In the *Sonnets*, Rilke claims that any poetry ('Gesang', song) is in effect the voice of Orpheus using the modern poet as a mouthpiece. The disembodied head is transformed into the voice of a successor poet. Within the imagery of the poem, the transformational act affects the forest, the animals, and the shelter created by the song of Orpheus. The forest is illuminated and dissolved, the animals are tamed and silenced, and the make-shift hut with its precarious doorposts becomes a metaphorical temple. In the sonnets that follow, Orpheus will be presented as the god of the turning-point, the cross-roads, the place where life and death meet.

In accord with this notion, Rilke returns in the first lines of his sonnet to an earlier poem of his own. The poem is 'Eingang', meaning both 'entrance' and 'beginning', the opening poem of *Das Buch der Bilder* [The Book of Images]. Composed in Berlin in 1900 at the height of Rilke's fascination with the 'art for art's sake' movement, it depicts three phases in the creative act as Rilke saw it at the time: initially, the monad-like subject is restricted to a single familiar room; then, stepping out of the house, the subject creates a world by willing it into existence; and finally, this world asserts its independence of the subjectivity that has projected it. The poem centres on the image of a black tree erected by the poet's creative perception. Rising against the sky, 'schlank, allein' (slender, alone), the dark tree represents the world as a whole (1: 371). A much later poem, 'Klage' [Lament] (1914), likens the failure of creative power to the destruction of a tree by storm (2: 84).

The very last sonnet to Orpheus Rilke wrote, at the end of February 1922, returns to the motif of the tree and links it with the motif of inspiring breath. Air is here conceived as the stuff of poetry itself: 'Atmen, du unsichtbares Gedicht!' (Breathe, you invisible poem! 1: 751). When he put the Orpheus sequence together, he placed this poem at the beginning of the second section, thus implicitly pairing it with the opening poem of the first section. This pairing emphasises the notion of poetry as a sacred force that Rilke had adopted from the Orphic tradition and more immediately from Valéry's early essay.

To make the link between Valéry's 'Paradox Concerning the Architect' and Rilke's rewriting of the Orpheus story is to understand something of the peculiar way in which modernism reappropriates the classics. Unlike some other modernist writers, Rilke does not explicitly reflect on the issue of literary reminiscence. Rilke's modernism is of another kind. It is a modernism whose synthetic origins dissolve in the distinctive voice he has created for himself.

DEAD POETS' COUNTRY

In *Die Zehnte Elegie* [The Tenth Elegy] (1: 721–726), completed several days after the first *Sonnet to Orpheus*, Rilke reworks the imagery of metamorphosis that he had developed while thinking about Orphic transcendence. Now, however, the transformation of nature is linked with a descent into the realm of the dead rather than a re-emergence into the world of the living. And the reflection on the relation between modernity and tradition is focussed on ancient Egypt rather than classical antiquity. Conceiving a landscape that, like Orpheus' aural architecture, eludes the descriptive capacity of ordinary language, Rilke seems increasingly aware of the almost outlandish character of his return to a belief in the power of poetic figuration.

With the unexpected composition of twenty-four of his *Sonnets to Orpheus* in the early days of February, 1992, a new beginning really seemed to have come about. Taking advantage of this sudden rush of words and images, Rilke took up his *Duino Elegies* again. Several whole elegies (the seventh and eighth), substantial parts of others (the ninth and tenth), and an addition to another (the sixth) emerged during this period of exceptional fecundity. Rilke rewrote *The Tenth Elegy*, originally begun in 1912, from its sixteenth line on. The new version includes a new theme: recollections from Rilke's trip to Egypt in late 1910 and early 1911. Although Rilke's trip had taken place a scant year before he began the *Duino Elegies*, there is no Egyptian imagery in the early part of the cycle.

Rilke's introduction of Egyptian motifs into the *Elegies* appears to have involved a re-evaluation of his experiences of 1910–12. Rilke's psychological state had been very poor when he embarked on the trip; he had fallen ill in the course of the journey and had to part with his travelling companions for a month; and although he had rejoined them later, he thought of the expedition with deep misgivings for many years. What little we know of his mental state between December 1910 and March 1911 is derived from his correspondence;[19] but we also have the testimony of his mother, whose letters to a friend during this period testify to her anxiety about what she terms his 'neurasthenia'.[20] Recollections of his trip to Egypt had begun to emerge again in late 1920 and the spring of 1921 in a rather peculiar sequence of poems *Aus dem Nachlaß des Grafen C.W.* [From the Posthumous Papers of Count C.W.] (2: 112–129), which Rilke felt had come to him by 'Diktat' (dictation). Revisiting Egypt in memory seems to have involved precisely the kind of self-cure that Rilke had long anticipated from his writing.

In Cairo, Rilke had spent some time reading the Egyptian *Book of the Dead*, a collection of texts intended as guides to the newly dead about how to conduct themselves on their journey beyond the tomb. *The Book of the Dead* was a title given in the nineteenth century to a collection of texts inscribed on cloth or papyrus and placed near the embalmed body of a dead person in Egyptian tombs or sarcophagi. The Egyptians believed that the dead person followed the sun-god Râ on his daytime journey across the sky and his night-time journey through the underworld. Once in the world beyond the grave, the deceased had to perform certain tasks and chant certain hymns in honour of various divinities. The god Osiris was of particular importance in this process, since he himself had died and been resuscitated. The dead person had to present himself before Osiris, in whose presence his heart, the seat of his consciousness, was weighed by forty-two judges. If the balance pans were even, the deceased was acquitted and released into the paradise-like 'field of reeds'. Some texts from *The Book of the Dead* describe landscapes from the realm beyond the grave, vast expanses of water to be traversed in a boat and fields in which the dead person was required to labour, sowing and reaping, moving sand, or digging canals. If one knew the right formulas, one could survive without being bitten by serpents or eaten by crocodiles, and ultimately emerge unscathed on the other side.

The trip through the realm of the dead is recreated in *The Tenth Elegy* in the form of a journey undertaken by a newly-dead youth guided by a female figure from a mythic race that the poem calls 'Laments':

Und sie leitet ihn leicht durch die weite Landschaft
der Klagen,
zeigt ihm die Säulen der Tempel oder die Trümmer
jener Burgen, von wo Klage-Fürsten das Land
einstens weise beherrscht. Zeigt ihm die hohen
Tränenbäume und Felder blühender Wehmut,
(Lebendige kennen sie nur als sanftes Blattwerk);
zeigt ihm die Tiere der Trauer, weidend, – und manchmal
schreckt ein Vogel und zieht, flach ihnen fliegend
durchs Aufschaun,
weithin das schriftliche Bild seines vereinsamten Schreis. –
Abends führt sie ihn hin zu den Gräbern der Alten
aus dem Klage-Geschlecht, den Sibyllen und Warn-Herrn.
Naht aber Nacht, so wandeln sie leiser, und bald
mondets empor, das über Alles
wachende Grab-Mal. Brüderlich jenem am Nil,
der erhabene Sphinx –: der verschwiegenen Kammer
Antlitz.
Und sie staunen dem krönlichen Haupt, das für immer,
schweigend, der Menschen Gesicht
auf die Waage der Sterne gelegt.

Nicht erfaßt es sein Blick, im Frühtod
schwindelnd. Aber ihr Schaun,
hinter dem Pschent-Rand hervor, scheucht es die
Eule. Und sie,
streifend im langsamen Abstrich die Wange entlang,
jene der reifesten Rundung,
zeichnet weich in das neue
Totengehör, über ein doppelt
aufgeschlagenes Blatt, den unbeschreiblichen Umriß.
(1: 724–725)

And gently she leads him through the Laments' vast
landscape,
shows him columns of temples or ruins
of fortresses where Lament-princes once
wisely ruled the land. Shows him the high   .
tear trees and fields of blossoming melancholy,
(the living know it only as softest leafage);
shows him the beasts of mourning, grazing, – and sometimes

a bird startles and, flying athwart their upturned gaze,
traces afar the written sign of its lonely cry. –
In the evenings she takes the youth to the graves of the
                                    elders
from the race of Laments, the sybils and prophets.
When night draws close, though, they walk more slowly,
                                   and soon
it rises up moon-like, the funeral monument watching
over all things. A brother to that on the Nile,
the noble sphinx –: the visage of
secret chambers.
And they are amazed by the kingly head that forever,
silently, lays the face of men
on the balance-pan of the stars.

His gaze does not grasp it, dizzy with
early death. But their gaze,
from behind the edge of the crown, frightens away the owl.
                                  And it,
brushing with slow-drawn stroke along his cheek,
that ripest contour,
traces softly in the new
death-hearing, over a double
unfolded page, the indescribable outline.

After conducting the youth through this quasi-Egyptian landscape, the Lament leaves him to pursue the final part of his journey by himself.

Late nineteenth-century and early twentieth-century studies of comparative religion tended to emphasise the similarity between the Egyptian *Book of the Dead* and the Orphic mysteries. Both Osiris and Orpheus are torn into pieces and subsequently brought back to life. Both the Egyptian cult of the dead and the Orphic cult aim to release the dead soul from an otherwise eternal round of metamorphoses, purifying it and allowing it to rest in peace without having to run another earthly course in a different body. We know that Rilke became familiar with the Orphic mysteries just a few years after his first acquaintance with the Egyptian *Book of the Dead*, mainly through attending lectures by Alfred Schuler, a pupil of Johann Jakob Bachofen. He had also read Mechthilde Lichnowsky's book on Egypt, *Götter, Könige und Tiere in Ägypten* [Gods, Kings, and Animals in Egypt].[21] Edouard Schuré, whose book *Les grands initiés* [The Great Initiates] (1889), had gone through ninety editions by the time of Rilke's final phase of work on the *Duino Elegies*, presents the mystic beliefs of eight religious movements, including

Orphism and the Egyptian death cult, in an attempt to show their underlying similarities.[22] Salomon Reinach, another popular author of the period, also develops the common features of Orphism and the Egyptian death cult in his widely-read *Orphée. Histoire Générale des Religions* [Orpheus. General History of Religions] (1909), in which he observes that there is 'an evident analogy between [the] tablets [found in Crete and southern Italy near the skeletons of Orphic initiates], guides to the dead on their voyage beyond the tomb, and the verbose Egyptian *Book of the Dead*'.[23] These turn-of-the-century exercises in comparative mythology need to be understood against the backdrop, on the one hand, of contemporary interest in spiritism, and, on the other hand, of the new archaeological discoveries in the ancient world, especially Egypt, that were being made throughout the last decades of the nineteenth century and into the twentieth century.

In *The Tenth Elegy*, Rilke invents a realm of the dead that reflects the Egypt he had visited in 1910–1911. Temples, ruins and a sphinx-like monument appear in a landscape whose vast night sky seems marked as if with a hieroglyphic inscription by an owl's cry. The sphinx, 'der verschwiegenen Kammer Antlitz' (the face of a secret chamber), rises up out of the desert like the moon. Its head is identified with that of Osiris, who weighs the hearts of the newly dead on a balance-pan. God of the night-time sun, Osiris is further suggested by the great funerary monument dominating the landscape as if it were the rising moon.[24]

Both the Egyptian cult of the dead and the Orphic mysteries have a relation to the stellar world: Râ and Osiris are sun and moon gods respectively, and the cult of Orpheus promised its adepts resurrection in the form of a constellation. *The Tenth Elegy* invents an entire list of new constellations, and one of *The Sonnets to Orpheus* (1: 737–738) is devoted to the first of these, the rider. The voyage recounted in *The Tenth Elegy* is a conflation of the Egyptian voyage beyond the tomb and Orpheus' descent into the underworld. And as if in recognition of the secret identity between the Osiris and Orpheus cults, the young traveller in *The Tenth Elegy* is brought to a fountain whose waters shimmer in the moonlight, recalling the rejuvenating spring from which the Orphic adept drinks in order to purify himself and thus escape the eternal round of metamorphoses.[25] The beginning of *The Tenth Elegy*, finally, recalls both the Egyptian and the Orphic passage through the underworld, as the speaker imagines how he will feel when (or if) he finally emerges:[26]

Daß ich dereinst, an dem Ausgang der grimmigen Einsicht,
Jubel und Ruhm aufsinge zustimmenden Engeln.
Daß von den klar geschlagenen Hämmern des Herzens
keiner versage an weichen, zweifelnden oder
reißenden Saiten. Daß mich mein strömendes Antlitz
glänzender mache; daß das unscheinbare Weinen
blühe. O wie werdet ihr dann, Nächte, mir lieb sein,
gehärmte. Daß ich euch knieender nicht, untröstliche
                                        Schwestern,
hinnahm, nicht in euer gelöstes
Haar mich gelöster ergab. Wir, Vergeuder der Schmerzen.

(1: 721)

That I might once, at terrible insight's exit,
sing joy and praise to consonant angels.
That none of my heart's clearly struck hammers
might fail on soft, hesitant, or
tearing strings. That my streaming face might make me more
radiant; that my obscure weeping might
blossom. Oh how dear you will be to me then, nights,
injured ones. That I did not accept you, inconsolable
                                        sisters,
more kneelingly, did not give myself up
in your dissolved hair. We, wasters of pain.

Appropriately transposing his instrument from the ancient lyre to the modern pianoforte, the speaker of these opening lines prays that his song will not be rendered useless by 'soft, hesitant, or tearing strings' as they are struck by the 'hammers' of his heart.[27]

Alongside its reworking of ancient mysteries, *The Tenth Elegy* also engages with literary tradition. Like the ruins in the landscape through which the young man passes, remnants of other texts emerge in the strange terrain of Rilke's elegy. Two important predecessors are alluded to in one of the poem's most puzzling passages: Dante and Goethe. The 'new stars' of this land of sorrow recall the stars of the southern hemisphere seen by Dante and Virgil as they emerge from their journey through the centre of the earth at the end of the *Inferno*. In Dante, the new stars incorporate a religious vision: one of the constellations, for example, takes the shape of a cross. Some of the new constellations in *The Tenth Elegy* – 'Puppe' (puppet or doll) and 'Fenster' (window), for example – belong to a peculiarly Rilkean cosmos; there is also the constellation 'Reiter' (rider) which is to recur in *The Sonnets to Orpheus*; but others resist interpretation in the terms of Rilke's imaginative universe, as if to insist on their fundamental strangeness:

Und höher, die Sterne. Neue. Die Sterne des Leidlands.
Langsam nennt sie die Klage: – Hier,
siehe: den *Reiter*, den *Stab*, und das vollere Sternbild
nennen sie: *Fruchtkranz*. Dann, weiter, dem Pol zu:
Wiege; Weg; Das Brennende Buch; Puppe; Fenster.
Aber im südlichen Himmel, rein wie im Innern
einer gesegneten Hand, das klar erglänzende '*M*',
das die Mütter bedeutet . . . –   (1: 725)

And higher up, the stars. New ones. Stars of suffering land.
The Lament slowly says their names: – here,
look: the *Rider*, the *Staff*, and that fuller constellation
is called: *Wreath of Fruits*. Then further, toward the pole,
Cradle; Pathway; Burning Book; Puppet; Window.
But in the southern sky, pure as in the palm
of a hand that's been blessed, the clear shining '*M*'
that signifies Mothers . . . –

Whatever the group as a whole may mean, the last in the list, 'that clear shining '*M*',/ that signifies Mothers...' is an obvious allusion to Goethe's Faust and his descent through a cleft which opens up in the ground with the help of Mephisto's magic arts to visit the strange, norn-like figures called the Mothers. Like Orpheus' journey into the underworld, Dante's and Faust's journeys are descents into lower regions; all three are led back out by a guide, be it Hermes, Virgil or Mephisto; and all three are in mourning for the loss of a beloved woman, Eurydice, Beatrice, and Gretchen/Helena.

The shining 'M' gives an important clue about the relation of the land of the Laments to the world with which we are familiar. We can imagine it as a reversal of the easily recognised constellation Casseopeia, which has the shape of a 'W'. Reversal, a phenomenon dear to Rilke, is one of the principles at work in the imaginary landscape Rilke has created here. The 'M' is also compared with the lines on the palm of a hand. Reading signs in the sky and signs in the hand (as in palm-reading) are linked in this metaphor.

Conflation is another principle: not merely the conflation of literary models we have already observed, but also a conflation of different sensory impressions and different cultural epochs. What grows in the land of the Laments is a projection of human emotions into vegetable and animal form: 'Tränenbäume' (tear trees), 'Felder blühender Wehmut' (fields of blossoming melancholy), 'Tiere der Trauer' (beasts of mourning; 1: 724). This strangely abstract vegetation – it reminds one of Paul Klee's 'Trauerblumen' [Flowers of Sorrow] (1917)[28] – contrasts implicitly with the plants mentioned at the beginning and end of *The Tenth Elegy*, the periwinkle and the hazel, which not only bear metaphoric significance, but also have a real existence in the familiar world.[29] As the youth proceeds through the countryside, he gradually learns to use his senses of sight and hearing differently, in accordance with the different physical laws in the land of the dead. His new mode of perception is synaesthesia, a concept Rilke adopts from the French Symbolists. Thus the youth 'hears' the cry of the owl as if it were a hieroglyph traced into his ear, a sound transformed into a visible shape. Even a casual glance at a hieroglyphic text shows many bird images, the most important being that of the human-headed bird 'ba' that the Egyptians figured as the soul or 'spiritual manifestation' of a dead person. As with the transposition of the poet's song from lyre to pianoforte, here too the medium has been modernised: the mark made by the owl's cry appears not on papyrus, as would befit the ancient Egyptian setting, but on the 'double unfolded page', the book in its modern form. Rilke was probably thinking here of Mallarmé's concept of the book as quintessentially a folded sheet of paper. Playing on the double meaning of the word 'Blatt' (page and leaf), the speaker comments that the 'Felder blühender Wehmut' (fields of blossoming melancholy) are known to the living 'nur als sanftes Blattwerk' (only as delicate leafage). By the same token, the bird's cry appears as a 'schriftliches Bild' (written sign) in the night sky.

The realm of Laments is a written world, a world that exists only by virtue of the existence of previous textual worlds. The royal figure who eternally weighs the newly dead is silent, like a picture on a papyrus scroll; similarly, the youth's footsteps give off no echo as he climbs the mountains of sorrow at the end of his journey. This silent landscape is capable of being read like a book. The idea of nature as a book has a long history. Rilke would have known it primarily through its development by the German Romantics, who liked to think of poets as prophets gifted with the ability to read the otherwise undecipherable hieroglyphs of the natural world.

More than the other *Duino Elegies*, the *Tenth* is an elegy about elegy itself. Not only is the youth's guide a 'Klage' (Lament), but the landscape is constituted almost entirely by different forms of sorrow, suffering, mourning and commemoration of the dead. In a quite remarkable way, the elegy still bears traces of its original conception in 1912/13, when Rilke was immersed in German classical literature. Three elegies from the grand tradition, by Schiller, Goethe and Hölderlin, serve as Rilke's models for his reflection on the elegiac mode: Schiller's poem 'Der Spaziergang' [The Walk] (1795/96), Goethe's 'Euphrosyne' (1799) and Hölderlin's 'Brot und Wein' [Bread and Wine] (1801). From Schiller's elegy, Rilke's *Tenth Elegy* picks up the central image of a symbolic walk through a landscape that motivates the poet to explore his relationship to ancient civilisations and past poetic traditions.[30] From Goethe's 'Euphrosyne', Rilke's poem adopts the the motif of the early dead, those snatched from life while still young; it also reworks Goethe's reflections in 'Euphrosyne' on problems of representation.[31] Hölderlin's 'Bread and Wine', finally, provides a model for the opening description of the busy city, the transition to open countryside, and the idea of landscape as a repository and embodiment of the divine. The implicit presence of these great German elegies enables *The Tenth Elegy* to reflect on the tradition of elegy itself and on the way it leads out of sorrow into spiritual peace.

At the same time, *The Tenth Elegy* contains a more contemporary note: the long description of an amusement fair at the edge of a big city (1: 722). With its shallow theatrical effects, its shrill music, its deceptive posters and its excessive emphasis on monetary gain, the fair is an expression of modern life in all its vulgarity and emptiness. At the same time, however, the fair is frankly a façade. To perceive it as such is to begin to penetrate the veil of appearances: 'gleich im Rücken der Planke, gleich dahinter, ists *wirklich*' (just at the back of the boards, just behind them, that's *real*). The youth must experience the fun fair with all its distracting mummery before he can embark on his journey of initiation through the realm of the dead.

The poem juxtaposes three essentially different motivic clusters – memories of past sorrow, a vision of modern life and a trip through the realm of the dead – without making more than a perfunctory attempt to link them coherently. Throughout the elegy, its allegoric nature is frankly displayed, and at its conclusion, a kind of moral expressed through metaphor is awkwardly appended.

We do not see the end of the youth's journey. Does he find his way to some equivalent of the ancient Egyptian 'field of reeds'? The poem's final section, with its imagined message from the dead about the nature of fortune or happiness, suggests that death is a way of totally re-conceiving positive experiences. This reconception is only indirectly accessible to those who have been left behind in the land of the living. Accordingly, the narrative peters out, disappearing, as it were, in the crevice between two kinds of understanding. Why does the action break off at this point?

Underlying the great German elegies of around 1800 was an attempt to conflate classical antiquity with modern times. The consolation for having been born into a later age was the recognition that 'die Sonne Homers, [...] sie lächelt auch uns' (Homer's sun [...] smiles for us, too).[32] Rilke substitutes ancient Egypt for the canonical poets' ancient Greece. Egyptian culture, however, puts up more formidable barriers to access. Reading Egyptian documents is as remote from us as identifying the stars of an unfamiliar sky. Its form of writing, hieroglyphs, is even more mysterious than the art of palm-reading, alluded to in the passage about the shining 'M'.

Hieroglyphs take a special place in Rilke's pseudo-Egyptian landscape. Unlike the Greek and Roman alphabets, which consist in representations of sounds, Egyptian hieroglyphs represent visual images. This makes them an appropriate sign system for the country Rilke is describing: a country where familiar modes of cognition are reversed. In the land of the Laments, sound is absent, or at least virtually absent. The young man has to relearn the art of hearing, and although the guiding Lament communicates with him in language, the landscape all around is silent. Even the footfall of the youth as he makes his final climb up the mountains cannot be heard. The cry of the startled bird becomes a 'written sign' against the sky, and later the flight of the owl, though somehow 'heard' by the newly dead youth, seems to be heard by means of its visible trace. This process, seemingly so mystifying, is in fact what we do every time we read silently. This explains why the 'krönliches Haupt' (kingly head) weighs the dead in the balance 'für immer, schweigend' (forever, silently): we are looking at a papyrus that represents this event. Literature is always 'forever' present, and works that use pictorial methods of representation are more remote from sound than those that use phonetic methods[33] and hence, as it were, more 'silent'.

Once we begin to see the narrative of *The Tenth Elegy* as not only the story of a newly deceased person's voyage through the realm of the dead, but also the 'voyage' of a modern reader perusing an ancient text, we can follow more surely its exploration of representation. The sphinx in the elegy is a 'brüderlich jenem am Nil' (brother to that on the Nile) because it is a representation of it, not the sphinx itself. The other elements of the landscape, trees, flowers, birds, and animals, are the principal elements in which hieroglyphs take their origin. In the *Book of the Dead*, the pictures representing the various stages of the dead person's voyage through the underworld are surrounded by hieroglyphic texts that repeatedly include stylised images of birds, plants and so forth. In Rilke's *Tenth Elegy*, the dead youth's hearing, still accommodating itself to the unfamiliar realm of the dead, apprehends a sort of pictogram of the owl's cry on a 'doppelt aufgeschlagenes Blatt' (doubly opened page). The imaginary landscape of Rilke's elegy is suspended somewhere between two kinds of representation: the visual, hieroglyphic language of an Egyptian papyrus and the phonetic language of a modern book. The language of the new stars is similar, combining pictorial images (the 'fuller' constellation of the 'wreath of fruits') with phonetic representation (the initial 'M' of the word 'Mothers'). The new constellations reveal, furthermore, that what can be named cannot always be interpreted. Unlike the cosmology of the ancient Greeks and Romans, the constellations of Lament country do not fit together into a system accessible to the reader. Sign and signified fall radically apart.

Rilke's move into abstraction is as much a return to the theoretical problems of his early years as it is a progression into modernism. *The Tenth Elegy* reinterprets a personal, psychological crisis (his trip to Egypt in 1911) as a crisis of representation. In so doing, it reverts, in effect, to what Hofmannsthal's fictive Lord Chandos had called 'die stumme Sprache der Dinge' (the silent language of things).[34] But it does so by recalling an ancient, hieratic language that, because of its primarily visual nature, seems to the modern mind to embody silence itself. At the same time, the elegy justifies its own procedure by giving preference to the language of images over the language of reason. But, unlike the decorative images of Rilke's early poetry, the images of *The Tenth Elegy* are stark, abbreviated and cryptic, like hieroglyphs themselves.

Hand in hand with the poem's resistance to meaning, however, goes an almost clumsy attempt to supply meaning. Walter Benjamin's declaration of allegory's modernist status seems less compelling when we think of this elegy's coded topography. The Valley of Laments, the rocky piece of Primal Suffering, the fields of Blossoming Melancholy, the Spring of Joy: all of these might have come straight out of *Pilgrim's Progress*. Despite superficial similarities, they are quite different from the 'creatures of silence' in the first *Sonnet to Orpheus*, which may be abstractions but are certainly not allegories.

The Tenth Elegy is located in the borderland between poetic convention and modernist innovation. In its final ambiguity, it resists deciding whether one can ever return from dead poets' country. Communication between the dead and the living takes place in the form of images, but these, it seems to say, can only ever be approximate. The last lines of the

elegy, cast in simple and almost prosaic language, are remote from the
hieratic texts evoked in the body of the poem:

> Aber erweckten sie uns, die unendlich Toten, ein Gleichnis,
> siehe, sie zeigten vielleicht auf die Kätzchen der leeren
> Hasel, die hängenden, oder
> meinten den Regen, der fällt auf dunkles Erdreich im
> Frühjahr. –
>
> Und wir, die an *steigendes* Glück
> denken, empfänden die Rührung,
> die uns beinah bestürzt,
> wenn ein Glückliches *fällt*.   (1: 726)
>
> But if they, the eternally dead, enlivened an image for us,
> look, they would point perhaps to the catkins of empty
> hazel, hanging, or
> mention the rain that falls on the sombre kingdom of earth
>   in springtime. –
>
> And we, who think of fortune *rising*,
> would feel that touching emotion
> that almost overwhelms us when
> something fortunate *falls*.

It is hard to know quite what to make of this anticlimactic conclusion.
One thing is clear, however: this part is merely hypothetical (in German,
it is couched in the subjunctive). Here in the ordinary world it is
impossible fully to imagine the radically different realm of the dead. The
magic moment of understanding that reaches beyond human language
and thought has not yet arrived: it is postulated, not actualised.

SIBLING ARTS

Written immediately after the tenth, *Die Fünfte Elegie* [The Fifth Elegy]
(1: 701–705) also postulates achievement rather than actualising it; indeed, its conclusion consists in a more extended set of hypotheses than
that of its predecessor. *The Fifth Elegy* has commonly been seen as a
vision of 'constant deterioration and fragmentation', characterised by a
'mood of negativity and despair'.[35] Certainly it paints a bleak picture of
the street acrobats it apostrophises and, by extension, of human life,
which, the elegy says, is only a little less 'flüchtig' (fleeting) than these
most transitory of all performers. Yet, like the tumblers themselves, the

poem models not only a downswing but also an upward one. Properly seen, the elegy enacts a complicated series of reversals, represented not only by the acrobatic figures of the street performers at the beginning, but also by the 'endlos' (endlessly) looping bows and ribbons of the hatmaker in the penultimate section. Almost everything in this poem is in motion, opening out and turning in upon itself, rising and falling, winding through multiple convolutions, alternating between surface and depth. The language is strange, abstract, manipulative; it is at once transparent and opaque, appealing and repellent, passionate and prosy. To follow this loop-the-loop act with one's mind's eye requires a special kind of mental gymnastics:

> Wer aber *sind* sie, sag mir, die Fahrenden, diese ein wenig
> Flüchtigern noch als wir selbst, die dringend von früh an
> wringt ein *wem, wem* zu Liebe
> niemals zufriedener Wille? Sondern er wringt sie,
> biegt sie, schlingt sie und schwingt sie,
> wirft sie und fängt sie zurück; wie aus geölter,
> glatterer Luft kommen sie nieder
> auf dem verzehrten, von ihrem ewigen
> Aufsprung dünneren Teppich, diesem verlorenen
> Teppich im Weltall. (1: 701)

> Who *are* they, though, tell me, the travelling ones, these just a little
> more
> fleeting than we ourselves, urgently, early, wrung
> by a will for *whose* sake, *whose?*
> never satisfied? Still, though, it wrings them,
> bends them, twirls them and hurls them,
> throws them and catches again; as if from greasily
> smoother air they come back down
> to the worn and thinner carpet (from their eternal
> landing), that forlorn
> carpet in the cosmos.

One of the strangest metaphors in the poem is the comparison of the acrobats' mat with sticking plaster on a wound:

> Aufgelegt wie ein Pflaster, als hätte der Vorstadt-
> Himmel der Erde dort wehe getan. (1: 701)

> Laid on like a bandage, as if the suburban
> heaven had hurt the earth there.

Rilke's most painstaking exegete, Jacob Steiner, comments that the passage contains 'reminiscences of [Rilke's] anthropomorphising, sentimental early work'.[36] Yet the image is, in fact, part of the elegy's complex system of reversals. The passage contains reminiscences of German Romanticism: in this case, of Eichendorff's poem 'Mondnacht' [Moonlit Night], which opens with a similar 'as if' construction: 'Es war, als ob der Himmel die Erde sanft geküßt' (It was as if heaven had quietly kissed the earth). Almost from the outset, then, Rilke reverses canonical poetic models in this elegy. For, like Eichendorff's lyric, this elegy, too, is a poem about love. Where Eichendorff's song, however, rises effortlessly on the wings of a still-positable unity between the human soul and its natural context, Rilke's elegy takes a more painful and laborious route toward transcendence. Union is seen as a mere moment of precarious bliss in *The Fifth Elegy*, and the world of nature is present only indirectly, in the form of metaphor.

At first, Rilke regarded *The Fifth Elegy* as an afterthought to the *Tenth*; then he decided to substitute it for an elegy on the relation of women to men that had originally taken fifth place in the sequence.[37] In many ways, the (new) *Fifth Elegy* is a continuation of the fun fair scene with which *The Tenth Elegy* opens. The visitor to the fair is bedazzled, seduced, and confused by its multiple sights and sounds, its glossy surface, its emphasis on spurious pleasures. The speaker imagines a place where true achievement can take place, where the performers' smiles are no longer just part of their act but a sign of true artistic and erotic consummation. Like *The Tenth Elegy*, *The Fifth Elegy* hinges upon a contrast between genuine and fake, real and illusory, the profoundly experienced and the merely performed. It also harks back to *The Second Elegy* and its image of lovers whose embrace seems to promise eternal existence, however much we and they know that this can never actually be achieved. And like *The Second Elegy*, the *Fifth* concludes with a passage in the optative, the wish for a place where such things could be so.

If we may see it for a moment in terms of biography, *The Fifth Elegy* looks back at one of the worst phases in Rilke's long period of depression and inability to complete the *Duino Elegies*, the time around 1915 when his initial enthusiasm over the outbreak of World War I had been dispelled, he expected to be conscripted for military service in Austria, and found himself increasingly unable to summon up his poetic talent. In this moment of suspension, he spent some time in the apartment of his friend Hertha Koenig. Hertha Koenig had acquired, at Rilke's suggestion, Picasso's large painting, *La Famille des Saltimbanques* [The Family of Acrobats] (1905), and Rilke was able to study it on a daily basis. He spent four months in her apartment, absorbing the details of

Picasso's picture, seeing friends, going to lectures and the theatre, but not writing much poetry.

Recollections from this period blend in *The Fifth Elegy* with earlier memories of street acrobats in Paris. In a two-and-a-half-page prose text written on July 14, 1907, Rilke had described a group of performers he had been following for over two years (6: 1137–1139). The focus of the prose piece is on an elderly weight-lifter who, unable to do gymnastics any longer, has been given the task of beating the drum. The shrunken figure of the former strong man, the carpet spread out on the pavement, the touching performance of the littlest acrobat, are among the elements from the prose text *Saltimbanques* [Acrobats] that Rilke carries over into *The Fifth Elegy*:

> Da: der welke, faltige Stemmer,
> der alte, der nur noch trommelt,
> eingegangen in seiner gewaltigen Haut, als hätte sie
> früher
> *zwei* Männer enthalten, und einer
> läge nun schon auf dem Kirchhof, und er überlebte den
> andern,
> taub und manchmal ein wenig
> wirr, in der verwitweten Haut.
>
> Aber der junge, der Mann, als wär er der Sohn eines Nackens
> und einer Nonne: prall und strammig erfüllt
> mit Muskeln und Einfalt. (1: 702)

> There: the fading, wrinkled lifter,
> the old one, now only drumming, receding
> in his powerful skin, as if it had earlier
> held *two* men, and one of them lay now, too soon,
> in the churchyard, this one surviving the other,
> deaf and sometimes a little
> confused, in the widowed skin.
>
> But the young one, a man as if he were son of a neck
> and a nun: full and strappingly filled
> with muscles and simpleness.

Nonetheless, the earlier prose text and the personal experience it is based on do not fully account for Rilke's deviation, in *The Fifth Elegy*, from Picasso's depiction of the acrobats. Critics have long puzzled over this problem. The little girl, in particular, is viewed from a different perspective, wears a dress of a different colour, and seems to be slightly older in the poem than in the painting:

> Du dann, Liebliche,
> du, von den reizendsten Freuden
> stumm Übersprungne. Vielleicht sind
> deine Fransen glücklich für dich – ,
> oder über den jungen
> prallen Brüsten die grüne metallene Seide
> fühlt sich unendlich verwöhnt und entbehrt nichts.
> Du,
> immerfort anders auf alle des Gleichgewichts
>   schwankende Waagen
> hingelegte Marktfrucht des Gleichmuts,
> öffentlich unter den Schultern.   (1: 703–704)

> You then, lovely one,
> you, wordlessly leapedfrogged
> by the most charming of joys. Perhaps
> your fringes are lucky for you –,
> or the green metallic silk
> over your young, full breasts
> feels itself endlessly coddled, lacking for nothing.
> You,
> serenity's market fruit,
> over and over, laid different ways on balancing scales of
>   poise,
> for show among shoulders.

Jacob Steiner is torn between the idea that Rilke may no longer have recalled certain details of the picture at a distance of six and a half years, and the recognition that his intensive habits of observation make such forgetfulness highly unlikely.[38] Naomi Segal argues that Rilke 'rear-ranged, re-clothed and repositioned' the acrobats because he was blend-ing images from several different works of Picasso with his own recollec-tions of street acrobats in Paris.[39] Kathleen Komar regards the discrepancies between poem and painting as changes wrought by a process of interiorisation: 'His initial response [to the painting]', she remarks, 'is not visual [...] but rather psychological.'[40]

The Fifth Elegy appears quite differently if we regard its depiction of the acrobats as a deliberate act of revision. Rather than describing a work of visual art, Rilke creates a counter-work by taking up some of the artwork's salient features and adapting them in specific ways.[41] In doing so, he conjures up a vision that essentially reverses the terms of the original painting. In this way, his elegy about reversal is itself contructed upon reversal. *The Fifth Elegy* reverses Picasso's terms in multiple respects.

First, Rilke extends the acrobats' existence in time, showing the 'fleeting ones' as they might appear several years later. The fat man in the red costume is older; his skin is wrinkled as if he once contained two men, one of whom has since died.[42] The young man to his left has been made older and stronger, though he is still as ascetic as in Picasso's painting: in the picture, he carries a tin drum balancing on his shoulder and the back of his neck, thus giving rise to Rilke's strange description of him as the son of 'a neck and a nun' (the word 'Nacken' refers specifically to the nape of the neck.) The little acrobat is still young, 'unreif' (unripe or immature), and although the soles of his feet burn as he leaps down from the others' shoulders (recalling the pain and the brimming eyes of the youngest acrobat in the 1907 prose text), he nonetheless knows how to end his performance with a smile. The little girl, whom we see from the back in the picture, has reached adolescence; she wears green metallic silk over her bodice, revealing the shape of her youthful breasts. These figures in the painting have been subjected to the force of time, as it were, extended in a temporal dimension. The harlequin figure on the left-hand side of the painting, usually interpreted as a representation of Picasso himself,[43] seems to be missing from *The Fifth Elegy*. It is not clear, furthermore, who the 'ihr' (you [plural]) are who are addressed as having once received suffering as if it were a toy (1: 702). Logic suggests that the pronoun refers to the two figures just mentioned, the lifter and the younger man, but there is no proof of this. The mysterious woman on the right-hand side of Picasso's painting, wearing a hat precariously perched on her head and seated just in front of a rather shadowy clay pitcher, has become, in Rilke's elegy, the hatmaker Madame Lamort; her straw hat decorated with roses has been converted into the image of 'die billigen Winterhüte des Schicksals' (the cheap winter hats of fate; 1: 705).

No longer set against a spare desert background, the acrobats of the elegy perform on a mat spread out on the pavement. Above all, they no longer stand forlorn, gazing into their own separate unfathomable distances, feet on the ground but ever poised for departure. In *The Fifth Elegy* the acrobats are seen in motion, working as a team, creating their human pyramid and juggling with whirling plates. The most important clue to what has happened here, in the transformation of painting into poem, is the speaker's evocation of a moment where the acrobats form the shape of a capital 'D', just as the figures do in Picasso's picture. The poem's speaker reads this letter as the initial of 'Dastehn' (standing there). Most critics are quick to leap from 'Dastehn' to 'Dasein' (existence). Yet although some of Rilke's best-known poetic formulations might seem at first glance to justify this association, there is no evidence in the elegy itself for equating 'Dastehn' with 'Dasein'. On the contrary. In the elegy, the figure D is created but for a moment before the impersonal force of dynamics 'rolls them again' into ever-changing constellations. 'Dastehn', standing there, refers to a particular moment in the gymnastic performance.

In the painting, of course, the figures stand for all time in the shape of a 'D'. Yet the fact that each of the acrobats is gazing in a different direction renders this suspension somewhat tentative. In addition, fleetingness is suggested by the little girl's left foot, which seems to have become transparent to the sand all around, and by the mysterious absence of the lower part of the fat acrobat's right leg. The figures' hands, too, seem full of incipient motion: the harlequin reaches behind his back, the boy with the drum steadies it on his shoulder, and the woman in the hat seems to adjust her shawl with an almost fluttering hand. The painting thus hints at movement; but as a painting, it can do no more than hint at it. Rilke's *Fifth Elegy*, in contrast, is in constant motion, as indicated by the sinuous syntax, the predominance of often quite forced enjambement, the proliferation of action verbs, and the constant, abrupt shifts in the viewer's gaze. The extravagant deployment of alliteration and assonance, the dashes and dots of suspension, the imagery of looping and twirling, all contribute to the impression of intense dynamic energy created by the poem.

In this respect, *The Fifth Elegy* enacts Lessing's characterisation of poetry as a medium uniquely capable of representing dynamism and temporality. Picasso's *Family of Acrobats* also does exactly what Lessing claims for painting in his essay *Laokoon* [Laocoon] (1766): it shows a single moment forever held in stasis. As a trained art historian, Rilke was of course familiar with Lessing's famous theory; we have already seen how Rilke alludes to the struggle between the sibling arts, verbal and visual, throughout the *New Poems*.[44] By reading the 'D' shape of the acrobats in Picasso's painting as an emblem of 'Dastehn', Rilke reminds the reader of his elegy that stasis is the quintessential property of painting, even when it represents those least static of beings, street performers. Since poetry lacks the proper means to do so, *The Fifth Elegy* does not even try to imitate the painting; instead, it creates a substitute form of representation that opposes the stasis of the picture by means of its constant motion. As a work of verbal art, *The Fifth Elegy* can properly convey movement and temporal change, and it fully exploits its potential to do so. What we see here, by setting Picasso's *Family of Acrobats* against Rilke's *Fifth Elegy*, is an almost textbook example of Lessing's distinction between painting and poetry.

Although they frequently treat poems depicting imaginary paintings, studies of ekphrasis – the verbal description of paintings – have failed to recognise what underlies Rilke's use of the technique here.[45] Despite his engagement in the ancient rivalry between the arts, Rilke does not argue here in favour of poetry and against painting. It is not as if he has discarded his earlier admiration of Picasso's picture. Indeed, while converting elements of the painting from their original stasis into relentless movement, Rilke still captures much of the sadness and alienation that pervades *The Family of Acrobats*. Acrobatics is exciting, but it also involves undoing figures that have just been created, dropping from heights that have just been attained, suffering pain and pretending to smile for the benefit of the audience. At the heart of the acrobats' alienation is the commodification of their performance.

The intrinsic sadness of acrobats was a theme frequently reworked in the nineteenth century. Baudelaire's prose poem 'Le vieux saltimbanque' [The Old Acrobat] (1861) describes an old acrobat, a 'ruin of a man', mute and immobile; Mallarmé's poem 'Le Guignon' [Misfortune] (1862) depicts a group of travelling acrobats, down at heel, full of bitterness, wandering through the desert whipped by the raging force of a cruel fate. Picasso's friend Apollinaire kept the motif alive in his 1909 poem 'Un Fantôme de Nuées' [A Ghost of Clouds], which paints the street performers in tones of sickly green and yellow, purple and 'rose pulmonaire' (pulmonary pink).[46] The pathetic tawdriness of acrobats had already become a common place.

In the same period, tumblers were increasingly used as symbols for the artist in general.[47] In Baudelaire's 'Old Acrobat', the narrator concludes that he has just had a premonition of his own later self, abandoned by friends and family, poverty-stricken and ignored as if he had never enjoyed poetic success.[48] Nietzsche, in *Also sprach Zarathustra* [Thus Spake Zarathustra] (1878) associated the acrobat not just with the artist, but also with the position of man in the universe and the nature of human freedom. Walking a tight-rope between animals and the superman, human beings hover precariously above an abyss. This perilous condition enables humans to experience freedom and greatness, even though they are bound eventually to fall. Nietzsche's image of the tightrope-walker was continued and adapted by Thomas Mann in *Felix Krull* (first part 1911), and parodied by Franz Kafka in 'Ein Bericht für eine Akademie' [A Report to an Academy] (1917).[49]

Does Rilke see the acrobat as identical to the artist, as an equivalent for human beings in general, or as a separate class of being? At the beginning of the elegy, the acrobats are described as 'just a little more/ fleeting than we ourselves'. Steiner rightly points out that the pronoun 'wir' (we) in the *Duino Elegies* almost invariably refers to humans in general.[50] Throughout *The Fifth Elegy*, the emphasis is on an element of unreality in the acrobats' performance – attested to by the smile that accompanies each new landing on the mat in spite of any physical pain. The acrobats' performance shines 'mit dünnster/ Oberfläche leicht scheinlächelnden Unlust' (from thinnest/ surface of delicate, seemingly smiling indifference; 1: 702); their art is a glossy covering over an empty centre. Fashion and the market place determine clothing and performance. The metaphors Rilke uses would have been readily recognised by Rilke's contemporaries as derived from aestheticist writing. The implicit link between the young girl, with her fringes and green metallic silk, and Madame Lamort, with her proliferating ornaments, suggests that both the acrobats and the hatmaker represent a false and superficial form of art:

> Plätze, o Platz in Paris, unendlicher Schauplatz,
> wo die Modistin, *Madame Lamort,*
> die ruhlosen Wege der Erde, endlose Bänder,
> schlingt und windet und neue aus ihnen
> Schleifen erfindet, Rüschen, Blumen, Kokarden,
> künstliche Früchte –, alle
> unwahr gefärbt, – für die billigen
> Winterhüte des Schicksals.   (1: 704–705)

> Squares, oh square in Paris, infinite stage,
> where the hatmaker, *Madame Lamort,*
> twists and winds
> the restless paths of the earth, endless ribbons,
> inventing new bows from them, ruffles, blossoms, cockades,
>   faux fruits –, and all
> unrealistically dyed, – for the cheap
> winter headgear of fate.

Madame Lamort is an intriguing figure. Kathleen Komar treats her as a kind of Madame Defarge and thus as a parody of the three fates who spin human lives, measure them, and then cut them short (Komar, p. 105). The name of Rilke's allegorical hatmaker derives most probably from a play by Rachilde, *Madame La Mort* [Madam Death], of 1891.[51] In the manuscript of the *Fifth Elegy* Rilke vacillates between spelling the hatmaker's name in two words, 'La Mort', as in Rachilde's play, or 'Lamort', as in the final version of his poem.[52] Rachilde's Madame La Mort is not, unfortunately, a hatmaker.

Rachilde's play is a symbolist drama in three acts. It tells the story of a young man, addicted to morphine, who decides to put an end to his life by smoking a poisoned cigar. As he falls under the influence of the deadly philtre, he is visited by two apparitions, his girlfriend, who tries to pull him back into life, and Madame Lamort, a mysterious figure in a grey veil who seduces him into opting for death. A drawing by Gauguin illustrating the temptress's shadowy form appears as the frontispiece to the published edition of the drama.[53] By introducing this variant of the allegory of death, Rilke interweaves the thematics of love and art with those of life and its surcease. The poem's roots in Rilke's depression of 1915 go some way toward explaining this linkage between the temptations of suicide, on the one hand, and erotic and creative impotence, on the other.

Even images from fertile nature are cast in a negative light in *The Fifth Elegy*. The onlookers surround the acrobats' carpet like petals around the centre of a rose: joining the crowd and leaving it again, they create a configuration that resembles blossoming and the shedding of petals:

> Ach und um diese
> Mitte, die Rose des Zuschauns:
> blüht und entblättert. Um diesen
> Stampfer, den Stempel, den von dem eignen
> blühenden Staub getroffnen, zur Scheinfrucht
> wieder der Unlust befruchteten, ihrer
> niemals bewußten, – glänzend mit dünnster
> Oberfläche leicht scheinlächelnden Unlust.   (1: 701–2)

> Oh and around this
> centre, the rose of beholding:
> blooms and sheds petals. Around this
> pestle, the pistil, touched by its own
> blooming pollen, made fertile again
> for the semblance of fruit of indifference,
> never aware of it, – shining from thinnest
> surface of delicate, seemingly smiling indifference.

This metaphor recalls a poem from the second part of the *New Poems*, 'The Group', written in early summer, 1908. Here an acrobat appears to arrange the facial expressions of his public like a bouquet of flowers, now drawing them close, now loosening them up, tidying up their ragged edges and binding them together (1: 593). But the rose petal metaphor in *The Fifth Elegy* is less positive. Here, the rose (contrary to botanical reality) is seen as self-fertilising. The second section of the *Fifth Elegy* draws on a tradition in which aestheticism was conceived as a self-reproductive phenomenon.[54] It emphasises the self-enclosed nature of this kind of art by means of multiple alliteration: 'Stampfer, Stempel, Staub' (pestle, pistil, pollen). The Romantic poet Novalis had called his collection of poetico-philosophic fragments *Blütenstaub* [Pollen] (1798), a word that Rilke expands here to the logically impossible form 'blühender Staub', 'blossoming pollen' or perhaps, if we read his German more literally, 'blossoming dust'. Whereas Novalis saw his fragments as pointing toward transcendence, continually combining and recombining to form a projected but never completely visualisable greater whole, Rilke conceives his 'rose of beholding' as a self-reflexive simulacrum of fruitfulness. The semblance of fruiting and the semblance of smiling come together here in a way that presages the blind smile of the boy acrobat and the artificial fruits on Madame Lamort's hats. Despite (or because of?) the precious tone and the high-flown syntax in which these lines are cast, they constitute a critique of aestheticism and its tendency towards artificiality. Yet the speaker also enjoys this excess of beauty even as he exposes its futility.

Only the final section of the *Fifth Elegy*, couched in the subjunctive of a possibly unfulfillable wish, projects a more genuine kind of achievement:

> Engel!: Es wäre ein Platz, den wir nicht wissen, und
>   dorten,
> auf unsäglichem Teppich, zeigten die Liebenden, die's hier
> bis zum Können nie bringen, ihre kühnen
> hohen Figuren des Herzschwungs,
> ihre Türme aus Lust, ihre
> längst, wo Boden nie war, nur an einander
> lehnenden Leitern, bebend, – und *könntens*,
> vor den Zuschauern rings, unzähligen lautlosen Toten:
> Würfen die dann ihre letzten, immer ersparten,
> immer verborgenen, die wir nicht kennen, ewig
> gültigen Münzen des Glücks vor das endlich
> wahrhaft lächelnde Paar auf gestilltem
> Teppich?   (1: 705)

Angel!: Should there be a square we knew not, and there,
on the untellable carpet, the lovers who here
never come to success would show their daring
high figures of heart swing,
their towers of eros, their
ladders long since merely leaning against one another
where ground never was, trembling, – and they *succeeded*,
before the spectators all round, numberless silent dead:
Would they then throw their last, long saved,
long hidden, unknown to us, eternally
valid good luck coin before the finally
truly smiling couple upon the sated
carpet?

The 'truly smiling couple' on the 'sated carpet' represent the inverse of the erotic and creative impotence figured and feared in the preceding sections of the poem.

Rilke had begun to develop the motif of the smile in the years just preceding the completion of the *Elegies*. In 1920, he composed four lines of not quite perfect Italian verse, a prose narrative in German, and a rhymed poem (also in German), on the theme, 'La Nascita del Sorriso' [The Birth of the Smile] (2:454–457). These sketches invent a new mythology to explain the phenomenon of smiling. Out of the original flux, Rilke writes, human beings were made, and spirit, which had hitherto been part of the flux, found itself enclosed in the clay shapes formed by human bodies. Angry at its captivity, spirit began to rage, caught on fire, and swept everything along with it in an immense holocaust. Seeing this, a god chose a maiden and a cool island arose beneath the two of them. Hearing the god's praise of the young woman's diaphanous beauty, spirit consented to dwell in her body – and so the smile was born. The important thing for *The Fifth Elegy* is the way in which 'The Birth of the Smile' transforms a gesture of communicative pleasure into a symbol of a more pervasive sense of balance. The smile, in this scheme of thought, represents a state of equilibrium between the human and the divine, the individual and the cosmos.

In *The Fifth Elegy*, the smile motif becomes almost a fetish. Although the passage about the 'rose of beholding' distinguishes between genuine and false acts of smiling, the subsequent discussion of the young acrobat deems even an inauthentic smile to have value. The choreography of performance requires an acrobat to smile as he or she lands on the mat; this kind of smile is not so much an expression of aesthetic pleasure or even just of relief at having accomplished a difficult gymnastic feat, but a sign that one portion of the act is over and the performer is ready to receive applause. Despite this elegy's disparagement of the 'market' culture or commercialisation of acrobatic performance, the speaker is nonetheless eager to salvage even this kind of smile and protect it against the threat of transience.

The task of preserving the acrobat's smile falls to the angel, who is exhorted to 'pluck' it and keep it in a vase:

> Engel! o nimms, pflücks, das kleinblütige Heilkraut.
> Schaff eine Vase, verwahrs! Stells unter jene, uns *noch*
> > > nicht
> offenen Freuden; in lieblicher Urne
> rühms mit blumiger schwungiger Aufschrift:
> > > 'Subrisio Saltat.'.   (1: 703)

> Angel! o take it, pluck it, the small-blossomed healing
> > > herb.
> Fashion a jar, and preserve it. Place it among those
> > > pleasures not *yet*
> open to us; in a lovely urn
> praise it with flourishing, florid inscription:
> > > 'subrisio saltat.'.

Continuing the image of wounded suburbia, for which the acrobats' carpet was to function as a glorified adhesive bandage, the smile now becomes a herb of healing to be preserved in an apothecary's jar. On a sheet of paper containing a list of corrections gathered while reading page proofs of the *Elegies*, Rilke comments that the Latin words that appear in this section of the poem were 'conceived as an inscription, as it were, on an apothecary's jar; abbreviation of *Subrisio Saltat(orum)*'.[55] The jar is to contain not just a single specific smile, but a kind of essence of acrobats' smiles. Rilke toyed with a number of different formulations before settling on this particular version of apothecary's Latin for his imaginary inscription. But the jar[56] is not merely a medicinal container with a florid Latin label; it is also described as a 'liebliche Urne' (lovely urn). Thoughts of death, and of urns containing ashes, complicate the metaphor Rilke creates here, bringing the hope of healing into conflict with the knowledge of transience. Thus the most fleeting of gestures comes to have a double significance, standing for both life and death. The jar passage functions, furthermore, as a hinge between the boy's landing on the mat and the hoisting aloft of the young girl on the acrobats' shoulders, presaging the moment a little later in the elegy where 'das reine Zuwenig' (the pure too little) reverses to become 'jenes leere Zuviel' (that empty too much).

Starting as early as the *New Poems*, Rilke had been interested in turning-points and reversals. Many of his poems from the Paris period enact the figure of reversal, usually seen as a process of transfiguration or transcendence. In his novel *Malte Laurids Brigge*, a moment of reversal is postulated, but deferred into the unreachable (though somehow also dreadfully near) future, which he calls 'die Zeit der anderen Auslegung' (the time of the other exegesis; 6: 756). In the novel, this moment never comes. Completing the elegy project was for Rilke an equivalent of the moment Malte had envisaged. Both postulated turning-points – Malte's and that of the speaker in *The Fifth Elegy* – contain an element of fear. Malte imagines that the reversal of all values will also involve a reversal in the process of signification: things will no longer be meaningful in any familiar way. The language of experience will have become foreign. Malte himself will no longer be a subject, even in the abjected sense in which he maintains his subject-position as the writer of the notebooks. If all is reversed, he must necessarily become an object.

The imagined reversal in *The Fifth Elegy* is more exalted. Still, the idea of pure inadequacy being transformed into empty plenitude is not easy to understand. The 'vielstellige Rechnung' (multi-digited calculation), we are told, is solved 'zahlenlos' (without number). Some readers conceive of this as a kind of long division that leaves no remainder or as a complicated problem involving fractions that cancel each other out.[57] Neither image makes much sense here. What Rilke seems to be thinking about is the problem of identifying the precise moment where the rising movement turns into a falling one, or vice versa. There is no way to fix the moment of reversal in one's mind's eye: at any given moment, the acrobat always seems to be either rising or falling. At first glance, the calculation metaphor does not seem completely appropriate to this idea, but what is in fact being calculated is the transformation of quantity into space, or perhaps more accurately, of time into space. The speaker's hope is to express numerically the 'space' or 'spot' where too little becomes too much, a hope which is, of course, perennially doomed to failure.

The 'spot' thus designated is the central term in a series of three words indicating location: 'Ort', 'Stelle' and 'Platz' (rendered in my translation as 'place', 'spot' and 'square' respectively). Of the three, 'Ort' is the most general term, whereas 'Stelle' refers to an exact point. 'Platz' means a place intended for the carrying on of some activity,[58] hence a city square or (as also here) a stage ('Schauplatz'). There is a fourth term in German for 'place' that does not occur in *The Fifth Elegy*, and that is 'Stätte', an elevated expression that refers to a sacred place or an edifice with spiritual associations. But the consecrated space is not absent. In effect, the carpet where the lovers consummate their relationship is the sacred place that completes the sequence of spatial designations invoked in this part of the elegy. Unlike the performers' mat, laid out on the city pavement, the lovers' carpet seems to be drawn from the realm of fairy tale: we are to imagine it hovering in the air. More literal-minded readers may see this as a metaphor for the carpet's metaphorical status. As such, it elaborates a motif familiar to the turn-of-the-century culture in which Rilke began his poetic career: one might think, for example, of Stefan George's *Teppich des Lebens* [Carpet of Life] or Henry James's 'Figure in the Carpet'. On this metaphorical carpet, the lovers perform metaphorical saltos, create metaphorical towers where one balances on the shoulder of the other, and climb metaphorical ladders whose feet rest on empty air. Their audience, though, is composed of 'numberless silent dead'; and the showplace of their performance is inaccessible to ordinary mortals. We can only imagine the feats of delicate balancing these metaphorical beings enact. The elegy attempts to render something of this equipoise in its juxtaposition of 'eternally' and 'finally' at the ends of two successive lines just before the conclusion:

> Würfen die dann ihre letzten, immer ersparten,
> immer verborgenen, die wir nicht kennen, ewig
> gültigen Münzen des Glücks vor das endlich
> wahrhaft lächelnde Paar auf gestilltem
> Teppich? (1: 705)

> Would they then throw their last, long saved,
> long hidden, unknown to us, eternally
> valid good luck coin before the finally
> truly smiling coupled upon the sated
> carpet?

All the same, this last section of the elegy is couched in the subjunctive, and it poses an unanswered and possibly unanswerable question. The triumphantly positive image of the elegy's concluding lines is an ideal to be borne in mind as a counter-image to the tawdry realities of the market-place depicted in the elegy as a whole. The subjunctives in which it is formulated indicate that it is no more than an image.

If we return now to the debate about the sibling arts that underlies *The Fifth Elegy*, we can see that Rilke has here reworked the Horatian theme of a 'monument more lasting than bronze'. Devoting most of the poem to a meditation on those 'just a little more fleeting than we ourselves', namely the acrobats, Rilke finally posits a couple even more fleeting still, namely the lovers. The acrobats are fleeting in the first instance because they are travellers, in the second because of the transience of their art. On another level, they are fleeting because they have become no more than a memory. As the speaker of the poem transforms them increasingly into creatures of the imagination, he makes them increasingly insubstantial. At that point, the imaginary lovers step in, just as the 'pure too little' reverses to become the 'empty too much'.

Rilke enacts here the process he describes at that crucial moment in his elegy: he has metamorphosed the real world into a realm of the imagination. In this realm, even money is no longer subject to devaluation, as it most frighteningly was for Rilke during the German inflation:[59] the dead onlookers' long-saved good luck coin turns out to be 'eternally valid'. The poetic process enacted here will later be described, in *The Seventh Elegy*, as a compensation for the constant degradation and vanishing away of external reality. Our task, as that elegy sees it, is to transform the external world by changing it into mental images. And, since individual consciousness is itself transient, these images must be preserved in the vision of the angel. The repeated invocation of the angel in *The Fifth Elegy*, significantly at the beginning of the passage about the apothecary's jar and again at the beginning of the passage about the imaginary lovers, is to be understood as a summons to the angel to take on this function of a meta-consciousness that can outlast the mortal consciousness of the poet. At the same time, we must not forget that the angel has already been figured as a symbol of art, particularly, as *The Second Elegy* makes clear, of autonomous art. Thus the angelic meta-consciousness in which images of external reality are to be preserved is also art, the medium that creates a 'monument more lasting than bronze'.

Leaving aside Rilke's highly fetishised private mythologies (those of the smile, the angel and the lovers), we can see that he has accomplished what was traditionally regarded as the proper task of the poet. In a complex act of revision, he turns the stasis of Picasso's painted acrobat family into the dynamic, temporal figures that had been understood, in the wake of Lessing's *Laocoon*, as the most appropriate subject for the verbal arts. Rilke's *Fifth Elegy* does not attempt to render in words what Picasso presents in painting; instead, it invents a new set of images that can only be rendered in poetry. In this sense, Rilke's modernism, his daring gymnastics on the very borders of what can be done with the German language, turns out to be rooted in a profoundly conservative ideology. Not only does it aim to preserve what is pre-eminently transient, it returns to an earlier conception of the proper distinction between painting and poetry, attempting to bear off the trophy in the ancient competition between the sibling arts.

THE BURDEN OF NARCISSUS

Rilke's sonnet on mirrors, the third poem in the second sequence of his *Sonnets to Orpheus*, continues to wrestle with the problem of painting and poetry. Conceptually, the 'mirror sonnet' is one of the most intriguing in this remarkable cycle. At the same time, it is also one of the most baffling:

> Spiegel: noch nie hat man wissend beschrieben,
> was ihr in euerem Wesen seid.
> Ihr, wie mit lauter Löchern von Sieben
> erfüllten Zwischenräume der Zeit.
>
> Ihr, noch des leeren Saales Verschwender –,
> wenn es dämmert, wie Wälder weit...
> Und der Lüster geht wie ein Sechzehn-Ender
> durch eure Unbetretbarkeit.
>
> Manchmal seid ihr voll Malerei.
> Einige scheinen *in* euch gegangen – ,
> andere schicktet ihr scheu vorbei.
>
> Aber die Schönste wird bleiben –, bis
> drüben in ihre enthaltenen Wangen
> eindrang der klare gelöste Narziß.   (1:752)

> Mirrors: the essence of what you are
> no one could knowingly start to define.
> Filled as by holes of a colander,
> Nothing but in-between spaces of time.
>
> You squanderers even of empty rooms –,
> when dusk descends, like forests wide...
> Like a sixteen-pointer the chandelier roams
> through your untreadable other side.

At times your paintings are made to last.
Some people seem to have gone inside –,
others you usher discreetly past.

But the most beautiful one will abide, –
till in her cheeks, contained over there,
Narcissus went in, dissolved and clear.

Most readings of the poem founder on the last tercet, especially on the two mysterious figures, the woman described only as 'die Schönste' (the most beautiful one), and 'der klare gelöste Narziß' (the dissolved and clear Narcissus). An effect of extraordinary compression is created in these concluding lines of the sonnet, but the reader is left with the feeling that something crucial has been left out. An appeal to the myth of Narcissus does not help substantially, for although it is easy to see why one might think of Narcissus in connection with mirrors, we still do not know who the 'most beautiful' woman is, why her cheeks are contained within the mirror, nor why Narcissus at the end is 'dissolved and clear'.

The 'mirror sonnet' incorporates motifs from several different domains. Underlying it is a whole lineage of Symbolist poetry on mirrors, as well as philosophical debates about the nature of mirror-space and mystic or esoteric traditions involving mirrors. It is hard to distinguish among the different elements that contributed to the sonnet's genesis: texts that may have been on Rilke's desk while he wrote, images stored in memory and cultural fashions that go beyond literature proper. My discussion of the poem will delineate something of the heterogeneous background against which it takes shape.

On one level, we can read the sonnet as a poetic enquiry into the properties of mirror-space, a topic much discussed in late nineteenth-century philosophy.[60] Lewis Carroll's *Alice Through the Looking-Glass* is the best known fictional enquiry of the time into this issue. In claiming that the 'essence' of mirrors has not been 'knowingly' described, the poem's speaker alludes directly to the philosophical treatment of mirror-space, its intrinsic qualities, and its relation to ordinary space. The implication is that philosophy has proved inadequate to the task of defining mirrors. How do we distinguish between virtual reality (the mirror image) and 'real' space? In empiricist philosophy, the enquiry into mirror-space was also linked with such problems as the status of dreams and hallucinations. Such phenomena are psychologically real for the experiencer; what enables any individual to know that they are not also real for others? Rilke had explored this question in a scene in *Malte Laurids Brigge*, where he describes a monkey perched on a mantelpiece, trying to grasp hold of a box he perceives in the mirror (6: 876). The monkey is unaware that mirror-space cannot be entered – or, to use the terms of the sonnet, is merely an image located in the 'Untretbarkeit', on the 'untreadable other side' of the glass.

While the philosophical discussion was concerned with space, Rilke's sonnet connects the mirror with time. But time itself, in the poem, is understood as a kind of space, just as music (a temporal form) had been linked with space in his poem 'To Music' and in the first *Sonnet to Orpheus*. The idea of 'Zwischenräume der Zeit', 'interstices' or 'in-between spaces' in time, is intriguing. A clue to what Rilke may have meant by it can be found in a text that might have been consigned to oblivion had not Rilke conserved its traces in a letter to his young friend, Balthus Klossowski, the second son of Rilke's friend Baladine Klossowska and later to become a well-known painter. Balthus was born in a leap year, on February 29. Writing to him on his birthday in 1921, Rilke consoles him with a whimsical thought drawn from a novel by an English writer named Algernon Blackwood whom he had met in Cairo.[61] Rilke explains Blackwood's idea as follows:

il prétend là que, toujours à minuit, il se fait une fente miniscule entre le jour qui finit et celui qui commence, et qu'une personne très adroite qui parviendrait à se glisser sortirait du temps et se trouverait dans un royaume indépendant de tous les changements que nous subissons; à cet endroit sont amassées toutes les choses que nous avons perdues.[62]

He claims there [in his novel] that, always at midnight, a miniscule crack opens between the day which is ending and the one which is beginning, and that a very agile person who could manage to slip through it would leave time behind him, and find himself in a realm independent of all the changes which we undergo; there, all the things we have lost are heaped up.

Rilke goes on to advise Balthus to slip through the crack at midnight on February 28 and 'prendre possession' (take possession) of his birthday. Amalgamating this idea with the notion of entering mirror-space, Rilke develops in his sonnet the metaphor for mirrors as interstices of time.[63]

Time is important in the *Sonnets to Orpheus*, since the entire sequence is an exploration, not only of the nature of death, but also of the problem of origins. Rilke shows, on the one hand, how the modern poet forms his notion of poetry and fulfills his vocation to write by listening to the voices of his predecessors, disseminated into nature like the dismembered Orpheus himself. But he also asks, on the other hand, how the modern poet can accede to a lineage that descends from Orpheus without in some sense destroying himself in the process. 'Ein Gott vermags. Wie aber, sag mir, soll/ ein Mann ihm folgen durch die schmale Leier?' (A God can do it. But how, tell me, is/ a man to follow him through the narrow lyre? 1: 732). The double realm of Orpheus, who had gone down to the underworld and back, cannot be completely recreated, even by a complicated arrangement of double mirrors, in the post-Orphic world. Like the Romantics, Rilke imagines Orphic song as pre-conscious or 'ahnend' (intimating; 1: 736), whereas modern song is inevitably conscious or 'wissend' (knowing), as he puts it in the 'mirror sonnet'. What Rilke proposes here is a return to a posture in which the poet would defer to the Orphic model and recapture a kind of beauty that belongs to an earlier epoch. By participating in Orphic song, modern poetry, in effect, slips through a 'crack in time' to reconnect with its own origins, just as Rilke encouraged Balthus to slip through a crack in time to get back to his leap-year birthday.

But the sonnet does not rest content with its initial description of mirrors: in the second quatrain, the speaker hazards another attempt at definition. Now mirrors are described as 'noch des leeren Saales Verschwender' (squanderers even of empty rooms). The image is amusing. We say that light, meaning electric current, is 'wasted' when a lamp is left on in an empty room. A mirror, however, is not a machine requiring electricity. Nor does the poem say that the mirror is wasted. Instead, it says that the 'empty room' is wasted. This conceit suggests that mirrors somehow draw energy from the things they reflect, much as sunlight fades curtains or upholstery fabric. It also implies a reversal of priorities, as if the objects were there for the purpose of the mirror, rather than the mirror for the purpose of reflecting them. The idea becomes more intelligible if we think of mirrors as a form of representation: for a poet, representation can become more important than the actual objects represented.

Allegorising art through the motif of an empty room reflected in a mirror has a long tradition in Symbolist poetry. Baudelaire's sonnet 'La Mort des amants' [The Death of the Lovers], for example, imagines death as a kind of sleep in an empty room, decorated with two mirrors that reflect the lamplight. Proposing that the 'twin lamps' are an allegory for the lovers' hearts, Baudelaire's sonnet claims that the reflections of the lamps in a mirror will guarantee the lovers' reanimation at some future time. Similarly, Mallarmé's famous 'sonnet in '-yx'' ('Ses pures ongles...', Her pure nails...) begins with an 'empty salon' illuminated by the allegorical figure of 'Anguish bearing a lamp'. A mirror with a highly decorative frame captures the image of a stellar constellation that seems to represent Orpheus' lyre spangled with drops of water from the underworld river Styx. The Belgian Symbolist Rodenbach, describing a moment when evening falls in a silent room, elaborates a visual and auditory complex involving a candelabra 'toujours vibrant comme un arbre d'échos' (still vibrating like a tree of echoes; Rodenbach, 1: 189).

Rilke's second quatrain compares the mirror with 'Wälder weit' (forests wide). The sudden shift from interior to exterior is facilitated by the chandelier, whose arms are visualised as the antlers of a stag (a 'sechzehn-Ender', sixteen-pointer). Woodland settings are, of course, intrinsic to the Narcissus story. In Ovid's version,[64] the spurned nymph Echo is absorbed into nature, living on in disembodied form in woods and caves. Her bones are turned into stone, and only her voice remains (*Metamorphoses* 3: 399). Nature becomes a visual and auditory record of her former presence. The myth of Narcissus thus haunts Rilke's poem long before Narcissus's name is actually mentioned.

With their reference to 'paintings', the final tercets of Rilke's sonnet turn to the problematic relation between mimesis and mirroring. Objects enter the 'untreadable' space of representation less indiscriminately than they enter mirror-space. Even the most naturalistic art is to some degree selective: mirrors, on the contrary, reflect everything that stands in front of them. Why does Rilke set up this limping analogy between art and the mirror?

I would argue that he is thinking here of a particular kind of 'mirror': the daguerreotype, advertised in its time as 'a mirror with a memory'.[65] An early form of photography, daguerreotypes use mercury vapors to fix onto glass images obtained by the action of light in a camera obscura. Viewed from one angle, the image can be clearly seen; from other angles, the image is either less distinct or the glass surface looks simply like a mirror. Rilke's 'Jugend-Bildnis meines Vaters' [Portrait of my Father in his Youth] (1906), from the *New Poems*, refers explicitly to this property of the daguerreotype: 'Du schnell vergehendes Daguerreotyp/ in meinen langsamer vergehenden Händen' (you quickly vanishing daguerreotype/ in my more slowly vanishing hands; 1: 522). The first part of the poem describes the image of his father in the daguerreotype; the second, the way the surface looks when held at a different angle, rendering the image almost invisible and revealing only the cloudy depths of the treated glass. The daguerreotype idea applies well to the tercets of the later 'mirror sonnet' in which the images of some people are captured while others are not. The daguerreotype vacillates, as it were, between being a kind of painting and a kind of dusky mirror. The 'most beautiful one' remains as an image in the daguerreotype; but if we were to hold the glass plate at a different angle and try to use it as a mirror, our own image would be 'dissolved'.

Late nineteenth-century poetry is full of images of dead women held captive in a mirror, a notion probably inspired by the daguerreotype. In Mallarmé's 'Her pure nails . . .' the mirror is described as containing the image of a dead woman.[66] In Mallarmé's prose-poem 'Frisson d'hiver' [Shiver of Winter] this image is elaborated further:[67]

Et ta glace de Venise, profonde comme une froide fontaine, en un rivage de guivres dédorées, qui s'y est miré? Ah! je suis sûr que plus d'une femme a baigné dans cette eau le péché de sa beauté; et peut-être verrais-je un fantôme nu si je regardais longtemps. (Mallarmé, p. 271)

And your Venetian glass mirror, deep as a cold fountain, in a bank of snakes from which the gilt has worn off, who is reflected there? Ah! I am sure that more than one woman has bathed away the sin of her beauty in that water; and perhaps I would see a naked ghost if I gazed for a long time.

This 'naked ghost', the phantom of some beautiful woman, purified of her seductive beauty, who may emerge in the mirror if one looks at it persistently, comes very close to Rilke's image.[68]

Georges Rodenbach repeatedly envisages mirrors as containing the images of the dead, especially of dead women. He imagines, for example, that one might be able to kiss their foreheads, still present in the clear surface of the mirror (Rodenbach, 1: 280). In a passage closely related to Rilke's mirror sonnet, the speaker of one of Rodenbach's poems seems to see his own soul becoming clearer and purer as he looks into the glass (Rodenbach, 2: 13).

Rilke's friend Rudolf Kassner draws on the tradition of the dead woman in the mirror in his chapter on Morris and Burne-Jones, subtit-led 'Die Bürde der Spiegel' [The Burden of the Mirrors].[69] Kassner writes that the figures in Burne-Jones's paintings look 'als hätten sie sich einmal in schönster und verruchtester Stunde vor den Spiegel gestellt, und der Spiegel hätte sie aufgefangen und gäbe sie nicht mehr zurück' (as if they had once stood before the mirror in their most beautiful and decadent hour, and the mirror had captured them and never given them back; p. 212–213). Kassner goes on to say:

Und sie können aus ihrer Schönheit nicht mehr heraus und sind starr geworden wie Glas an der Bürde der Spiegel, sie sind überhaupt nur noch Spiegel. [. . .]

Narcissus ertrank in seinem Spiegel, und die Jünglinge und Mädchen Burne-Jones' sind an ihm Kunstwerke geworden. Und ihre Augen leben … Ihre Augen sehen aus dem Bilde heraus, sehnen sich heraus … (p. 213)

They cannot get back out of their beauty and have become as still as glass from the burden of the mirrors, they are no longer anything but mirrors. [...] Narcissus drowned in his mirror, and Burne-Jones's youths and maidens have become artworks as a result of theirs. And their eyes live … Their eyes stare out of the painting, longing to escape …

Rilke most certainly knew this passage.

The motif of the dead woman in the mirror was also used in Pre-Raphaelite poetry. In Rossetti's poem 'The Portrait', for example, a painting of the dead beloved (presumably his wife, Elizabeth Siddell) gives rise to the fancy that the speaker's own image might live on in the mirror after his death:

> This is her picture as she was:
> 　It seems a thing to wonder on,
> As though mine image in the glass
> 　Should tarry when myself am gone.
>
> 　　　　　　　　　　　(Rossetti, p. 111)

Rossetti's sonnet sequence *The House of Life*, which Rilke had read with admiration very early in his poetic career,[70] contains an even more remarkable poem in which the image of the self merges with that of a loved woman who is dead. The poem is the first one in a cluster of four entitled 'Willowwood'. The poet describes himself as sitting beside a 'woodside well', communicating silently with the allegorical figure of Love, depicted as a (male) winged Cupid. As the two exchange glances in the water at their feet, a strange metamorphosis takes place: the sound of Love's lute becomes the voice of the poet's dead wife, his eyes become hers, and the ripples in the water become the undulating strands of her beautiful hair. 'His eyes beneath [i.e. below the surface of the water] grew hers' is how Rossetti puts it (p. 66). The change of sex whereby the eyes of a male cupid become those of a dead woman, is the reverse of the process in Rilke's sonnet where the woman's cheeks, contained in the mirror, are penetrated by the male Narcissus.

We know, from Rilke's review of Pater, that he was familiar with the Diederichs edition of Rossetti. In that edition, however, the switch from male to female is not rendered, since the allegorical figure of Love is given its German grammatical gender, which is feminine. The transformation of Love's eyes into those of the dead woman is not reproduced at all. Instead, the full strangeness of Rossetti's conceit is avoided: 'Bekannt die Augen unten in der Flut!' (Familiar the eyes in the flood below!)[71] Stefan George does better, however, in his translation of Rossetti's sonnet. Here, 'Love' becomes 'Amor' and can thus be assigned a masculine pronoun. His version of the line runs: 'Ich weinte und sein aug ward ihrem gleich' (I wept, and his eye became like hers).[72] It would be surprising if Rilke had not known George's translation.

Nineteenth-century mirror mania was often expressed through the motif of Narcissus. Taking a cue from Rilke's two Narcissus poems of 1913, scholars have gained some ground in resolving the puzzles of his 'mirror sonnet' by referring to Valéry's project on the same theme, 'Narcisse parle' [Narcissus speaks] (1891) and 'Fragments du Narcisse' [Fragments of Narcissus] (1919–26).[73] The adjective 'clear', for example, may recall Valéry's repeated use of the word 'pur' (pure) in connection with the image of Narcissus in the water.[74]

Rilke was almost certainly thinking about Valéry's 'Narcissus speaks' during the composition of his *Sonnets to Orpheus*. In the eighth sonnet of the first sequence, he addresses the 'Nymphe des geweinten Quells' (nymph of the spring wept dry; 1: 735), a motif that adapts Valéry's address to the nymph of the fountains at the beginning of 'Narcissus speaks' and his offering of his tears at her shrine (Valéry, p. 82). Valéry's poem bears a Latin motto, 'Placandis Narcissae Manibus' (To placate the shades of Narcissa). Rilke probably did not know what to make of this, but it certainly must have suggested the idea of a female equivalent of Narcissus.[75] The sexual imagery Rilke introduces at the end of his sonnet – Narcissus 'penetrates' the beautiful woman's image in the mirror – may also be related to Lou Andreas-Salomé's study of Narcissism as a psychological problem: 'Narzißmus als Doppelrichtung' [Narcissism as Double Directionality] (1921).[76] Lou's thinking about 'femininity' and 'masculinity' had long been an ingredient in Rilke's understanding, not only of sexual difference, but also of the poetic vocation.

Underlying Rilke's image of Narcissus penetrating the mirror is an idea not unlike Mallarmé's question, in the final stanza of his poem 'Les Fenêtres' [The Windows], whether it might be possible to break through the glass and escape from reality into mirror-space, specifically allegorised as the realm of art or poetry (Mallarmé, p. 33). The speaker sees himself transformed into an angel plunging through mirror-space; he imagines his own death and rebirth as a star in some other sky.

Rilke ingeniously recreates mirror-space in the final tercet of his 'mirror sonnet' by diverging from normal syntax: Rilke delays the subject until the end of the clause, keeps a separable verb together in a position where it would normally be separated, and places the verb following the conjunction 'bis' (until) into the past tense in a context that requires the present. Just as mirror-space differs from real space by laterally inverting its image, so the conclusion of Rilke's sonnet uses syntax that obeys laws unknown to those of ordinary grammar.[77]

In Orphic tradition, with which Rilke had become familiar through a disciple of Bachofen in 1915, it was believed that having a person's image in a mirror meant having him or her in your power.[78] In Bachofen's book on the concept of eternal life in Orphic belief, there is a two-page description of the mirror motif as used on Greek vases, together with a discussion of some of the Orphic beliefs which he believed were manifested in these decorations. Bachofen quotes classical sources who regard the mirror as an image of the transparent, light-filled ether in which the divine sees its purest likeness; in the mirror of Dionysus, he claims, the Orphics believed that the soul recognises its 'lichtreines Bild' (light-pure image).[79] Bachofen left many traces in Rilke's later poetry.[80] The 'clear' Narcissus of Rilke's last tercet may be related to the Orphic purification rites that Rilke had read about in Bachofen.

All of this still does not explain what is meant by the 'most beautiful' woman who remains in the mirror. Could it be Narcissus' female lover, Echo, transformed after her death into a voice that remains in woods and caves? As the 'image [or semblance] of a voice' (*Metamorphoses* 3: 385), Ovid's Echo is peculiarly appropriate to Rilke's sonnet on mirrors. Furthermore, her final dissemination into nature and continued existence as a disembodied voice has its parallel in the dismemberment of Orpheus, whose singing head, borne on his lyre, floats down the river toward Lesbos in the *Metamorphoses* (11: 51–55).[81] In the *Sonnets to Orpheus*, Rilke describes the originary poet as himself disseminated into nature: 'Denn Orpheus ists. Seine Metamorphose/ in dem und dem. Wir sollen uns nicht mühn// um andre Namen. Ein für alle Male/ ists Orpheus, wenn es singt.' (For it is Orpheus. His metamorphosis/ in this and that. We should not try to search// for other names. Once and for all/ it is Orpheus, whenever there is singing.; 1: 733).[82] In Rilke, Orpheus himself has become a kind of Echo.

Equating the Orpheus myth with the myth of Echo and Narcissus has important consequences for the theory of poetry that Rilke develops in the *Sonnets to Orpheus*. In Ovid's version of the Narcissus tale, a connection between visual and aural 'images' is made as the voice of Echo calls upon Narcissus to unite with her while Narcissus himself longs only to unite with his image in the water. Rilke's 'mirror sonnet' explores this relation between image and echo. Its opening lines allude to the rivalry between the visual and the verbal (can one describe mirrors?), an allusion continued by the direct mention of painting at the beginning of the first tercet. If the 'most beautiful' woman in the second tercet is also in some sense Echo, then the idea of auditory mimesis is also implicitly present.

By linking image and echo, Rilke resolves a problem that had long preoccupied him: the disparity between his desire to mirror the world of concrete reality and his consciousness of the allusive dimension of his poetry. Once image and echo are conceived as two versions of a single phenomenon, the two modes of creation – imitating nature, and imitating other writers – seem less violently at odds with one another. Orpheus, the originator, and Echo, the imitator, are not as far apart as they might seem. By conceiving of Orpheus and Echo as somehow equivalent – as male and female versions of a mythical process of disembodiment in which only voice remains as an emanation of nature – Rilke collapses the conventional opposition between original and derivative speech. Inspired simultaneously by Orpheus and Echo, the 'mirror sonnet' draws on previous tradition yet is anything but imitative.

A TEXTUAL TOMB

Rilke's incipient modernism emerges most strongly in a small group of little known poems written toward the end of his life. Suggestive, abstract and elliptical, full of innovative compound words and sudden syntactic turns, the poems of 1924/25 frankly display their aspiration to the condition of pure poetry. Perhaps not accidentally, these texts are also products of Rilke's orientalism, the penchant for the exotic that he had inherited from the French symbolists and that had been reinforced by his trip to Egypt in 1911 and his study, then and later, of ancient religions and esoteric cults. The poems are 'Mausoleum' (2: 500–501), written in October 1924, 'Idol' (2: 185–86) and 'Gong' (2: 186–87), written in November 1925. The first poem refers to Asia Minor; the second two invoke the far east by their common use of the gong motif, although the reference to the cat as an idol in the first line of the poem by that name suggests an Egyptian setting. 'Mausoleum' is, to my mind, the richest and most daring of the three poems. Oddly enough, it has scarcely been studied at all; and yet it is one of Rilke's most entrancing poems, well worth discovering for its own sake:

Königsherz. Kern eines hohen
Herrscherbaums. Balsamfrucht.
Goldene Herznuß. Urnen-Mohn
mitten im Mittelbau,
(wo der Widerhall abspringt,
wie ein Splitter der Stille,
wenn du dich rührst,
weil es dir scheint.
daß deine vorige
Haltung zu laut war ...)
Völkern entzogenes,
sterngesinnt,
im unsichtbaren Kreisen
kreisendes Königsherz.

Wo ist, wohin,
jenes der leichten
Lieblingin?
: Lächeln, von außen,
auf die zögernde Rundung
heiterer Früchte gelegt;
oder der Motte vielleicht,
Kostbarkeit, Florflügel, Fühler ...

Wo aber, wo, das sie sang,
das sie in Eins sang,
das Dichterherz?
: Wind,
unsichtbar,
Windinnres.   (2: 500–501)

King's heart. Seed of a high
ruler-tree. Balsam-fruit.
Golden heart-nut. Urn-poppy
right in the midst of the middle vault,
(where the echo splits off
like a splinter of silence
whenever you move
as it seems to you
that your previous
stance was too loud ...)
hidden from nations,
star-minded,
king's heart revolving
in the invisible orbiting.

Where is, where has it gone,
the heart of the delicate,
most cherished woman?
: smile, from the outside,
laid on the hesitant curve
of joyous fruits;
or the precious parts, perhaps,
of the moth, wing dust, antennae...

Where, though, where, that which sang them,
that sang them together,
the poet's heart?
: wind,
invisible,
inside of wind.

One might wish to claim that 'Mausoleum' creates a 'modernist' impression simply because it is unfinished; but in fact there are good reasons for regarding it as a completed poem.[83] Certainly, in comparison to the first version (2: 499–500), the clean copy shows that the text has been carefully worked over. The five- and six-stress lines of the first version, which recall the verse forms of the *Duino Elegies* without fully actualising their rhythms, are shorter and pithier; and the poem, in particular the ending, has a firmer structure. The short-line form, as well as some of the imagery, recalls earlier poems of Rilke's such as 'Soul in Space' and 'To Music', but the execution of this poem is more accomplished.

The word 'mausoleum' is derived from the name of a Carian King, Mausolos, whose widow (who was also his sister), Artemisia, had an elaborate tomb contructed for him in Halicarnassus after his death. The large temple-like building, almost 50 metres high, was one of the seven wonders of the world; described in ancient times by Pliny, it stood for many centuries before being demolished in an earthquake in 1304. British excavators discovered some parts of the monument (sections of the frieze around its base and a large statue of King Mausolos, among other objects) in 1857, and transferred these finds to the British museum. When Rilke was writing his poem, the site had still not been completely excavated; in fact, it was not until 1977 that Danish archaeologists finished work on the location. In Rilke's day, however, scholars had already developed quite accurate ideas about the monument's external structure, which, because of its airy use of columns, had been said in antiquity to be 'suspended in air'.[84] After the collapse of the Mausoleum, the site was littered with thousands of blocks of stone and marble, and some of the stones were removed in the sixteenth century to fortify a nearby castle. Rilke's poem brilliantly imitates the fragmentary character of the ruined Mausoleum. In Rilke's day, the entrance to the tomb chamber had been completely covered over by earth, and although tomb robbers had gained access by other means, the entry staircase cut in living rock was not uncovered until the Danish excavation.[85] Rilke and his contemporaries could only imagine the king's tomb-chamber.

Although the monument itself had long been in ruins, the story of Artemisia and the erection of the Mausoleum was well known. Goethe uses it, for example, as one of the tableaux vivants enacted in *Die Wahlverwandtschaften* [Elective Affinities] (1809). The sorrowing Artemisia is usually presented as a paradigm of mourning, the widow who grieved so much that she felt obliged to erect a monument more extravagant than any other in existence.

Rilke's poem situates itself in the tradition of Mallarmé's 'tombeaux', poems about monuments over a grave or vault that are also themselves monuments to and tombs of dead poets.[86] Mallarmé wrote three poems of this type: one on the tomb of Edgar Allan Poe, written in connection with the erection of a monument on Poe's tomb; one on Charles Baudelaire, written for a memorial volume intended to raise money for a monument to Baudelaire; and one on Verlaine, published on the first anniversary of his death in 1897. All three poems are sonnets that simultaneously commemorate the dead poets and mourn the death of poetry, or at least its diminution, since the departure of the three great predecessors. We know that Rilke was familiar with this group of texts, since he had translated the poem on Verlaine in 1921;[87] and the *Sonnets to Orpheus*, as a 'Grab-Mal' (grave-stone) for a young dancer and a memorial to the lost predecessor Orpheus, are another indication of Rilke's interest in the idea of poetry as a kind of textual tomb.

Rilke's studies of archaeological discoveries in Greece, Asia Minor and Egypt, and recollections of his 1911 trip to Egypt doubtless also contributed to his choice of an exotic setting for his 'tomb poem' of 1924, 'Mausoleum'. The Carian funeral monument was a particularly appropriate choice for a poem about the possible death of poetry, since the edifice was designed to encase, and thus completely conceal, the body of King Mausolos within a temple-like structure.[88] This notion permitted a ready linkage with the tradition of hermetic poetry represented by Mallarmé. Rilke's poem, with its short lines of irregular length, does not, however, imitate the form of Mallarmé's 'tomb' poems, all of which are sonnets.[89]

The three sections of the poem, each shorter than the one that precedes it, focus on three different hearts: the heart of the king; the heart of his sorrowing widow; and the heart of the poet. In accordance with the poem's emphasis on silence, no names are mentioned. Mausolos and Artemisia become as anonymous as the unnamed poet who celebrated their story. The heart of the king is concealed in the innermost sanctuary of the monument, which appears to be conceived as a set of vaults within vaults. We will return in a moment to this image, which has important consequences for Rilke's conception of poetry and the poetic tradition. First, we need to examine the way in which Rilke unfolds the theme of the dead heart.

The king's heart is presented through a fourfold set of imagery: as a seed of a tree, a fruit, the kernel of a nut and (a metaphor for the king's ashes in their funeral urn) as poppyseeds. In the space of three lines, the royal heart has gone through four metamorphoses, all of them suggesting the possibility of future growth or resurrection but the last (poppy) also hinting at an ultimate forgetting. This idea is picked up in the last lines of the first section, where the king's heart is described as removed from 'nations' and oriented toward the stars, orbiting invisibly with the planets. This cosmic imagery recalls Rilke's interest in ancient cults, in which the dead were conceived as having an astral afterlife. The poem also appears to allude to the Egyptian belief, mentioned in *The Tenth Elegy*, that the heart of a deceased person was weighed on a scale in the presence of Osiris. If the balance pans were even, the dead person was allowed to continue on his journey beyond the tomb to the paradise-like 'field of reeds'; if not, the heart of the deceased was torn into bits. The king's heart appears to have passed the test, since it has attained a kind of identity with the circling planets.

Entering the dead centre of the mausoleum, a modern visitor feels like an intruder. Unlike the king's heart, multiply contained within the succession of vaults and the spheres of the planets, the visitor's body seems too alive and too loud. It is as if the only possible posture, in this innermost of sanctuaries, is that of a figure on an ancient scroll, forever making the same silent gesture. Even sounds – the sounds made by the visitor's movements – create the impression of silence, a silence that is not whole like the heart and the building that surrounds it, but curiously splintered. The visit to the inner temple is placed in parentheses which situate it within the description of the dead king's heart in much the same way as the king's heart is itself situated within the mausoleum. But the marks of suspension at the end of the parenthetical section suggest that this enclosure is not really complete: the thought breaks off, and the notion that the modern visitor is an intruder is not pursued further.

The problem of enclosure and openness, inward- and outward-directedness, is made even more acute by the fact that the visitor's thoughts are expressed in the second person, making the parenthetical section of the poem a kind of interior monologue or self-contemplation and drawing us into the reflections of the speaker as if we were present together in the mausoleum. Expanding one's cultural horizons by visiting ancient monuments also involves reflection on one's own customs. Past and present are uneasily in tension here, the past a hermetic collection of objects, the present a series of awkward sounds and movements, as suggested by the contrast between the solid concentration of nominal and adjectival expressions in the lines on either side of the parenthesis and the almost unchecked sequence of subordinating conjunctions within the parenthesis. The living visitor from the present can only appear clumsy in this confrontation with the splendid objects left behind by a mysterious and hieratic past.

The second and third sections of the poem, with their opening questions ('Wo ist, wohin?' Where is, where? and 'Wo aber, wo?', Where, though, where?) recall the second part of Hölderlin's 'Hälfte des Lebens' [Middle of Life] (1805), with its desperate cry, 'Weh mir, wo nehm' ich, wenn/ Es Winter ist, die Blumen und wo/ Den Sonnenschein und Schatten der Erde?' (Alas, where shall I find, though, when/ It is winter, the flowers and where/ The sunshine and shadow of earth?). Hölderlin's language is also echoed by Rilke's use of the word 'Leiblingin' (most cherished woman), a word formation characteristic of his predecessor. 'Middle of Life' is a poem about the coming of winter after a glorious late summer; but is is also about the epigone's fear of losing his powers in an epoch when the wellsprings of creativity seemed to have dried up. The last section of Rilke's 'Mauseoleum', by calling for the 'Dichterherz' (poet's heart) that might celebrate and, as it were, recreate and reunite the royal couple, directly alludes to Hölderlin's anxiety about his poetic vocation and about the ability of poetry to fulfill its noble calling in the modern age. The final section of 'Mausoleum' also alludes to Hölderlin's poem in its reference to wind in the last three lines, which recall the ending of 'Middle of Life' with its weather-vanes emptily rattling in the wind. Like Hölderlin's poem, 'Mausoleum' ends on a note of cryptic pessimism.

But 'Mausoleum' also has links with Rilke's own earlier works. Artemisia, the loving wife who created the mausoleum, is assimilated implicitly to Rilke's pantheon of women lovers: Teresa von Avila,

Gaspara Stampa, Marianna Alcoforado, Héloise, Louise Labbé, Marceline Desbordes, Bettina von Arnim and many others. In *Malte Laurids Brigge* the young poet writes on the margin of his notebook: 'Geliebtsein heißt aufbrennen. Lieben ist: Leuchten mit unerschöpflichem Öle. Geliebtwerden ist vergehen, Lieben ist dauern' (To be loved is to burn up. To love is to shine with inexhaustible oil. To be loved is to be transitory, to love is to last; 6: 937). The great women lovers whom Malte praises in his jottings are also great women writers; the eternal flame of their passion is the source of the literary monuments they have created, which last beyond the death of the men who failed to requite their love. No wonder the prodigal son, whose return is narrated at the end of *Malte*, does not wish to be loved; as one who is 'furchtbar schwer zu lieben' (terribly hard to love; 6:946) he has, at least, a chance of 'shining with inexhaustible oil'. In Rilke's scheme of things, enduring love is a kind of monument, and hence intimately linked with the creation of poetry. Thus it is curious that he does not seem to have discovered Queen Artemisia until so late in his life. As a grieving lover who built an extraordinary monument for her husband, Artemisia is an ideal embodiment of creativity predicated on irreparable loss. If Orpheus' song in mourning for his wife becomes a kind of temple, Artemisia's temple in memory of her husband becomes, as we shall see, a kind of song.

Mausolos' heart has been preserved by embalming – hence the reference at the beginning of the poem to the 'Balsamfrucht' (balsamfruit), a kind of apple that has only the name in common with balsam, the mixture of resin and ethereal oils used to preserve corpses. But this is a poem where objects, however solid and permanent they at first appear, are also somehow disturbingly identical with other objects. Balsam apples spring open when ripe, a fact that belies the idea that the king's heart is perennially enclosed in the centre of the tomb. Artemisia's heart is not enclosed, but neither has it completely disappeared, as the speaker at first fears. Instead, it is dispersed into other things ('aufgeteilt', as the first version of the poem has it; 2: 500). These things are natural objects, in contrast to the artifact that contains the king's heart. The speaker names two possibilities out of what we must assume to be many: the bloom on pieces of fruit or the dust on the wings and antennae of moths. Rilke calls the moth's wings 'Florflügel'. Derived from Latin, the word 'Flor' not only means flowering, floral display or decoration, but also has two other meanings: a plush or velvet surface and a black mourning band. Here, of course, the beauty of the wings and their soft powdery surface are meant; but mourning is not far absent. Balancing mourning is the smile, which appears here on the velvety surface of fruit like a reminder of the bloom on a healthy, smiling cheek. The speaker sees these delicate surfaces, so easily ruined by a careless hand, as jewels of nature, akin to the precious artifacts that decorate the mausoleum and contain the heart of the king.

To put it differently, two contrasting types of beauty are presented in the first and second sections of the poem: the enclosed and enduring beauty of man-made artifacts and the diaphanous, ephemeral beauty of the natural world. The most precious object of the first section, the king's heart, is hidden away at the centre of the mausoleum; the precious objects in nature, the fruit and the moth, bear their beauty delicately on their external surfaces. The static and silent mausoleum is contrasted with the constant play and movement of nature, the autonomous art object with the organic.

The moth is traditionally a symbol of transitoriness, though it is also linked, as in Goethe's poem 'Selige Sehnsucht' [Blissful Longing], another poem on an oriental motif, with the idea of metamorphosis. Artemisia's heart has, as it were, transmigrated into nature, appearing as beauty or bliss, with its characteristic signature, the smile. The oddly placed colon before the word 'Lächeln' (smile), as later before 'Wind' (wind), seems less a way of mediating between two halves of a thought structure than the sign of a silence, a pause in which meaning may be located, but not in any way that can be translated into words. If in Rilke's 'Archaic Torso of Apollo' the smile of the statue has been displaced into its body, in 'Mausoleum' the smile of Artemisia is disseminated into nature itself, where it can no longer 'speak' in a recognisably human way.

But what is a smile doing here in a poem of mourning? In *The Fifth Elegy* the smile was an image of lovers' bliss, but it was also a sign of successful transformation, the moment of orgasm being equated with the moment 'where the pure too little/ ungraspably metamorphoses –, and leaps/ into that empty too much' (1: 704). The 'truly smiling couple' on the 'untellable carpet' at the end of *The Fifth Elegy* smile because they have proved their power to build imaginary edifices, as if they were acrobats creating a human pyramid. Smiling, to put it briefly, has to do with poetic potency: the ability to create a successful work of art.

In the final section of the poem, the poet's heart is invoked as the one that can bring together the dissociated hearts, reuniting the dead king and queen. The two concepts of art presented in the first two sections (art as artefact, art as nature) are now replaced by a more modernist idea of the creative process as the reconstitution of something broken or dismembered (art as reconstructed ruin). Nonetheless, the poet is still seen, in accord with ancient tradition, as a singer. But inspiration, traditionally imagined as a breath or a wind, is present only in an obscure and paradoxical way: as 'Windinneres', the 'inside of wind'. The image recalls Rilke's earlier notion, 'the other side of the air'.

In an edition of *The Flowers of Evil* presented to Anita Forrer on April 14, 1921, Rilke inscribed a six-line poem about Baudelaire. In it, he describes the French poet's work as an attempt to bring together what is falling apart, to purify the ruined state of the world, and to turn the destructive into something aesthetically whole (2: 246). Baudelaire, presented as one who unifies what has been sundered, is not too different from the poet in 'Mausoleum'. But the poet in 'Mausoleum' is absent – or perhaps present only on the other side of the wind.

Singing things back together is something that does not fully succeed for the poem 'Mausoleum' itself. Is it possible, this poem asks, to create a poem that will properly function as a monument? The poem answers the question negatively, and it does so in several ways, not least by its own disjointed structure. It does so, too, by its movement from naming to questioning and from images of presence to images of absence. It also does so, finally, by identifying the inner sanctuary of the mausoleum, where the king's heart is preserved, with the empty inside of wind, where the poet's heart is sought, but not necessarily found. 'Mausoleum' asks an important question about hermetic poetry: is it a precious container for meaning that is hidden deep inside, like the kernel in the fruit, or is it merely a surface which, when turned inside out, will prove to contain nothing?

In Mallarmé's 'tombeaux' (tomb poems), the text becomes an elaborate sepulchre for a dead predecessor, constructed as a verbal double of the actual tomb the poet is contemplating, as well as of the dead poet's self-made tomb, his poetic works. In each of Mallarmé's 'tomb poems', the dead poet is explicitly named, each time toward the end of the sonnet (in the eleventh line in fact). The erection of the poetic tomb takes much the same course in each of the three poems. The poet piles up block after block of seemingly dislocated imagery in an ostensible effort to create a monument for his predecessor. Ultimately, however, the dead poets refuse to remain buried, or at least to be buried once again in the tomb-poem their successor is constructing. At the end of each of the 'tomb poems', the dead poet makes his presence felt beyond the bounds of the sepulchre: Poe in the form of a falling meteorite, Baudelaire in the form of a noxious but also 'tutelary' gas ('poison tutélaire'), and Verlaine in the form of a stream of water inconspicuously trickling through the grass near his tombstone.

Rilke retains some of these features of the 'tomb poem' genre as Mallarmé developed it, but discards others. Like Mallarmé, he piles image upon image at the beginning of the poem as if placing stone upon stone. But he does not name a particular poet, and even the rather obvious echoes of Hölderlin in the last two sections of the poem do not mean that the poem is 'about' Hölderlin. Indeed, Rilke takes care to preserve the anonymity of the poet whose heart is sought in the last section of 'Mausoleum'. And although the king's heart has been assimilated to the rhythms of the cosmos, there is no stellar apparition at the end of the poem, as there is in Mallarmé's poem on Poe. We are led to expect that the secret of poetry will emerge when we crack this hermetic nut, but no pithy kernel comes to light; and the inside of the wind that blows in the last lines of the poem seems less like an inspiration for new poetry than an intimation that the obscure may turn out to be ungraspable.

To readers of German, 'Mausoleum' seems to anticipate the spare and decisively modernist poetry of Paul Celan. Those texts by Celan that show the closest affinities with 'Mausoleum', predominantly in the volumes *Sprachgitter* [Speech Grille] (1959) and *Die Niemandsrose* [The No-Man's Rose] (1963), were in fact written in a period of intense interest in Rilke's works, especially his late poetry.[90] What Celan appears to have seen in poems like 'Mausoleum' is that here Rilke has gone further than ever before in his attempt to distill the essence of poetry.

Despite its allusions to earlier poetry, 'Mausoleum' is one of Rilke's most original creations. It recognises that modern poetry is constructed from blocks of material that no longer fit smoothly together. It is not the result of divine inspiration or the bursting forth of emotion into song, but an awkwardly poised agglomeration of disparate elements. And although there is a speaking subject here who meditates about his intrusion into the secret chambers of the past and poses unanswerable questions about the presence of love and poetry in the modern world, this speaker is ultimately occluded by the sheer weight of the nominalised objects that surround him in the textual conglomerate: the king's heart, the smile, the wind. Individual identity is effectively obliterated from 'Mausoleum', but what is the point of a monument when we cannot name the person it honours? Rilke's poem knows this, and it remains obstinately silent.

Conclusion: restorative modernism

T. S. Eliot conceived of the poet's mind as a 'receptacle' designed to 'form a new compound' from 'numberless feelings, phrases, images'.[1] Paul Valéry wrote that works whose relation to earlier works are so complicated that 'nous nous y perdons' (we lose ourselves in them) are the ones that we believe to have come 'directement des dieux' (directly from the gods).[2] Rilke's poetry fits well with these descriptions of the catalytic principle.

Nonetheless, Rilke does not seem to have shared their scepticism about the nature of creativity. Even during his Rodin phase, when he saw hard work as paramount and accepted no excuses for laziness, his poems attempt to force the appearance of inexplicable moments during which the object is illumined or transformed: the moment when the hydrangea seems to renew its colours, the flamingos stalk off into the imaginary, or the statue of Apollo seems to admonish its viewer. Though inspiration was not the initiating factor in these poems, something that goes beyond the speaker's sheer willpower is what turns a mundane observation into a work of poetry. During his crisis of 1910–14, inspiration is more overtly at issue. The *Poems to Night*, the poems to the future beloved, and the *Duino Elegies* all circle around this topic with unconcealed desperation.

It cannot have helped that Rilke's primary sponsor during this period, Princess Marie von Thurn und Taxis, called him 'Dottor Serafico'. Increasingly, Rilke waited for voices to speak to or through him, and made this idea one of the central thematic concerns in his writing. When poetry that comes by 'Diktat' (dictation) fails to live up to his standards, he attributes it to someone else, as in the sequence *From the Posthumous Papers of Count C.W.*; when Rilke is satisfied with it, he takes credit for what he also claims to have received from an exterior voice, as in the *Sonnets to Orpheus*.

His shift from Rodin's belief in the power of hard work to Marie von Thurn und Taxis's assumption that the Dottor Serafico relied on inspi-

ration accounts for some of the writing troubles Rilke experienced
during the years of the *Elegies*. His publishers, the Kippenbergs, who
knew what an incentive marketplace forces had provided during his
Paris years, were well aware that it was not wise to give him large
advances directly. But others helped out, including Werner Reinhart,
who bought Rilke the stone house at Muzot where he composed the
final *Elegies* and the *Sonnets*. This kind of support meant that Rilke could
return to the notion of inspiration – or perhaps one should say, inspiration with a bad conscience.

Rilke's move from the market to the patronage system was not,
however, the only reason for his change of creative strategy during the
second decade of the twentieth century. Nor was what he, his mother
and Lou Andreas-Salomé, along with several doctors, regarded as his
psychosomatic illness. The crisis went well beyond the personal. It was
the crisis of an era. Rilke's ability to project his own psychological
confusions and depressions onto the despair of an epoch played a
major part in his literary success. The *Duino Elegies* are a case in point:
many readers saw them as a spiritual guidebook through a time of
darkness that continued to linger in the aftermath of the First World
War.

In Munich during the war years, Rilke saw more theatre and opera
than ever before and frequented the company of great minds, literary
and political. He absorbed contemporary culture from a different, more
consumer-oriented perspective than he had done in Paris. In 1921, when
he made a new home for himself in Switzerland, he immediately began
to pile his writing desk with recent publications. These were predominantly in French, procured through an avid correspondence with Paul
Morisse and his wife, who owned a French bookstore in Zurich.[3] Rilke
not only ordered books at a 'breathtaking' pace:[4] he subscribed to a wide
array of French literary journals and magazines. His discovery of Valéry
was perhaps the most important event of that period, and although they
also met in person, the real impact of Valéry on Rilke was transmitted
through his poems and essays. Feeling settled at last may have helped,
but the intense course of reading that Rilke pursued during his first six
months at Muzot is surely one of the capital elements in his poetic
renewal.

His reading during that time includes a number of modernist writers:
Proust, Supervielle, Soupault, Breton, St. John Perse and others. In
letters to his booksellers, to Marie von Thurn und Taxis and to other
friends, he writes perceptively about them, just as he had in his early

book reviews about Thomas Mann or his early art criticism about Neo-Impressionism. He was impressed by Giraudoux's imagination, exalted by Valéry's mastery of language. In Proust's *La Prisonnière* [The Prisoner], he admired 'ces présences latentes de la vie' (those latent presences of life) and the almost disembodied narrative voice, 'de moins en moins un être vivant' (less and less a living being).[5]

Rilke's form of modernism is a very particular kind that is both elegiac and restorative. He did not participate in the various experimental movements that constituted the avant-garde of the teens and twenties. The Futurists were remote from him because of their enthusiasm for modern machinery, which Rilke believed had alienated modern man from simple and more satisfying craftsmanship. He was familiar with Expressionist poetry, notably that of Georg Trakl, whose daring, visionary work he much admired; he also read poetry by Georg Heym, Else Lasker-Schüler, Alfred Wolfenstein, and Johannes R. Becher. He knew personally the Expressionist dramatist and political activist, Ernst Toller, through his connections with the political group around Walter Rathenau. He was delighted to discover the paintings of Franz Marc at the 1916 retrospective in Munich: he praised Marc's work as particularly unified, uncompromising, and pure.[6] He admired Kokoschka, with whom he became friendly during his Munich years, when they worked side by side at the war archive. Still, he was reluctant to delve too deeply into the more painful aspects of Kokoschka's works, for fear of exacerbating his own depressive tendencies.[7]

While Rilke admired the early Picasso, he did not care for his Cubist works or the Cubist movement generally, which he regarded as willful and distorting, helpful only if it remained a studio technique for exploring the structure of objects.[8] While Rilke found Cézanne's paintings interesting precisely for certain techniques that seem to presage abstract art – blank spots, unfinished effects, relational structures created by colours – he tended to resist art where representation disappeared entirely. During the war years, however, he was fascinated by Paul Klee's multi-coloured paintings, which seemed to capture his own experience of a world collapsing.[9] What some critics have read as Rilke's subsequent rejection of abstraction in Klee is really his response to the horrified reactions of his friend Baladine Klossowska, who found this kind of art highly disturbing. In a much discussed letter, he gently tries to show her how the 'Ausfallen des Gegenstands' (loss of the object) can be a real experience – as it was for him during the war and is for others now living in urban centres.[10] He would probably not have agreed with a recent critic's view that abstraction, for Klee, 'never meant a renunciation of the representational mode'[11]; but Rilke's insistence, in *The Seventh Elegy*, on the 'Bewahrung der noch erkannten Gestalt' (retention of still recognisable shape; 1: 712) in the object allows for precisely the kinds of abstraction most common in Klee's art, those where vestigial forms from the world of experienced reality still remain.

Typographical innovations such as Apollinaire's *Calligrammes* and Mallarmé's *Un Coup de Dés* [A Throw of the Dice] seem to have had little impact on him: the only text Rilke wrote in a fanciful shape was a small poem in the shape of an Easter egg in March 1921. Significantly enough, this poem explores the Romantic motif of birdsong, which is understood not as unequivocally natural, but rather as something that must be practised to be fully achieved:

O
das Proben
in allen Vögeln geschiehts.
Horch, die kleine Treppe des Lieds,
und oben:
noch nichts

doch
der Wille
so groß schon und größer das Herz;
sein Wachsen im Raume unendlich gewährts
die Stille:
des Lichts.   (2: 462)

O
practising
in all birds it goes on.
Listen, the little ladder of song,
and at the top:
not quite

still
the will
so great already and greater the heart;
growing in space to forever assert
the silence:
of light.

The Easter egg form (perhaps intended for the back and front of an egg-shaped card) draws attention to the difference between birds' eggs as they occur in nature and the frankly artificial and culturally determined character of Easter eggs. The poem's final praise of silence as a higher form of song indicates its Symbolist heritage, as does its synaesthetic linking of auditory and spatial concepts (the 'little ladder of song') and its identification of silence with a visual phenomenon, light. Still, we should not give too much weight to the calligrammatic form of this presumably occasional poem.

Rilke speaks at times with horror of the experimental art movements. In 1913, he writes to a friend of 'die heutigen, in abgeleiteten Spielereien abgelenkten jungen Maler' (today's young painters, distracted by derivative game-playing).[12] He seems to have resisted Dada, and although he read and admired the Surrealists, even his more inventive metaphors are in a different register. Sound poetry, chance, found objects, automatic writing and the many other techniques used by Dadaists and Surrealists to circumvent the problem of inspiration in a belated age are methods he never seems to have considered, if indeed he knew about them. Rilke's death in 1926 prevented him from knowing some of the works that have since come to define modernism. In the writings of Valéry, Supervielle, Soupault and others, he was most impressed by their attempt to create through poetry a kind of counter-reality. He focussed on their innovations in language and metaphor, not on their theoretical views about how to make a poem. His fanciful suggestion, in 'Ur-Geräusch' [Primal Noise], that one might play the cranial grooves on a phonograph, is an idea that might well have been generated by Max Ernst; but the philosophy underlying Rilke's idea is very different from that of Ernst's 'frottages'. Rilke's image, in his first *Sonnet to Orpheus*, of the 'high tree in the ear' and his description of an acrobat in *The Fifth Elegy* as 'the son of a neck and a nun' are perhaps as close to Surrealism as he ever comes.

It is easy to see why Valéry, among all the high modernists, appealed to Rilke. His sense of belatedness, his obsession with tears, his evocation of silence, his interest in figures like Orpheus and Narcissus meshed well with Rilke's own concerns of the period. Valéry's often exclamatory style (especially in 'Le Cimetière marin' [The Graveyard by the Sea], the first of his poems Rilke translated) had the seraphic tone that Marie von Thurn und Taxis was encouraging in Rilke himself. But unlike Valéry, Rilke did not direct his restorative efforts toward classical antiquity. The neo-classical element that is so decisive in Valéry – as also in his contemporaries Eliot and Pound – is almost entirely missing in Rilke, even when he addresses classical themes, as in his poems about

Apollo, Orpheus and Narcissus. Rilke's most classicising texts in fact rely mainly on Symbolist or aestheticist modulations of antique motifs. Without Rodin's sculptures, Mallarmé's Orphism and Valéry's Narcissus there would be fewer recollections of classical antiquity in Rilke's works. Rilke's version of Valéry's symbolist essay on the Orphic architect of antique times produces one of his most strikingly modernist sonnets.

Rilke's experiments with imagery are the most innovative elements in his work, beginning as early as *The Book of Hours* and continuing into his *Duino Elegies, Sonnets to Orpheus* and certain poems from the last years of his life. Many of Rilke's unusual images have aestheticist origins: Phryne as a symbol for autonomous art; the angel as a muse; the smile on a torso; and the woman's face that Narcissus penetrates in the mirror. But Rilke makes something new of them. In his most daring poetry he aims to develop poetic correlatives for the realm of the imaginary. The topography of the 'heart's mountains', the 'other side of the air', Orpheus' temple of sound, the Laments' hieratic geography and the 'worldinnerspace' of poetic projection represent Rilke's conception of something that lies beyond the realm of empirical experience. More than any other aspect of his poetry, this network of images moves Rilke well along the path toward abstraction, despite his ambivalent relation to abstract painting.

Rilke's poetic success springs from his way of combining two contradictory gestures: on the one hand, his texts summon the reader to feel directly addressed; on the other, they deny access to what they imply is an impenetrable secret at their heart. The appellative structures of his poetry mediate between the ancient figure of apostrophe and a modern desire to cross the boundary between art and life. His 'Archaic Torso of Apollo', with its concluding image of a star bursting its borders as the statue confronts its viewer with a stony imperative, models this effect most clearly. *The Duino Elegies* speak from an unstable vantage-point that calls forth identification with their meditative argument but also overwhelm their readers with a proliferation of hermetic metaphors. Rilke's use of abstract figures has a related effect, allowing us to fill them with our own mental associations while implying that they are part of a language we still must attempt to master.

Filling his mental crucible with recent publications was certainly a conscious part of Rilke's poetic strategy in the early nineteen-twenties. He continued to fashion his career into his final years, continuing his carefully composed correspondence and writing his own epitaph. The epitaph takes a haiku-like form unusual in his work:[13] it is an unrhymed three-line poem that depends on multiple meanings impossible to reproduce in English:[14]

> Rose, oh reiner Widerspruch, Lust
> Niemandes Schlaf zu sein unter soviel
> Lidern.   (2: 185)

> Rose, oh pure contradiction, desire
> to be nobody's sleep under so many
> eyelids.

The text takes shape around a cluster of ideas and images dear to the Symbolists: the mystic rose as a symbol for poetry, the poem as essentially contradictory, the invisible author beneath a decorative surface, absence as more significant than presence, privileging of the mind's eye over the bodily eye. The poem reverses an earlier poem, called 'Schlaflied' [Lullaby], from the *New Poems*, in which the speaker imagines himself whispering or rustling like a linden-tree over the grave of a lost loved one and laying words 'wie Augenlider' (like eyelids) over the dead woman's breast and limbs while she 'sleeps' (1: 631). In much the same way as the speaker of 'Lullaby' imagines the dead woman hearing from the grave, so the epitaph is designed to let the dead Rilke 'speak' from beyond the grave. By calling death sleep (while knowing that it is not), the epitaph reactivates a traditional trope; but by continuing to speak, it negates even its claim of sleeping. It declares the persistence of desire – the essential constituent of life – into the condition of death, but it displaces this desire from a human agent into the rose, as if the voice from beyond the grave were also identical with nature. As in poems like 'To Music', or the 'mirror' sonnet, Rilke's epitaph hovers between naming (or defining) and addressing the rose. Unlike classical epitaphs that address the reader, this poem ignores the reader and speaks only to or of the rose. If nobody is there, who engages in this speech act, and, above all, who gasps 'oh pure contradiction'? Rilke continues to control our responses even from his gravestone.

Convention would see this as an appropriate stopping-place. But much of Rilke's poetry from his final years is in a lighter vein. Here are some little French verses written in September 1926 (four months before Rilke's death) and found in his papers among clean copies of completed poems. The verses are addressed to a brand of eraser called 'Nigrovorine':

A Nigrovorine qui s'en va...

Tu fais 'non' de ton corps, et *non*,
comme on fait *non* de la tête.
Pour entendre si l'on répond,
parfois tu t'arrêtes.

Tu te consumes, petite martyre,
grise dévote;
pour qu'elle expire
tu frottes la faute!

En sa plus secrète nature
tu l'irrites et tu l'agaces,
et tu mets à sa place
la pure fin de ta trace pure.   (2: 685)

To Nigrovorine, disappearing...

'No', you declare,
with a bodily shake.
Sometimes you stop:
is that a mistake?

Consuming yourself,
little grey martyr,
is error's death
really fair barter?

You underhand tease!
Dare you put in its place,
pure and simple, the end
of your own pure trace?

This witty little text takes the opposite tack from the epitaph, casting a less than devout eye on the cult of pure poetry, absence and negativity. The Symbolists' desire to remove from their poetry any trace of all too physical reality is given bodily form in the eraser Nigrovorine. The act of rubbing out an error is visualised as the shaking of the eraser's body, akin to the shake of a head saying 'no'. Claiming a superior kind of purity, the eraser becomes a 'little grey martyr', its body physically diminishing as it performs its task of eliminating mistakes. Death, perhaps because it is only present in metaphor, is treated with a light touch. The 'death' of error is bought at the price of the eraser's self-consumption, while the 'end' of the eraser's 'pure trace' is just as much a blank as the trace itself. Pure poetry as a kind of religion-substitute is here gently mocked.

Still, this kind of scepticism is rare in Rilke's works. Irony, pervasive in Pound and Eliot, was foreign to him. Nor was he really interested in the Mallarméan notion of erasure. Rilke's process of self-creation was in fact a life-long project of restoration. Avoiding the avant-garde gesture of making a break with the past, Rilke revived elements from tradition and recombined them according to his own catalytic methods. Much of his poetry is written as if he longed to be one of the 'early dead' whom he celebrated in his poetry. Their voices infiltrated his poetry, repeatedly causing the self-construction project to break down. In an epoch that tried, sometimes in quite paradoxical ways, to control the creative act, loss of control was devastating. The rift between conscious construction and its ever-threatening collapse is what makes Rilke such an eloquent witness to the first decades of the modernist era.

Notes

INTRODUCTION: RILKE'S WRITING DESK

1 *Rainer Maria Rilke – Ellen Key, Briefwechsel. Mit Briefen von und an Clara Rilke-Westhoff*, ed. Theodore Fiedler (Frankfurt and Leipzig: Insel, 1933), p. 212.

2 Harold Bloom speaks in his early chapters of a poet's 'deliberate misinterpretation' of another's work (*The Anxiety of Influence* (Oxford University Press, 1973, repr. 1975), p. 43), but subsequently turns to a more Freudian understanding of poetic creativity according to which the 'poetic father has been absorbed into the id, rather than into the superego' (p. 80).

3 For example Cynthia Chase, '"Viewless Wings": Intertextual Interpretation of Keats's "Ode to a Nightingale"', in *Lyric Poetry: Beyond New Criticism*, ed. Chaviva Hošeck and Patricia Parker (Ithaca and London: Cornell University Press, 1985), p. 213.

4 See Russell Berman, *Cultural Studies of Modern Germany* (Madison: University of Wisconsin Press, 1993), p. 10.

5 Rilke's works are cited according to *Sämtliche Werke*, ed. Ernst Zinn, 6 vols. (Frankfurt: Insel, 1955–1966). References are given in parentheses, with volume number followed by page number.

I FASHIONING THE SELF

1 Louis Menand, *Discovering Modernism. T. S. Eliot and his Context* (Oxford and New York: Oxford University Press, 1987), pp. 117–118.

2 With the exception of Tineke Ritmeester, 'Heterosexism, Misogyny, and Mother-Hatred in Rilke Scholarship: The Case of Sophie Rilke-Entz (1851–31)', *Women in German Yearbook 6: Feminist Studies and German Culture*, ed. Jeanette Clausen and Helen Cafferty (New York, 1991), 63–81.

3 See Claudia Nelson, *Boys will be Girls. The Feminine Ethic and British Children's Fiction, 1857–1917* (New Brunswick and London: Rutgers University Press, 1991).

4 See Mark M. Anderson, *Kafka's Clothes. Ornament and Aestheticism in the Habsburg Fin de Siècle* (Oxford: Clarendon Press, 1992).

5 I adopt this formulation from David Miles, '"Pleats, Pockets, Buckles and

Buttons": Kafka's New Literalism and the Poetics of the Fragment', in B. Bennett, A. Kaes and W. J. Lillyman, eds., *Probleme der Moderne: Studien zur deutschen Literatur von Nietzsche bis Brecht* (Tübingen: Niemeyer, 1983), pp. 331–42.

6 Marie von Thurn und Taxis, *Erinnerungen an Rainer Maria Rilke* (Frankfurt: Insel, 1966), pp. 43–46.

7 Robert Jensen, *Marketing Modernism in Fin-de-Siècle Europe* (Princeton University Press, 1994), p. 10.

8 *Briefe an einen jungen Dichter* (Leipzig: Insel, 1929), p. 26.

9 See Kathleen L. Komar, 'The Mediating Muse: Of Men, Women and the Feminine in the Work of Rainer Maria Rilke', *The Germanic Review*, LXIV (1989), 129–133.

10 *Renaissance Self-Fashioning. From More to Shakespeare* (Chicago University Press, 1990), p. 9.

11 Letter to Robert Heinz Heygrodt, 24 December, 1921 in *Briefe aus Muzot 1921 bis 1926* (Leipzig: Insel, 1935), p. 62.

12 Still, Prague left traces in Rilke's work beyond this first volume. See Egon Schwarz, 'Die Prager Gesellschaft in Rilkes Frühwerk', *Saggi di Letteratura Praghese* (Naples: Instituto Universitario Orientale, 1987), 1–18.

13 For example, 'When I entered the University' (I: 33–34), which plays on Faust's well-known monologue in his study.

14 Joseph von Eichendorff, *Gedichte, Epen, Dramen* (Stuttgart: Cotta, 1978), pp. 166–167.

15 In German, the verb 'rieseln' means both 'ripple' and 'rustle'.

16 The book was doubtless the volume of poems *What Life has Given* (1883).

17 See Anna A. Tavis, *Rilke's Russia. A Cultural Encounter* (Evanston, Illinois: Northwestern University Press, 1994), pp. 14–18.

18 See Karl Webb, *Rainer Maria Rilke and Jugendstil: Affinities, Influences, Adaptations* (Chapel Hill: University of North Carolina Press, 1978).

19 I quote the poems in their first version of 1897, not in the second, revised edition of 1909.

20 Verlaine conceived of the poet's 'soul' as 'landscape'. Baudelaire developed the motif further in his poem, 'L'Ennemi' [The Enemy], in *Les Fleurs du Mal* (1861), and it was continued by Huysmans in his novel *A rebours* [Against Nature] (1884).

21 See Ralph Freedman, *Life of a Poet: Rainer Maria Rilke* (New York: Farrar, Straus and Giroux, 1996), p. 75.

22 Published in *Die Nation*, 1892. It was based on those poems of George's that had been privately printed in the late 1880s.

23 In the original edition of *To Celebrate Myself*, both opening and closing sections consisted of a poetic epigraph followed by seventeen other poems. The frame around the poems on young women was thus symmetrical.

24 *Lebensrückblick*, ed. Ernst Pfeiffer (Frankfurt a.M.: Suhrkamp, 1968), p. 9.

25 Aris Fioretos, 'Prayer and Ignorance in Rilke's Buch vom mönchischen Leben', *The Germanic Review* LXV (1990), 171–177.

26 It was gleaned from her intensive reading of Akim Lvovitch Volynsky. See Tavis, *Rilke's Russia*, esp. pp. 26–27.

27 See Fioretos, 'Prayer and Ignorance', pp. 171–177.

28 Leo Tolstoy, *What is Art?*, trans. Richard Pevear and Larissa Volokhonsky (Harmondsworth: Penguin, 1995), p. 37.

29 See Tavis, *Rilke's Russia*, p. 37.

30 The text is quoted here according to the original version of 1899 (3: 291).

31 Rilke does not use an exclamation mark. Letter to Anton Kippenberg, August 1912, in *Briefe an seinen Verleger* (Leipzig: Insel, 1934), I: 141.

32 See Donald Prater, *A Ringing Glass. The Life of Rainer Maria Rilke* (Oxford: Clarendon Press, 1986), p. 57; Freedman, *Life of a Poet: Rainer Maria Rilke*, p. 108.

33 In the later version of the text, Rilke changed the cornet's first name, radically altered the 'quotation' from the seventeenth-century chronicle, and made a number of smaller changes.

34 See Rilke's letter to August Sauer, 11 January, 1914, in which he writes at length about Stifter and says that Stifter's *Studien*, among other texts, had 'preoccupied [him] for a long time.'

35 *Before the Battle*, watercolour on paper, mounted on canvas, $16\frac{3}{4} \times 11$ in., Museum of Fine Art, Boston; *Lady Affixing a Pennant*, watercolour on paper, $5\frac{5}{8} \times 5\frac{5}{8}$ in., Tate Gallery, London; *Going to Battle*, pen and ink and grey wash on vellum, $8\frac{7}{8} \times 7\frac{11}{16}$ in., Tate Gallery, London; *The Knight's Farewell*, pen and ink, Ashmolean Museum, Oxford.

36 The passage on mediaeval tapestries in *Malte Laurids Brigge* and his reliance on Froissart's chronicles for his retelling, in the same novel, of the story of Gaston Phöbus and part of the story of Charles VI of France, are a case in point.

37 It appeared in *Appreciations*. Page numbers cited in the following refer to *Selected Writings of Walter Pater*, ed. Harold Bloom (New York: Columbia University Press, 1974); here, p. 190.

38 Carolyn Williams, *Transfigured World. Walter Pater's Aesthetic Historicism* (Ithaca and London: Cornell University Press, 1989), p. 47. My summary of her argument is drawn largely from pp. 57–67.

39 The journal was *Deutsche Arbeit*. Kafka's characteristic use of the pronoun 'one' (German: 'man') does not appear until after 1904, with the exception of the undatable text, 'Wish to become a Red Indian', which appeared in the collection *Meditation* (1913) but was clearly written much earlier. The text can profitably be read as a parody of Rilke's *Cornet*.

40 I am thinking here, for example, of the opening paragraph of Musil's story 'Tonka' (1924).

41 Achim von Arnim, *Werke*, vol. 1, *Hollin's Liebesleben. Gräfin Dolores*, ed. Paul Michael Lützeler (Frankfurt a.M.: Deutscher Klassiker Verlag, 1989), pp. 396.

42 Felix Wittmer, 'Rilkes "Cornet"', *Publications of the Modern Language Association* XLIV (1929), 911–924, reprinted in Rüdiger Görner, ed., *Rainer Maria*

Rilke (Darmstadt: Wissenschaftliche Buchgesellschaft, 1987), pp. 11–25.

43 In fact, Pászthory's setting does not really resemble Schönberg's atonal pieces (I am grateful to Peter Bloom for musicological advice about this piece). Rilke himself disliked Pászthory's setting, which he described as making his text appear moth-eaten (letter to Katharina Kippenberg, 13 October, 1916; on this, see Harry E. Seelig, 'Rilke and Music. Orpheus and the Maenadic Muse', in *Rilke-Rezeptionen. Rilke Reconsidered*, ed. Sigrid Bauschinger and Susan L. Cocalis (Tübingen and Basel: Francke, 1995), p. 69).

44 Manfred Engel gives the clearest explanation for this paradox when he speaks of the novel's 'double optics'. See *Malte Laurids Brigge. Kommentierte Ausgabe* (Stuttgart: Reclam, 1997), p. 347.

45 See, in particular, Ulrich Fülleborn, 'Form und Sinn der Aufzeichnungen des Malte Laurids Brigge. Rilkes Prosabuch und der moderne Roman', in *Unterscheidung und Bewahrung. Festschrift für Hermann Kunisch zum 60. Geburtstag* (Berlin, 1961), pp. 147–169; Ernst Fedor Hoffmann, 'Zum dichterischen Verfahren in Rilke's *Aufzeichnungen des Malte Laurids Brigge*', *Deutsche Vierteljahrsschrift* 42 (1968), 202–230; Judith Ryan, '"Hypothetisches Erzählen": Zur Funktion von Phantasie und Einbildung in Rilkes *Malte Laurids Brigge*', *Jahrbuch der Deutschen Schillergesellschaft* (1971), 341–374; Anthony R. Stephens, *Rilkes Malte Laurids Brigge. Strukturanalyse des erzählerischen Bewußtseins* (Herbert Lang: Bern and Frankfurt, 1974). On Rilke's theory of art as developed in Malte, see Gertrud Höhler, *Niemandes Sohn. Zur Poetologie Rainer Maria Rilkes* (Munich: Fink, 1979).

46 On French influences, see Maurice Betz, 'Über die Aufzeichnungen des Malte Laurids Brigge', in *R. M. Rilke in Paris* (Zurich: Arche, 1958), pp. 67–91; on Scandinavian sources see Hans Aarsleff, 'Rilke, Herman Bang, and Malte', *Actes du IVe Congrès de l'Association Internationale de Littérature comparée* (1964), 628–636, and Børge G. Madsen, 'Influences from J. P. Jacobsen and Sigbjørn Obstfelder on R. M. Rilke's *Die Aufzeichnungen des Malte Laurids Brigge*', *Scandinavian Studies* 26 (1954), 105–114; Helmut Naumann discusses Rilke's reading of the 'Dame à la licorne' tapestries in *Malte-Studien. Ansätze zu einem neuen Verständnis Rilkes* (Rheinfelden: Schäuble, 1985), pp. 95–148.

47 Anthony Stephens argues that the concept of personality developed in *Malte Laurids Brigge* is that of a double surface surrounding an inner kernel (see *Rilke's Malte Laurids Brigge*, esp. pp. 100–108).

48 *Briefe an einen jungen Dichter*, p. 43.

49 On their relation, see Theodore Fiedler's foreword to *Rainer Maria Rilke – Ellen Key Briefwechsel*, pp. vii–xviii.

50 *Niels Lyhne*, in *Jens Peter Jacobsens sämtliche Werke* (Leipzig: Insel, n.d.), p. 417.

51 See Aarsleff, 'Rilke, Herman Bang, and Malte', p. 631.

52 *Ibid.*, p. 629.

53 *Ellen Olestjerne* (Frankfurt: Fischer, 1985), p. 149. Page numbers in the following discussion refer to this edition.

54 The passage is also a reworking of André Gide's novel *Le Retour de l'enfant prodigue* (1907).

2 ARTS AND CRAFTS

1 Brigitte Bradley regards Rilke's 'Ding' as analogous to T. S. Eliot's 'objective correlative'. See *R. M. Rilkes Neue Gedichte. Ihr zyklisches Gefüge* (Bern: Francke, 1967), p. 12. In *Umschlag und Verwandlung* (Munich: Winkler, 1972), I argue that the *New Poems* are dependent on the operations of creative subjectivity.

2 *Briefe 1906–7* (Leipzig: Insel, 1930), p. 405.

3 *Ibid.*, p. 390.

4 John Hollander calls this phenomenon 'notional ekphrasis'. *The Gazer's Spirit: Poems Speaking to Silent Works of Art* (Chicago and London: The University of Chicago Press, 1995), pp. 7–29.

5 See Gisbert Kranz, *Das Bildgedicht in Europa: Zur Theorie und Geschichte einer literarischen Gattung* (Paderborn: Schöningh, 1973) and *Das Bildgedicht. Theorie, Lexikon, Bibliographie* (Cologne and Vienna: Böhlau Verlag, 1981), esp. pp. 1158–1159.

6 Rilke owned Martin Luther's translation of the Bible; he also read the Kautzsch translation which had been recommended to him by Lou Andreas-Salomé. See *Rainer Maria Rilke – Lou Andreas-Salomé Briefwechsel*, ed. Ernst Pfeiffer (Frankfurt: Insel, 1989), Lou's letter to Rilke, 9 November, 1903, p. 123.

7 Grant Henley argues that certain of Rilke's Biblical poems can be linked to Rilke's personal struggle over loss and mourning during this period ('Aus der Fülle des Herzens: Rilke's Biblical Poetry in the *Neue Gedichte, Anderer Teil*', *Neophilologus*, forthcoming).

8 Stephen Gauster demonstrates that prophecy, in Rilke's Biblical poems, can be seen as a figure for poetry ('Of Poets, Prophets, and Platinum: Harold Bloom, T. S. Eliot and the Problem of Influence and Originality in Rilke's Biblical Poems'; unpublished paper).

9 In *Die Bücher der Hirten- und Preisgedichte der Sagen und Sänge und der hängenden Gärten* (1895; 6th Impression, Berlin: Georg Bondi, 1920), p. 27.

10 Two other motifs in Rilke's poem, the fruiting tree of section two and the star of section three, also occur in George's poem.

11 Peter Paul Rubens had also chosen to represent the elderly David, but in his painting the aged musician, dressed in a rich ermine collar, is shown playing the harp, his eyes fixed upon the distance as if in a visionary act (*King David*, oil on canvas, 85 × 69 cm, Frankfurt). See Philippe Junod, *La Musique vue par les peintres* (Lausanne: Edita S.A., 1988), p. 94–95.

12 'Rilkes Weg ins 20. Jahrhundert', in *Interpretationen zu Rainer Maria Rilke*, ed. Egon Schwarz (Stuttgart: Klett, 1983), p. 64.

13 Alfred Doppler comments on this effect in 'Die poetische Verfahrensweise in Rilkes *Neuen Gedichten*' (1976), reprinted in Görner, ed., *Rainer Maria Rilke*, p. 346.

14 The series of poems 'Der Alchimist', 'Der Reliquienschrein', 'Das Gold', and 'Der Stylit' (1: 576–580) is a good example of this tendency.

15 Ed. A. van Bever and Paul Léautaud (Paris: Mercure de France, 1900).
16 Ed. G. Walch (Paris: Delagrave, 1906).
17 Cf., for example, Gustave Kahn's 'Le vieux mendiant' and A.-Ferdinand Herold's 'La Cathédrale' (*Poètes d'Aujourd'hui*, 1: 211–212, 168) and Iwan Gilkin's "La Capitale" and Valmy-Baysse's "La Phtisique" (*Anthologie des poètes français contemporains*, 3: 124, 523).
18 Paris: Charpentier, 1896.
19 *A Life of Picasso*, vol. 1 (1881–1906) (New York: Random House, 1991), p. 216.
20 'Flower Pots', Oil on canvas, 97 x 88 cm., Collection Mrs John Hay Whitney. For Blanche's 'Blue Hydrangeas', see Arthur Edwin Bye, *Pots and Pans, or Studies in Still-Life Painting* (Princeton University Press, 1921), plate facing p. 142. Unfortunately this book does not give the date or location of this painting. A reproduction of 'La Petite Fille aux hortensias', along with a helpful commentary, can be found in *Jacques-Emile Blanche, peintre (1861–1942)*, catalogue of the musée des Beaux-Arts, Rouen, and the town of Brescia (Paris: Editions de la Réunion des musées nationaux, 1997), pp. 82–83.
21 'Un Professeur de beauté', in *Contre Sainte Beuve* (Paris: Gallimard, 1971), p. 516.
22 See Debora L. Silverman, *Art Nouveau in Fin-de-Siècle France. Politics, Psychology, and Style* (Berkeley: University of California Press, 1989), p. 234.
23 *The Flowers Personified; being a translation of Grandville's 'Les Fleurs animées'*, trans. N. Cleaveland (New York: R. Martin, 1847–49). See also Silverman, pp. 232, 234–35, and 268–69.
24 *Anthologie des poètes français contemporains*, 3: 45.
25 *Jacques-Emile Blanche, peintre (1861–1942)*, pp. 82–83.
26 August Stahl suggests that the poem may have been inspired by an actual potted hydrangea Rilke owned. *Rilke. Kommentar zum lyrischen Werk* (Munich: Winkler, 1978), pp. 214–215.
27 See his letter to Clara Rilke, 18 October, 1907, in which he refers to the manuscript as 'die blauen Blätter' 'the blue sheets of paper'. *Briefe 1906–1907*, p. 389; see also editor's note, *Sämtliche Werke*, 1: 526.
28 Rilke's trip to Belgium took place from 29 July – 16 August, 1906.
29 Letter of 27 July, 1906 to Clara Rilke, *Briefe aus den Jahren 1906–1907*, p. 57. He was doubtless familiar with Emile Verhaeren's poems on Flemish topics, 'Les Flamandes' (1883) in *Oeuvres* (Geneva: Slatkine, 1977).
30 Two quatrains have become four; one tercet has become a quatrain and the final tercet remains in conventional form; but the volta is displaced to the beginning of the fourth quatrain.
31 This motif has eluded the explanatory efforts of several critics. See Heidi Heinemann, '"O wenn er steigt, behangen wie ein Stier": Rilkes Gedicht "Der Turm"', *Publications of the English Goethe Society* 32 (1963), 46–73; H. W. Belmore, '"Behangen wie ein Stier": Eine Entgegnung auf H. Heinemann (mit Berichtigung von H. Heinemann)', *Publications of the English Goethe Society* 33 (1963), 1–9; and Brigitte Bradley, *R. M. Rilkes Neue Gedichte*, pp. 135–137.

32 Dante Gabriel Rossetti, *Poems and Translations 1850–1870* (London: Oxford University Press, 1913), pp. 154–156.

33 Rilke was familiar with Rodenbach: he mentions him in his essay 'Furnes' (5: 1006), and alludes to his famous novella *Bruges-la-morte* in his poem 'Quai du Rosaire' (1: 534) and in his correspondence (*Briefe aus den Jahren 1906–1907*, p. 64).

34 Page references to *The Carillon Player* are to the French *Le Carilloneur* (Paris: Charpentier, 1897); here, pp. 26–27.

35 The painting is in the Dahlem museum in Berlin; Rilke doubtless saw it when he was living in Berlin in 1899–1900.

36 The poem was withdrawn from the collection in 1861 and subsequently published in Brussels in three different editions between 1864 and 1869. See Claude Pichois's commentary, in Charles Baudelaire, *Oeuvres complètes*, vol. 1 (Paris: Gallimard, 1975), pp. 812 and 1123.

37 Baudelaire, *Oeuvres complètes*, vol. 1, p. 150.

38 Rilke is shown to have adapted various themes and motifs from Baudelaire (L. de Sugar, *Baudelaire et R. M. Rilke. Etude d'influence et d'affinités spirituelles* (Paris: Nouvelles Editions Latines, 1954), pp. 61–79), and is said to have learned from him how to merge the subjective and the objective (K. A. J. Batterby, *Rilke and France. A Study in Poetic Development* (Oxford University Press, 1966), p. 128) and the beautiful and the ugly (Paul de Man, *Allegories of Reading. Figural Language in Rousseau, Nietzsche, Rilke, and Proust* (New Haven: Yale University Press, 1979), p. 23).

39 Larousse, Pierre, *Grand dictionnaire universel du XIXe siècle* (Paris, 1866–1879; repr. Paris: Slatkine, 1982), 10: 1: 402.

40 This passage is actually a double allusion: there is also an echo of Novalis' fragment about the person who miraculously succeeded in lifting the veil of Isis, only to see 'Wunder des Wunders – sich selbst' (wonder of wonders – himself). Novalis [Friedrich von Hardenberg], *Schriften*, ed. Paul Kluckhohn and Richard Samuel (Stuttgart: Kohlhammer, 1960), 1: 110.

41 The flamingos in the Jardin des Plantes belong to what ornithologists term the Old World flamingo (phoenicopterus ruber roseus). Their outer feathers are extremely pale, flushed with only the slightest tinge of pink; their underfeathers are bright red and black. When they are asleep or at rest, all that can be seen is their delicate colouring; as soon as they move, however, their vivid underfeathers become visible.

42 Georges Rodenbach, whose work Rilke studied in preparation for his trip to Belgium in 1906, uses a related image of 'cygnes en fleur' (blossoming swans) in his poetry. *Oeuvres* (Geneva: Slatkine, 1978), 2: 225, 229, 235.

43 The section of the Jardin des Plantes that contains the flamingos has remained much the same as it was when Rilke visited it in 1907–1908 (unlike the wild animal cages, which were rebuilt in the 1920's). The birds are kept uncaged (their wings are clipped) on a grassy area through which runs a small stream; behind this area, partly hidden by trees, is the 'Grande Volière', an enormous metal cage in which a variety of other birds are kept.

It is characteristic of the poem's ambiguous treatment of external reality that these details are only sketchily represented.

44 Brigitte Bradley (*Rainer Maria Rilke. Der Neuen Gedichte anderer Teil* (Bern: Francke, 1976), p. 205) and Karl-Heinz Fingerhut (*Das Kreatürliche im Werke Rainer Maria Rilkes. Untersuchungen zur Figur des Tieres* (Bonn: Bouvier, 1970), p. 165) regard this process more positively.

45 Joachim Heusinger von Waldegg, 'Jean-Léon Gérômes "Phryne vor den Richtern"', *Jahrbuch der Hamburger Kunstsammlungen* 17 (1972), 124.

46 Helmut R. Leppien, 'Genre im Kostüm', in *Ein Hamburger sammelt in London* (Hamburg-Altona: Dingwort, 1984), p. 39.

47 James Rolleston, 'The Poetics of Quotation: Walter Benjamin's Arcades Project', *Publications of the Modern Language Association* 104 (1989), 119.

48 Charles Baudelaire, *Critique d'art*, ed. Claude Pichois (Paris: Colin, 1965), p. 74; P. Brunel, 'Lesbos', in Max Milner, ed., *Baudelaire: Les Fleurs du mal. L'Interiorité de la forme* (Paris: Sedes, 1989), p. 88.

49 Oil on canvas, 80 × 128 cm., Hamburger Kunsthalle.

50 *Larousse du XIXe siècle*, 12: 2: 901.

51 See Waldegg, 'Gérômes "Phryne"', p. 123, and Gerald M. Ackermann, *La Vie et l'oeuvre de Jean-Léon Gérôme* (Paris: ACR Edition, 1986), pp. 55–56. Rilke was familiar with Falguière's bronzes (see *Briefe 1902–1906*, pp. 23, 241, 270).

52 Stoullig, *Les Annales du théâtre et de la musique*, 29e année 1903 (pub. 1904), pp. 124–125; 31e année 1905 (pub. 1906), p. 16.

53 *La Vie Parisienne*, 16 January, 1909, p. 54.

54 In *La Vie Parisienne*, 7 August, 1909, p. 573.

55 Théophile Gautier, *Abécédaire du salon de 1861* (Paris: Dentu, 1861), p. 178.

56 Waldegg, 'Gérômes "Phryne"', p. 123.

57 Ackermann, *Gérôme*, pp. 55–56.

58 Pencil, 88 × 131 mm., private collection. Chappuis dates the sketch 1870–1874 (p. 298).

59 *Briefe 1906–1907*, p. 315.

60 *Briefe 1902–1906*, p. 120; *Briefe 1906–1907*, p. 91.

61 Paris, n.d. (1899), 6: 860.

62 *Larousse du XIXe siècle*, 12: 2: 901.

63 For a more detailed discussion of the composition and use of colour in this painting see Leppien, p. 41.

64 Letter to Clara Rilke, 13 June, 1907, *Briefe 1906–1907*, p. 267.

65 One of these paintings, 'La Chemise enlevée' (ca. 1765–72; oil on canvas, 36 × 43 cm., Louvre), shows a small cupid mischievously undressing a lovely young woman lying on a bed. This treatment of the theme of beauty unveiled contrasts sharply with Gérôme's treatment of the theme in his 'Phryne'.

66 In this respect, the Apollo differs from Walter Benjamin's definition of aura in his essay on Baudelaire. There, the object invested with aura 'opens its eyes', not to send a message to the poet, but to draw him with it

into the distance. *Schriften*, ed. Rolf Tiedemann and Hermann Schweppenhäuser (Frankfurt: Suhrkamp, 1974), 1: 2: 647n.

67 Letter to Lou Andreas Salomé, 10 August, 1903, in *Rainer Maria Rilke – Lou Andreas-Salomé Briefwechsel*, p. 103.

68 *Oeuvres*, pp. 519–523.

69 Wolfgang Schivelbusch, *Lichtblicke. Zur Geschichte der künstlichen Helligkeit im 19. Jahrhundert* (Munich and Vienna: Carl Hanser, 1983; repr. Frankfurt: Fischer, 1986). Some early electric lamps, modelled on gas lamps and often the result of converting gas lamps to electricity, also had a switch that turned; but it did not create the effect of a dimmer switch (p. 71).

70 I am grateful to Egon Schwarz for pointing this out. Gerhard Wahrig, *Deutsches Wörterbuch*, defines 'Glassturz' as a protective glass cover for an art object or clock (p. 567). Rilke uses the word in this sense in *Malte* (6: 781, 6: 906, 6: 909).

71 *Oeuvres*, p. 70.

72 See Charles Chassé, 'Les thèmes de l'éventail et de l'éclairage au gaz dans l'oeuvre de Mallarmé', *Revue des sciences humaines* 61–64 (1951), 333–344; Jean Pommier, '"Le Tombeau de Charles Baudelaire" de Mallarmé', *Mercure de France* 332 (1958), 656–675, and 'Ou que le gaz récent...', *Synthèses* 22, nos. 258–259 (1968), 96–98.

73 The principal contenders were André Gide and Jean-Marc Bernard, who conducted the debate through a series of polemical articles and open letters in the *Nouvelle Revue Française*. The debate was taken up again in 1912 and 1913. See D. Hampton Morris, *Stéphane Mallarmé: Twentieth-Century Criticism 1901–1971* (Missippi: Romance Monographs, 1977), pp. 14–15. Mallarmé resurfaces in Rilke's works precisely at this moment of renewed interest.

74 Ross Chambers, *Opposition et melancholie. Les débuts du modernisme en France* (Paris: Corti, 1987).

75 William Waters notes that 'there is something oddly anatomical about the image'; he goes on to speak of the 'loose housing' which 'contributes to the eyes' uncomfortably detached quality'. 'Answerable Aesthetics: Reading "You" in Rilke', *Comparative Literature* 48 (1996), p. 138.

76 Martina Lauster's 'Stone Imagery in the Sonnet', *Comparative Literature* 45 (1993), 146–174, emphasizes the 'hardness' of form in Baudelaire and Rilke.

77 See esp. 5: 218–219. On the importance of surfaces, see 5: 150 and 5: 167.

78 On the function of Rilke's Venice experiences as an impulse for poetic creativity, see Richard Exner, '"Dieser Streifen Zwischen-Welt" und der Wille zur Kunst: Überlegungen zu Rilke in Venedig', *Blätter der Rilke-Gesellschaft* 16/17 (1989/90): 57–78.

79 Joachim W. Storck, 'Rilkes frühestes Venedig-Erlebnis', *Blätter der Rilke-Gesellschaft* 16/17 (1989/90), 22–23.

80 See letter to Dory von der Mühll, April 1921, *Briefe an Schweizer Freunde*, ed. Rätus Luck (Frankfurt: Suhrkamp, 1990), p. 161.

81 John Ruskin, *Les Pierres de Venise*, trans. Mathilde P. Crémieux, preface by Robert de la Sizeranne (Paris: H. Laurens, 1906). Two years later,

Sizeranne also published a substantial collection from various works of Ruskin, *Pages choisies* (Paris: Hachette, 1908), with a thirty-page introduction that surveyed Ruskin's life, works, and opinions.

82 Sizeranne speaks of Ruskin's rehabilition of the concept of work and his promulgation of art for all (John Ruskin, *Les Pierres de Venise*, p. xvii).

83 *The Queen of the Air. Being a Study of the Greek Myths of Cloud and Storm* (1869; rep. New York: Charles E. Merrill and Co., 1891), p. 233.

84 Elizabeth Helsinger, *Ruskin and the Art of the Beholder* (Cambridge: Harvard University Press, 1982); and Susan Phelps Gordon, 'Heartsight Deep as Eyesight: Ruskin's Aspirations for Modern Art', in *John Ruskin and the Victorian Eye*, ed. Harriet Welchel (New York: Harry N. Abrams, 1993).

85 *Modern Painters* (London: 1860), vol. 5, p. 177.

86 Helsinger, *Ruskin*, p. 307, n. 22.

87 Ruskin spells the word 'incrusted'; I have normalised his spelling.

88 On this issue, see John D. Rosenberg, *The Darkening Glass: A Portrait of Ruskin's Genius* (New York: Columbia University Press, 1961), pp. 85–87.

89 Helsinger, *Ruskin*, p. 162.

3 WRITING TROUBLES

1 Letter to Artur Hospelt, 11 February 1912, in *Briefe aus den Jahren 1907 bis 1914* (Leipzig: Insel, 1933), p. 197.

2 For example, two famous paintings by Orazio and Artemisa Gentileschi, both titled 'Judith and Maidservant with the Head of Holofernes', painted in 1610–12 and 1630 respectively. In Rilke's day, Orazio Gentileschi's painting was in Genoa, Artemisia Gentileschi's painting in Naples; they are now in the Wadsworth Atheneum, Hartford, Conn., and in Detroit, respectively. So, too, Carlo Saraceni's 'Judith with the Head of Holofernes' (ca. 1615–20; then in Venice; now in the Dayton Art Institute). For a fuller listing of paintings depicting the Biblical Judith, see Mechthilde Hatz, *Frauengestalten des Alten Testaments in der bildenden Kunst von 1850 bis 1918. Eva, Dalila, Judith, Salome* (Diss. Heidelberg, 1972), pp. 393–399.

3 Luca Giordano's painting on the ceiling of the Certosa of San Martino, Naples (1704), as well as Carlo Maratti's mosaic in St. Peter's, Rome (1677–1686), depict this moment.

4 For an interesting discussion of Klimt's 'Judith I' in its contemporary context and in terms of its reception today, see Patrick Werkner, 'Frauenbilder der Wiener Moderne und ihre Rezeption heute', in *Expressionismus in Österreich. Die Literatur und die Künste*, ed. Klaus Amann and Armin A. Wallas (Cologne, Weimar, Vienna: Böhlau, 1994), pp. 138–148.

5 On the late nineteenth-century tradition from which Oscar Wilde's play emerges (Gustave Moreau, Karl-Joris Huysmans, and Stéphane Mallarmé) see Françoise Meltzer, *Salome and the Dance of Writing. Portraits of Mimesis in Literature* (Chicago and London: Chicago University Press, 1987), chapter 1, pp. 13–46.

6 Judith and Salomé were ninth-century British anchoresses, related to one another as aunt and niece. See *Oxford Dictionary of Saints*, ed. David Hugh Farmer (Oxford, New York: Oxford University Press, 2nd ed. 1987), p. 242.

7 See Carola Hilmes, *Die Femme Fatale: Ein Weiblichkeitstypus in der nachromantischen Literatur* (Stuttgart: Metzler, 1990), and Bram Dijkstra, *Evil Sisters: The Threat of Female Sexuality and the Cult of Manhood* (New York: Knopf, 1996).

8 *Geschlecht und Charakter. Eine prinzipielle Untersuchung* (Vienna and Leipzig: Wilhelm Braumüller, 3rd edition, 1904), pp. 378–379. The English translation seriously misrepresents this passage, taking several words to mean their opposites. See Otto Weininger, *Sex and Character*, authorized translation from the sixth German edition (London: William Heinemann; New York: G. P. Putnam's Sons, 1912), p. 279.

9 Rilke had begun to read Weininger in 1905 (see letter of 31 March, 1905, in *Rainer Maria Rilke – Lou Andreas-Salomé Briefwechsel*, p. 200).

10 Sigmund Freud and Josef Breuer, *Studien über Hysterie* (Frankfurt: Fischer, 1970), p. 175.

11 See André Pierre Brouillet's famous medical painting, 'A Clinical Lesson of Doctor Charcot at the Salpêtrière' (1887), now in the Countway Library of Medicine at Harvard University. Other hysterical body positions were illustrated in Paul Richer's *La Grande hystérie*; see George Frederick Drinka, *The Birth of Neurosis. Myth, Malady and the Victorians* (New York: Simon and Schuster, 1984), p. 82. For an analysis of Freud's attempt to 'read the hysterical body' in the Dora case, see Peter Brooks, *Body Work. Objects of Desire in Modern Narrative* (Cambridge: Harvard University Press, 1993), pp. 234–244.

12 Sander Gilman, 'Sigmund Freud and the Sexologists: A Second Reading', in *Reading Freud's Reading*, ed. Sander Gilman, Jutta Birmele, Jay Geller, and Valerie D. Greenberg (New York and London: New York University Press, 1994), p. 61.

13 Quoted by Jens Malte Fischer in 'Kundry, Salome und Melusine: Verführung und Erlösung in der Oper der Jahrhundertwende', in Helmut Kreutzer, ed., *Don Juan und Femme Fatale* (Munich: Fink, 1994), p. 145.

14 See Sander Gilman, 'Opera, Homosexuality, and Models of Disease: Richard Strauss's *Salomé* in the Context of Images of Disease in the Fin de Siècle', in *Disease and Representation. Images of Illness from Madness to AIDS* (Ithaca and London: Cornell University Press, 1988), esp. pp. 162–166.

15 Letter of 28 February 1911, in *Briefe an seinen Verleger* (Leipzig: Insel, 1934), 1: 99.

16 *Encyclopedia Britannica*, 11th edition (New York: Encyclopedia Britannica Company, 1910), 14: 211.

17 The chapter is titled 'Das erotische Wahngebilde' (*Die Erotik* (Frankfurt: Rütten & Loening, 1910), pp. 21–25).

18 See Biddy Martin, *Woman and Modernity. The (Life)styles of Lou Andreas-Salomé* (Ithaca and London: Cornell University Press, 1991), esp. pp. 52–53.

19 Patrick Werkner interprets Klimt's 'Judith I', for example, in terms of contemporary theories of hysteria ('Frauenbilder der Wiener Moderne').

20 *The Oxford Study Bible. Revised English Bible with the Apocrypha*, ed. M. Jack Suggs, Katherine Doob Sakenfeld and James R. Mueller (New York: Oxford University Press, 1992), p. 1083.

21 I am grateful to Margret Guillemin for this very suggestive idea.

22 Lou Andreas-Salomé also argued for a positive re-interpretation of Narcissism as a creative impulse. See Karla Schultz, 'In Defense of Narcissus: Lou Andreas-Salomé and Julia Kristeva', in *The German Quarterly* 67 (1994), 185–196.

23 Leipzig: Diederichs, 1900, p. 45–46.

24 'William Morris und Edvard Burne-Jones. Die Bürde der Spiegel', in *Die Mystik, die Künstler und das Leben. Über englische Dichter und Maler im 19. Jahrhundert* (Leipzig: Diederichs, 1900), pp. 193–219.

25 For scholarly treatment of angelology, see Erik Peterson, *Das Buch von den Engeln: Stellung und Bedeutung der heiligen Engeln im Kultus* (Leipzig: J. Hegner, 1935); D. P. Walker, *Spiritual and Demonic Magic. From Ficino to Campanella* (London: The Warburg Institute, 1958); Loren T. Stuckenbruck, *Angel Veneration and Christology: A Study in early Judaism and in the Christology of the Apocalypse of John* (Tübingen: Mohr, 1995); and David Keck, *Angels and Angelology in the Middle Ages* (New York: Oxford University Press, 1997). See also Harold Bloom, *Omens of Millenium. The Gnosis of Angels, Dreams, and Resurrection* (New York: Riverhead Books, 1996), esp. pp. 85–90, on the 'answering angel' in Kabbalist theory.

26 It has been suggested that El Greco's paintings may have contributed to the conception of the angel in the *Duino Elegies*. Rilke had conceived an enthusiasm for El Greco's 'Toledo' as early as 1908, and admired other paintings by him on a visit to Munich in 1911; he did not visit Toledo until winter 1912/13. On Rilke's Toledo experience, see Fatima Naqvi-Peters, 'A Turning-Point in Rilke's Evolution: The Experience of El Greco', *Germanic Review* 72 (1997), 342–362.

27 From *Der Teppich des Lebens*. Stefan George, *Gedichte*, ed. Ernst Klett (Stuttgart: Klett-Cotta, 1983), p. 32.

28 Marie von Thurn und Taxis recounts this episode in her *Erinnerungen an Rainer Maria Rilke*, pp. 48–49.

29 The compound verbs 'aufsingen' and 'aufschreien' ('to sing upward' and 'to cry upward').

30 See Mrs. (Anna) Jameson, *Legends of the Madonna as Represented in the Fine Arts* (London: Longman, Roberts & Green, 4th edn. 1864), p. 84.

31 Ernst Zinn explains that the phrase 'von Holzglut zu Holzglut/ geben wir schwächern Geruch' refers to the process of smoking with amber (1: 792).

32 Mechthild is included in the list of women lovers in *Malte Laurids Brigge*, those in connection with whom Malte comments that 'to love is: to burn with inexhaustible oil' (6: 937).

33 Two years later, he wrote the poem 'Zu der Zeichnung, John Keats im Tode darstellend' [On the Drawing representing John Keats on his Deathbed] (2: 75).

34 Kassner, *Die Mystiker, die Künstler und das Leben*, p. 114. Kassner cites the last six lines of the second stanza of Keats's ode (p. 115). Earlier in the chapter, Kassner lists 'On a Grecian Urn' as one of Keats's most admired poems (p. 111). Kassner regards Keats, furthermore, as a 'brother' of Niels Lyhne (p. 103), an identification that would certainly have attracted Rilke's attention.

35 Similarly, Michael Minden suggests that the last two sections of *The Second Elegy*, consisting of eight and six lines respectively, recall the octave and sestet of a sonnet, while lacking a sonnet's rhymes. See 'Elegy Two', in *Rilke's 'Duino Elegies': Cambridge Readings* (London and New York: Duckworth and Ariadne Press, 1996), p. 31.

36 Ulrich, Fülleborn *Das Strukturproblem der späten Lyrik Rilkes* (Heidelberg: Winter, 1960); Stephens, Anthony, *Rainer Maria Rilke's 'Gedichte an die Nacht'. An Essay in Interpretation* (Cambridge University Press, 1972).

37 See Hölderlin's poem 'The Rhein', with its constant repetition of the key words 'pure' and 'heavenly'. Rilke had been introduced to Hölderlin's works in 1910 by Norbert von Hellingrath. See Werner Günther, 'Rilke und Hölderlin', *Hölderlin-Jahrbuch* 1951, 121–157, and Herbert Singer, *Rilke und Hölderlin* (Köln und Graz: Bohlau, 1957).

38 See Friedrich Ohly, 'La Poesia come necessario frutto di una sofferenza', in *Geometria e memoria. Lettera e allegoria nel Medioevo*, trans. Lea Ritter Santini (Bologna: Società editrice il Mulino, 1984), pp. 53–89. Rilke refers to the traditional connections among poetry, pearls, and suffering in the *Duino Elegies* ('Perlen des Leids', 1: 723).

39 The image of the moon recalls Brockes' meditation on the relative merits of moonlight and starlight, the earthly and the transcendent in 'Kirschblüte bei der Nacht' [Cherry Blossom by Night] as well as Hölderlin's description of the rising moon in the first stanza of 'Brot und Wein' [Bread and Wine].

40 In his 'Fragments' (jottings originally intended to serve as the basis for his projected encyclopaedia), Novalis had noted: 'Fülle der Zukunft – Zeitenfülle überhaupt' (fullness of the future – fullness of time altogether).

41 Eudo C. Mason, *Rilke, Europe and the English-speaking World* (Cambridge University Press, 1961).

42 'The Dramatic Monologue and Related Lyric Forms', *Critical Inquiry* 3 (1976), p. 150.

43 Mason, *Rilke, Europe, and the English-speaking World*, p. 41.

44 Robert Langbaum, *The Poetry of Experience. The Dramatic Monologue in Modern Literary Tradition* (London: Chatto and Windus, 1957), pp. 75–108.

45 To be more accurate, the poem is an imitation of the Schlegel-Tieck Shakespeare translation, as the quotation in the last line of the original indicates ('und das ist wenig').

46 See Judith Ryan, *The Vanishing Subject: Early Psychology and Literary Modernism* (Chicago University Press, 1991), pp. 57–61.

47 *Gedichte. Dramen I. Gesammelte Werke* (Frankfurt: Fischer, 1979), p. 22.

48 Kassner refers indirectly to Browning's 'Caliban' when he says that Browning is at his strongest when he 'combines Caliban and Prospero' (*Die Mystik*, p. 234).

49 *The Power of Genre* (Minneapolis: University of Minnesota, 1985), p. 57.

50 *Briefwechsel mit Katharina Kippenberg* (Wiesbaden: Insel, 1954), p. 679.

51 On Rilke's links with Klopstock (and, in passing, with Hölty), see Friedrich Wilhelm Wodtke, *Rilke und Klopstock* (Diss. Kiel, 1948), pp. 15–51. Rilke's knowledge of Mallarmé was long-standing: he mentions him in his second letter to Clara Rilke after his 1902 arrival in Paris. See *Briefe aus den Jahren 1902–1906* (Leipzig: Insel, 1930), p. 24. Rilke read at least some of Keats's poems in a German translation given to him in 1911. See Ingeborg Schnack, *Rainer Maria Rilke. Chronik seines Lebens und seines Werkes* (Frankfurt: Insel, 1975), p. 380.

52 Ironically, Goethe's 'Gegenwart' is itself the result of an intertextual reversal in which Goethe reworks a contemporary song. See Ernst Ribbat, 'Poetik im Liebesgedicht. Johann Wolfgang Goethe: "Gegenwart"', in *Poetik und Geschichte. Viktor Žmegač zum 60. Geburtstag*, ed. Dieter Borchmeyer (Tübingen: Niemeyer, 1989), pp. 208–210.

53 Mason, *Rilke, Europe and the English-speaking World*, p. 144.

54 He was later to claim that his unpublished sequence of poems *From the Posthumous Papers of Count C. W.* (1920) and his *Sonnets to Orpheus* (1922) had been 'dictated'.

55 See Judith Ryan, '"Une chute antérieure de plume": Mallarmé's "Le Démon de l'analogie"', *French Studies* XLVII (1993), 33–42.

56 Orpheus is occasionally associated with birds. See Charles Segal, *Orpheus. The Myth of the Poet* (Baltimore: Johns Hopkins University Press, 1989), p. 13.

57 John Keats, *The Complete Poems*, ed. John Barnard (Harmondsworth: Penguin, 1988), p. 348 (lines 65–66). Kassner quotes two passages from 'Ode to a Nightingale' in his chapter on Keats in *Die Mystik* (pp. 95–115) and includes the poem in his list of Keats's most 'admired' odes (p. 111); he does not, however, quote the lines 'perhaps the self-same song…'.

58 See Cynthia Chase, '"Viewless Wings"; Interpretation of Keats's "Ode to a Nightingale"', in Hošek and Parker, eds., *Lyric Poetry*, pp. 208–225; John Hollander, *The Figure of Echo, A Mode of Allusion in Milton and After* (Berkeley, Los Angeles, London: University of California Press, 1981), pp. 94–95; and Thomas McFarland, *Originality and Imagination* (Baltimore and London: The Johns Hopkins University Press, 1985), pp. 137–143.

59 It is not surprising that Rilke subsequently supported Annette Kolb's efforts to found an international magazine that would work actively for peace (Leppmann, *Rilke. A Life*, p. 299).

60 August Stahl, in collaboration with Werner Jost and Reiner Marx, *Rilke-Kommentar zum lyrischen Werk* (Munich: Winkler, 1978), p. 288.

61 Heinz von Lichberg, ed., *Das deutsche Herz. Gaben deutscher Dichter. Für den Alice-Frauenverein* (Hessischer Landesverein vom Roten Kreuz) zu seinem fünfzigjährigen Bestehen (Berlin: Georg Stilke, 1917).

62 Gerard Noel, *Princess Alice. Queen Victoria's Forgotten Daughter* (London: Constable and Co., 1974), p. 137.

63 Eleonore was the proprietor of the Third Grand Ducal Hessian Life Guards, Infantry Regiment No. 177, known as the 'Grand Duchess'. see Melville Henry Massue, Marquis of Ruvigny and Raineval, ed., *The Titled Nobility of Europe: An International Peerage, or 'Who's Who,' of the Sovereigns, Princes, and Nobles of Europe*, (London: Burke's Peerage, 1980).

64 Maria von Ewald, ed., *Großherzogin Eleonore und ihr Werk* (Darmstadt: Verlag L. C. Wittich, 1938), pp. 52, 56 and 64.

65 See Maria von Ewald, *Großherzogin Eleonore*, p. 29.

66 See E. A. Wallis Budge, *The Egyptian Book of the Dead (The Papyrus of Ani)* (New York: Dover, 1967 (rpt. of 1895 original)), p. 318. See also Richard H. Wilkinson, *Reading Egyptian Art. A Hieroglyphic Guide to Ancient Egyptian Painting and Sculpture* (London: Thames and Hudson, 1992), p. 99. Wilkinson explains that the 'ba' was 'the spiritual aspect of the human being which survived – or came into being – at death' (p. 99); it was depicted as 'a human-headed (i.e. individualised) being, with the body of a bird, usually a falcon' (*ibid.*).

67 See Klaus Michalowski, Jean-Pierre Corteggian, and Alessandro Roccati, *L'Art de l'Egypte* (Paris: Citadelles & Mazenod, 1968/94), p. 104; Carol Andrews, ed., *The Ancient Egyptian Book of the Dead* (Austin: University of Texas Press, 1990) pp. 68, 85, 87, 89, 90, 91; Sue D'Auria, Peter Lacovara, and Catharine H. Roehrig, *Mummies and Magic. The Funerary Arts of Ancient Egypt* (Boston Museum of Fine Arts; Museum of Fine Arts, Texas, 1988); and Richard H. Wilkinson, *Reading Egyptian Art* (London: Thames and Hudson, 1992), p. 98.

68 Leppmann, *Rilke. A Life*, p. 276.

69 'The Man Who Was Tired of Life', in *The Literature of Ancient Egypt. An Anthology of Stories, Instructions, and Poetry*, new edn, ed. William Kelly Simpson (New Haven and London: Yale University Press, 1973), pp. 201–209.

70 It also suggests Jung's 'anima' and 'animus'. Jung's *Wandlungen und Symbole der Seele* appeared in 1912. I do not know whether Rilke was familiar with it.

71 Salomon Reinach, *Orphée. Histoire Générale des Religions* (Paris: Alcide Picard, 1909), p. 122.

4   THE MODERNIST TURN

1 Hermann Meyer, 'Die Verwandlung des Sichtbaren', in Görner, ed., *Rainer Maria Rilke*, p. 173.

2 *Abstraktion und Einfühlung. Ein Beitrag zur Stilpsychologie* (Munich: Piper, 7th edn, 1919), pp. 17–19.

3 Worringer, *Abstraktion und Einfühlung*, p. 25.

4 Meyer, 'Die Verwandlung', p. 160.

5 *Kairuan oder eine Geschichte vom Maler Klee und von der Kunst dieses Zeitalters* (Munich: Kurt Wolff, 1921), pp. 121 and 110.

6 Letter to Wilhelm Hausenstein, 23 February, 1921, reproduced in Hermann

Meyer, 'Die Verwandlung des Sichtbaren', in Görner, ed., *Rainer Maria Rilke*, p. 183.

7 Letter of 23 February, 1921, reproduced in Herman Meyer, 'Die Verwandlung des Sichtbaren', in Görner, ed., *Rainer Maria Rilke*, p. 183.

8 See Marilyn Vogler Urion, 'Emerson's Presence in Rilke's Imagery: Shadows of Early Influence', *Monatshefte* 85 (1993), 153–169.

9 *Complete Works*, Concord Edition, 10 vols., *Essays, Second Series* (Boston: Houghton, 1903), 3:8. Urion identifies the German translation Rilke used as that of Oskar Dähnert in the Reclam edition of Emerson's *Essays* ('Emerson's Presence in Rilke's Imagery', p. 155); the key phrase in this passage appeared as 'jene Region [...], wo die Luft Musik ist' (p. 158).

10 See Fioretos, 'Prayer and Ignorance', p. 172.

11 See Leppmann, *Rilke. A Life*, p. 337.

12 See Jonathan Culler, who writes of that 'special temporality which is the set of all moments at which writing can say "now"'. 'Apostrophe', in *The Pursuit of Signs* (Ithaca, London: Cornell University Press, 1981), p. 149.

13 Hans Jürgen Tscheidel, 'Orpheus und Eurydike. Ein Beitrag zum Thema: Rilke und die Antike' (1973), reprinted in *Rainer Maria Rilke*, ed. Görner, pp. 299–300.

14 Leppmann, *Rilke. A Life*, p. 352.

15 Valéry, *Oeuvres*, ed. Jean Hytier (Paris: Gallimard, 1957), I: 1541.

16 To be sure, an early version of 'Orpheus' had appeared in 1891 in Pierre Louÿs' exclusive poetry magazine *La Conque* available only by subscription and at an elevated price. It is difficult to determine whether Rilke might have seen this (possibly via André Gide) in 1921/22.

17 *L'Ermitage*, vol. 2, no. 3 (1891), 129–133; reproduced in Valéry, *Oeuvres* 2: 1402–1405. 'Paradoxe sur l'architecte' was dedicated to André Gide (p. 1405).

18 There was one missing syllable in the prose version, which Valéry supplied for the verse version ('hauts', in line 8; see Valéry, *Oeuvres*, I: 1540).

19 See, for example, Rilke's letter to Anton Kippenberg, 25 February, 1911, in *Briefe an seinen Verleger* (Wiesbaden: Insel, 1949), I: 114, and his letter to Lou Andreas-Salomé, 28 December, 1911, in *Ausgewählte Briefe*, I: 328.

20 Fifty-five letters from Sophia Rilke (Entz) to Olga Theurner, 1908–1927, are in the Houghton Library of Harvard University (bMS Ger 58.3 [17–35]). See letters of 30 August, 1910, and 10 March, 1911.

21 Mechtild Lichnowsky, *Götter, Könige und Tiere in Ägypten* (Leipzig: Kurt Wolff Verlag, 1912). Lichnowksy's book is highly impressionistic; it is not a scholarly study.

22 *Les grands initiés* (repr. Paris: Perrin, 1960).

23 Paris: Picard, 1909, p. 121.

24 'Grab-Mal' (funeral monument) is the same term Rilke uses in the subtitle of *The Sonnets to Orpheus* when he describes them as a monument for Wera Ouckama Knoop (I: 727). This is only one of several links between *The Tenth Elegy* and *The Sonnets to Orpheus*.

25 On this spring, see Reinach, *Orphée*, p. 122.

26 The individual scrolls placed beside Egyptian mummies were entitled 'Livre de la sortie au jour' 'Book of coming out into the daylight'. Georges Jean, *L'Ecriture mémoire des hommes* (Paris: Gallimard, 1987), p. 33.

27 The image of 'tearing strings' of the heart may have been suggested by the conclusion of Goethe's elegy 'Euphrosyne', in *Werke*, ed. Erich Trunz (Munich: Beck, 1982), 1: 195.

28 Watercolour and pen, 23 × 14.6 cm., Bayerische Staatsgemäldesammlung, Munich.

29 Roger Paulin notes that both the periwinkle and the hazel are 'magic plants that remind us of the primitive links between divination and poetry' ('Elegy Ten', in *Rilke's Duino Elegies: Cambridge Readings*, p. 178; see also p. 189).

30 See Theodore Ziolkowski, *The German Elegy*. Also based on Schiller's 'The Walk' is Rilke's poem 'Exposed on the Heart's Mountains' (1914), which uses the metaphor of a symbolic walk up a mountainside as an allegory for the poet's feeling that he is moving beyond the capability of language to express his emotions.

31 See Jacob Steiner, 'Rilke und Goethe', *Blätter der Rilke-Gesellschaft* 18 (1991), p. 29.

32 Friedrich Schiller, *Sämtliche Werke*, ed. Gerhard Fricke and Herbert G. Göpfert (Munich: Hanser, 1987), 1: 234.

33 There is a small phonemic element in Egyptian hieroglyphs. I do not know if Rilke knew about this. See Jean, *L'Ecriture mémoire des hommes*, p. 28.

34 'Ein Brief', *Gesammelte Werke in Einzelausgaben* (Frankfurt: Fischer, 1951), *Prosa*, 2: 22.

35 Kathleen Komar, *Transcending Angels. Rainer Maria Rilke's Duino Elegies* (Lincoln and London: University of Nebraska Press, 1987), p. 89.

36 Jacob Steiner, *Rilke's Duineser Elegien* (Bern and Munich: Francke, 1962), p. 106 (my translation).

37 Rilke turned the other poem into a separate entity and gave it the title 'Gegen-Strophen' (2: 136–138), but did not publish it during his lifetime.

38 *Rilkes Duineser Elegien*, p. 102.

39 'Elegy Five', in *Rilke's 'Duino Elegies': Cambridge Readings*, p. 76.

40 Komar, *Transcending Angels*, p. 91.

41 Christina Pugh, in *Revising the Pictorial: Ekphrasis and the Nature of Modern Lyric* (Diss., Harvard, 1998), discusses the way in which ekphrastic poetry in general reworks its pictorial models.

42 Though it has been suggested that this figure, in the poem, is equivalent to the elderly acrobat of the prose text, Père Rollin, the 1907 piece is presented as aged, but also as suffering from dementia; the wrinkled skin and shrivelled appearance are not at issue in the prose text.

43 John Richardson points out that Apollinaire had recently acclaimed Picasso as 'Harlequin Trismegistus'. See *A Life of Picasso*, vol. 1, 1881–1906 (New York: Random House, 1991), p. 386.

44 See also Ralph Freedman, 'Rainer Maria Rilke and the "Sister Arts",

Literary Theory and Criticism, Festschrift Presented to René Wellek in Honor of his Eightieth Birthday, ed. Joseph P. Strelka (Bern: Peter Lang, 1984), 2: 821–847, esp. pp. 840–844.

45 Rilke's procedure here is different from what John Hollander terms 'notional ekphrasis'. See *The Gazer's Spirit* (Chicago University Press, 1995) pp. 7–32.

46 Guillaume Apollinaire, *Calligrammes. Poèmes de la Paix et de la Guerre (1913–1916)* (Paris: Gallimard, 1925), p. 55.

47 See Jean Starobinski, *Portrait de l'artiste en saltimbanque* (Geneva: Albert Skira, 1970).

48 Baudelaire, *Oeuvres complètes*, p. 157.

49 For a more extended discussion of this metaphor in the four authors, see Marion Faber, *Angels of Daring. Tightrope Walker and Acrobat in Nietzsche, Kafka, Rilke and Thomas Mann* (Stuttgart: Akademischer Verlag Hans-Dieter Heinz (Stuttgarter Arbeiten zur Germanistik, no. 72) 1979).

50 Steiner, *Rilkes Duineser Elegien*, p. 103. J. P. Stern calls the poetic persona of the *Elegies* the 'historical we'. See *The Dear Purchase; A Theme in German Modernism* (Cambridge University Press, 1995), p. 5.

51 I am grateful to Karl S. Guthke for suggesting this connection. Rachilde was the pseudonym of Marguerite Eymery Vallette, co-founder with her husband, Alfred Vallette, of the Mercure de France. It was at her instigation that the journal was given a cover in her favourite colour, mauve.

52 See *Materialien zu Rainer Maria Rilkes 'Duineser Elegien'*, ed. Ulrich Fülleborn and Manfred Engel (Frankfurt: Suhrkamp, 1980), pp. 344, 345.

53 Rachilde, *Théâtre* avec préface de l'auteur (Paris: Nouvelle Librairie Parisienne, Albert Savine, 1891).

54 George's poem about the sterile second blossoming of the almond, 'Wir schreiten auf und ab...', (in *Gedichte*, ed. Ernst Klett (Stuttgart: Klett-Cotta, 1983), p. 23) exemplifies this tendency. Proust's use of the orchid is more complex: the motif is linked with heterosexual intercourse, but also with the idea of art for art's sake; see *Du côté de chez Swann* (Paris: Gallimard, 1954), p. 261. At the turn of the century, the question of whether orchids self-pollinate was being hotly debated.

55 *Materialien zu Rainer Maria Rilkes 'Duineser Elegien'*, vol. 1, p. 284.

56 In the elegy it is first called a 'Vase'; but Rilke uses the same word in his term for 'apothecary's jar' – 'Apotheker-Vase' – in his note to the page proofs cited above.

57 Komar uses both terms, 'leave no remainder' and 'cancel itself out' in her reading of this passage (*Transcending Angels*, p. 103).

58 I use here the definitions given in R. B. Farrell, *A Dictionary of German Synonyms* (Oxford University Press, 1953, repr. with corrections 1955), pp. 255–256.

59 See the passage about money in *The Tenth Elegy*, 1: 722.

60 See Bruce Kuklick, *The Rise of American Philosophy. Cambridge, Massachusetts, 1860–1930* (New Haven and London: Yale University Press, 1977), p. 345. Kuklick is referring here to the neo-realist work of Edwin Holt.

61 E. C. Mason identifies the novel as *The Education of Uncle Paul* (1909). *Rilke, Europe and the English-speaking World*, p. 88.

62 *Ausgewählte Briefe*, 2: 222–223.

63 Mason cites this passage but does not make the connection between Blackwood's fanciful notion and Rilke's 'mirror sonnet'. *Rilke, Europe and the English-speaking World*, pp. 88–89.

64 Rilke had read Ovid. See Hans-Jürgen Tschiedel, 'Orpheus und Eurydike', p. 286.

65 Asa Briggs, *Victorian Things* (Chicago: The University of Chicago Press, 1988), p. 124. Ernest Hello, in *L'Homme* (Paris: Victor Palmé, 1872) described photography as having the same structure as memory (pp. 173–174).

66 *Oeuvres*, pp. 68–69. On 24 June 1926, Rilke wrote some lines in French that recall Mallarmé by invoking a cluster of images characteristic of the French poet: star, mirror, shell, fingernails, bones (Rilke, 2: 734). Rilke's fragment appears to apostrophize Mallarmé.

67 Rilke was certainly familiar with this text; see Rilke's French poem 'Comme un verre de Venise' of 1924 (2: 522).

68 On this motif in Mallarmé, see Léon Cellier, *Mallarmé et la Morte qui parle* (Paris: Presses Universitaires Français, 1959), esp. pp. 75–76. Mallarmé's image of the dead, nude woman in the mirror was later picked up by Valéry, significantly in his poem, 'Narcissus speaks'. Here, the youth describes his image in the water as 'a naked fiancé' who is also the 'shade of a dead person' (*Oeuvres*, pp. 82–83), thus explicitly alluding to Mallarmé's image.

69 *Die Mystik, die Künstler und das Leben*, pp. 193–219.

70 Rilke's 1902 review of Pater's *Renaissance*, in which he describes Rossetti as 'der Dichter unverge ßlicher Sonette' (5: 599), is one indication of his interest in the English poet. In the same essay, he refers to translations published by the Verlag Eugen Diederichs in Leipzig. The Diederichs edition of Rossetti appeared as *Das Haus des Lebens. Sonettenfolge*, trans. Otto Hauser (Leipzig: Eugen Diederichs, 1900).

71 *Ibid.*, p. 51.

72 Stefan George, *Werke* (Munich and Dusseldorf: Helmut Küpper, 1958), p. 345.

73 When Rilke composed his sonnet on mirrors in February 1922, the full three-part version of Valéry's Narcissus project had not appeared. He would certainly have known the versions of part I published in the *Revue de Paris*, September 1919, and the *Nouvelle Revue Française*, June 1921.

74 Heinz Mitlacher, 'Die Entwicklung des Narzißbegriffs', *Germanisch-Romanische Monatsschrift* 21 (1933), p. 379. See also Maja Goth, *Rilke und Valéry. Aspekte ihrer Poetik* (Bern: Francke, 1981), p. 123.

75 In a talk Valéry gave on his Narcissus poems in 1941, he explained that he had seen the motto on a marble plaque in a garden at Montpellier. According to local tradition, it was the grave of the poet Edward Young's daughter, whose name was Narcissa (Valéry, *Oeuvres*, 1: 1559–1560). On the

notion of a 'true feminine incarnation' of Narcissus, see Bram Dijkstra, *Idols of Perversity. Fantasies of Feminine Evil in Fin-de-Siècle Culture* (Oxford and New York: Oxford University Press, 1986), pp. 143–159.

76 On Lou Andreas-Salomé's ideas on Narcissism, see Martin, *Woman and Modernity*, p. 201. On sexuality in Rilke's poem, see Lorna Martens, *Shadow Lines. Austrian Literature from Freud to Kafka* (Lincoln and London: The University of Nebraska Press, 1996), p. 100–111.

77 See Martens, who makes the point that 'mirror logic can presumably annul the normal temporal relations involved in cause and effect' (*Shadow Lines*, p. 111).

78 M. L. West, *The Orphic Poems* (Oxford University Press, 1983), p. 136.

79 Johann Jakob Bachofen, *Die Unsterblichkeitslehre der orphischen Theologie auf den Grabdenkmälern des Altertums*, in *Gesammelte Werke*, ed. Emanuel Kienzle *et al.* (Basel: Benno Schwabe, 1958), 7: 70.

80 For example, Rilke's poem 'Das (nicht vorhandene) Kindergrab mit dem Ball', which alludes to Bachofen's discussion of the symbol of the ball (pp. 63–67).

81 Ovid follows the story of Narcissus and Echo with the tale of Pentheus, another case of dismemberment. This may also account for Rilke's linking of the Narcissus with the Orpheus myth. Another motif from Ovid that may be present in Rilke's sonnet on mirrors is the hunted stag, with which Orpheus is compared in the moments before his death at the hands of the Maenads (*Metamorphoses*, 11: 25–27).

82 For a more detailed exposition of Rilke's relation to Ovid, see Segal, *Orpheus*, pp. 118–154.

83 See, for example, Joachim W. Storck, 'Poesie und Schweigen. Zum Enigmatischen in Rilkes später Lyrik', *Blätter der Rilke-Gesellschaft* 10 (1983), 116–118, which treats the text as a finished poem. Although Ernst Zinn places it under the heading 'drafts', Rilke nonetheless thought enough of the poem to make a clean copy of it, intending originally to send it to Katharina Kippenberg in late 1925 with a small collection of poems consisting of his 'Improvisationen aus dem Capreser Winter' (composed in 1906/7); in the end, however, he removed the page containing 'Mausoleum' from the cluster. Zinn's argument that Rilke was not satisfied with the poem (2: 792) is not the only conceivable reason for the removal of the text from this convolute; much more likely is the fact that, apart from the motif of wind, the Capri poems and 'Mausoleum' have little in common.

84 *Encyclopedia Britannica* (New York: Encyclopedia Britannica, 1911), vol. 12, p. 838, col. 1.

85 Kristian Jeppesen, *The Maussolleion at Ancient Halicarnassus* (Ankara: Dönmez, n.d.), pp. 16, 20.

86 In contrast to Mallarmé's dense and complex 'Tombeaux', Rilke's own poems in French on the theme of 'tombeaux' (2: 601, 629, 638), are relatively slight reflections on the motif of gravestones.

87 *Übertragungen* (Leipzig: Insel, 1930), p. 350. Rilke also translated Mallarmé's

poem on his daughter's fan (see *Übertragungen*, p. 345–46); another Mallarmé translation, of 'Le vierge, le vivace, et le bel aujourd'hui . . .', which Rilke sent to Dory von der Mühll in 1919, appears to have been lost (see 2: 790–791).

88 The cross-section diagram in Jeppesen's *The Maussoleion at Ancient Halicarnassus*, p. 8, places the king's tomb at the very lowest depth of the monument, not in its exact centre, as Rilke's poem suggests.

89 There are some sonnet-like features, however: the first section is 14 lines long and the second and third sections together are 14 lines long. Disregarding the absence of rhyme, the first section is constructed like an 'embracing' sonnet with a parenthetical sestet enclosed in two quatrains; the second half of the poem consists of an octave followed by a sestet.

90 The second volume of Zinn's edition of Rilke, containing Rilke's unpublished poems and drafts as well as poems published apart from Rilke's major poetic cycles, appeared in 1957, two years before Celan's *Sprachgitter*. Traces of Rilke's influence can be found in Celan's earlier works, notably in *Mohn und Gedächtnis* (1952); but the short-lined forms, full of unusual compound nouns and adjectives, do not emerge fully in Celan's poetry until after the appearance of Zinn's volume two.

CONCLUSION: RESTORATIVE MODERNISM

1 'Tradition and the Individual Talent', in *Selected Prose of T. S. Eliot*, ed. Frank Kermode (London: Faber & Faber, 1975), p. 41.

2 'Lettre sur Mallarmé' (1927), *Oeuvres*, 1: 634–35.

3 See Renée Lang, 'Rilke and his French Contemporaries', *Comparative Literature* x (1958), 136–43.

4 'Breathtaking' is Renée Lang's word ('Rilke and his French Contemporaries', p. 138).

5 Letter to Mme Morisse, 8 March, 1924. Quoted in Lang, 'Rilke and his French Contemporaries', p. 139.

6 He visited the posthumous Franz Marc exhibition in September 1916 with Karl Wolfskehl and Rudolf Kassner. See *Rilke und die bildende Kunst seiner Zeit*, ed. Gisela Götte and Jo-Anne Birnie Danzker (Munich and New York: Prestel, 1996) p. 89.

7 Hermann Meyer, 'Die Verwandlung des Sichtbaren' in Görner, ed., *Rainer Maria Rilke*, p. 156.

8 Manja Wilkens, 'Etappen einer Genieästhetik. Lebensstationen und Kunsterfahrungen Rilkes', in *Rilke und die Bildende Kunst seiner Zeit*, p. 22.

9 *Rilke und die bildende Kunst seiner Zeit*, p. 90.

10 Letter of 28 February, 1921. Hermann Meyer reads this letter as, in the last analysis, a rejection of Klee's art and of abstraction in general ('Die Verwandlung des Sichtbaren', p. 163). Annette Gerok-Reiter rightly argues against Meyer's reading of the letter and shows how Rilke himself moves towards a new understanding of artistic representation. *Wink und Wandlung:*

Komposition und Poetik in Rilkes 'Sonette an Orpheus' (Tübingen: Niemeyer, 1966), p. 231 n. 63.

11 O. K. Werckmeister, *The Making of Paul Klee's Career 1914–1920* (University of Chicago Press, 1989), p. 241.

12 Letter to Kurt Becker, 24 March, 1913 (*Briefe 1907–14*, p. 286).

13 It resembles several poems that he calls 'Haï-Kaï' written in both German and French in 1920 and 1926 (2: 245, 638, and 745). While they do not conform to familiar definitions of haiku, based on syllable count, they do correspond to Rilke's description of 'Haï-Kaï' in a letter to Sophy Giauque as 'miniscules unités poétiques' that have been described as 'un bref étonnement' ('a brief astonishment') (*Ausgewählte Briefe*, 2: 489).

14 The German word for 'pure', 'reiner', is a homonym of Rilke's adopted first name 'Rainer'; the word for 'eyelids', 'Lider', is a homonym of the word for songs, 'Lieder'.

Index of Rilke's works

General index